THE BEST OF SAIL TRIM

ADLARD COLES NAUTICAL
London

Published by Adlard Coles Nautical
an imprint of A & C Black (Publishers) Ltd
35 Bedford Row, London WC1R 4JH

First published in Great Britain
in hardback by Adlard Coles 1975
Reprinted 1977, 1978, 1979, 1981, 1982, 1983
Paperback edition 1989
Reprinted 1990
Reprinted by Adlard Coles Nautical 1992, 1994, 1996, 1998

ISBN 0-7136-3594-0

A CIP catalogue record for this book is available from the
British Library.

Printed and bound in Great Britain by
MPG Books Ltd, Bodmin, Cornwall

Contents

I. ON THE MAIN

Mainsail on the Wind   3
Pointers for pointing
Herb Hild

Shaping Up the Main   6
Elements of draft and twist
John Marshall

The Mainsail Leech   15
Key to shape and power
Bruce Dyson

How to Trim a Cat   19
Tips on the full-batten main
Don McKibbin

II. GENOAS & JIBS

Halyard Hoist and Sheet Lead   25
The basics of genoa set
Norris Strawbridge

Adjusting a Genoa   27
More basics of headsail trim
Peter Schoonmaker

Genoa Overlap   33
Getting the most from LP
John R. Stanton

Jib Adjustment   38
Clew position on small boats
Steve Colgate

Jib Sheeting Angles   42
Considerations of the fairlead
Bruce Dyson

III. THE SPINNAKER

Fundamentals of Spinnaker Handling   47
Set, trim, and takedown
Steve Colgate

Fouls and Their Prevention   56
Some twists on spinnaker tangles
Bruce Cameron

Spinnaker and Mainsail Interaction   60
Downwind components of air flow
John R. Stanton

IV. WIND & SAILS

The Effects of Apparent Wind   67
Velocity and direction in points of sail
Steve Colgate

Steering and Sail Trim   73
Gaining a feel for "the groove"
Bruce Goldsmith

Sail Balance on the Wind   77
Coordination of main and headsail trim
Arvel Gentry

Sail Trim When Beating   89
Influences of the jib on the main
Peter Sutcliffe

Light Air Adjustments   92
The delicate art of zephyr sailing
Steve Colgate

Close Reaching with Multiple Headsails   96
Aerodynamic effects of auxiliary sails
John R. Stanton

Maximum Thrust on a Broad Reach   100
Factors that contribute to speed made good
John R. Stanton

The Spinnaker on a Broad Reach   104
Angle of attack and pole trim
John R. Stanton

Downwind in Heavy Air   109
Pushing a boat in wind and waves
Richard T. duMoulin

Hooking and Twisting   113
Leech control in various winds
Steve Falk

V. WHEREWITHALL

Basic Equipment for Mainsail Trim   121
The gear that shapes the sail
Peter Sutcliffe

Rudiments of Luff Tension   125
Some considerations of draft control
Steve Colgate

The Boom Vang   128
Preventing mainsail twist
Don McKibbin

The Traveller and Backstay   131
Mainsail flatness and optimum speed
Steve Colgate

The Jib Cunningham   136
Correct installation and varieties of use
John Welch

Upgrading the Power System   140
Simple, low-cost ways to more efficiency
Charles Booz

VI. CHANGING SAIL

When to Shorten Down   147
Calculating sail-carrying capability
Gabriel M. Giannini

Wind Strength and Sail Area   151
How to determine optimum combinations
Arthur Edmunds

The Virtue of "Jiffy" Reefing   157
A fast system for shortening the main
Peter M. Sutter

Which Headsail When?   161
Systematized sail changing
Richard duMoulin

On-the-Wind Headsail Changes   164
The techniques of fast handling
Richard duMoulin

Spinnaker Changing on Big Boats   168
Procedures used on Windward Passage
Don Vaughn

Spinnaker Takedowns in High Winds   170
Rigging and handling for smooth dousing
Warwick M. Tompkins, Jr.

Watch Out for Heavy Weather   174
Mainsail and spinnaker trim in a breeze
Steve Colgate

VII.   THE SAIL LOCKER

Optimize Your Sail Plan   179
Pointers on applying the IOR rule
Bob Barton

Sail Plans and Performance   183
Aspect ratios and efficiency
John R. Stanton

Heavy Weather Genoas   189
Design considerations of #2 and #3
Charles Ulmer

The Star-Cut   192
A spinnaker for the racing wardrobe
Hubert Dramard

The Close-Reaching Spinnaker   196
Construction and selection of the star-cut
Tony Johnson

Filling In the Foretriangle   200
The case for multiple headsails
John R. Stanton

The Double Head Rig   205
Jib topsail and genoa staysail
Arvel Gentry

Roller Furling Headsails   211
The answer to simplified sailing
Herb Hild

Triple Roller Headsails   214
A cruising rig with strings attached
Charles H. Vilas

Care and Maintenance of Synthetic Sails   222
A regimen for hale and hearty Dacron
Bernard A. Goldhirsh

VIII.   THEORY

Is High Aspect Ratio Efficient?   231
A cruising man casts his doubts
Murray L. Lesser

Some Basics of Sail Dynamics   235
Forces applied to a mainsail
John R. Stanton

Interaction of Sails on the Wind   240
Extreme sail plans and their performance
John R. Stanton

How Sails Really Work   247
Beginning to question old principles
Arvel Gentry

Boundary Flow and the Headsail   251
Continuing to question old principles
Arvel Gentry

How a Sail Gives Lift   256
Additional questions about old principles
Arvel Gentry

Another Look at Slot Effect   262
Yet further questioning of old principles
Arvel Gentry

More on the Slot Effect   268
Final questions about old principles
Arvel Gentry

On the Main

Mainsail on the Wind

Pointers for pointing   Herb Hild

Remember the last time your boat was cranked up on the wind and you felt you could defend the America's Cup? It felt great didn't it? But can you honestly say how or why you suddenly had the beautiful seat-of-the-pants top performance feeling?

If you can admit you really weren't sure what you were doing, you really don't understand all the complexities of mainsail shape and trim. But keep right on reading, for I've sailed with a lot of top drawer sailors and few knew much about the correct shape of a sail for a given set of conditions. Many *thought* they knew but they were still far from the heart of the matter.

Is there a simple answer? No, there is not. It is impossible to provide a set of short solutions for a perfect mainsail shape because every boat is different and, even on one boat, every situation is different. As any old salt will tell you: different ships — different splices.

Today, one of a sailmaker's most important jobs is to show his customers how to set and trim their sails to get the most out of them. Time and again, the average sailmaker hears complaints about poor performance or poor setting of a sail, only to find in the majority of cases that a visit to the boat, a short sailing trip accompanied by some basic education on cloth tension and trim, has resulted in a good looking well performing sail — and a much happier owner.

The techniques and controls will vary somewhat depending on whether you cruise or race, but even the cruising man with the simplest rig can sharply improve the performance of his mainsail with a few straightforward adjustments.

On a typical well-equipped racer, the available controls should include a halyard, boom vang, adjustable gooseneck, foot outhaul, mainsheet, mainsheet traveller, zipper foot, Cunningham hole and leech line. Bendy masts and booms are also possible control areas, but they are generally restricted to smaller boats.

The zipper foot and Cunningham hole are both really only of interest to the racing sailor. Both are essentially devices to obtain extra draft control but at the same time, keep the maximum sail area permitted by the boat's rating measurements.

Why is it necessary to cut a sail to its maximum measurement? All cloth stretches, and that is the racer's dilemma. A full-cut sail, the best type for light weather, will stretch beyond the black measurement bands when it is tensioned in heavy weather.

However, a sail made small enough for heavy weather will be undersized in balmy breezes. By adding a zipper foot and Cunningham, a big full-cut mainsail can alternately be tensioned and flattened within its measurement bands in any type of weather.

The cruising man can wring practically as good a response from his mainsail with just a halyard, outhaul, mainsheet and traveller. He won't have that feeling of inner serenity from knowing that everything has been done to guarantee maximum boat speed — but then his pocketbook won't hurt as much either.

Given a well cut sail, the racing skipper who knows how to control draft and shape will be well on the way towards a series of first places. Tension is the key to good control of draft and shape. And tension can be applied by any of the controls we've discussed, with the exception of the zipper.

There are essentially three areas of adjustment on the mainsail — the *luff*, the *leech* and the *foot*. To alter *luff tension* there is the halyard, the adjustable gooseneck and the Cunningham hole. The sailor who doesn't have the latter two can find happiness with a halyard, although most boats these days make it easier to control luff tension by using an adjustable gooseneck controlled by a downhaul. For the racing sailor with a sail cut to maximum dimensions, the Cunningham provides a simple, if unattractive, way of tensioning the luff.

Changing *leech tension* is accomplished by trimming in, or easing the mainsheet. Moving the mainsheet traveller athwartships together with mainsheet trim provides additional control.

Always remember that stretching any one side of the sail produces several other effects. Sailcloth tends to gather on the side that is being stretched, while it goes slack on the opposite side. This change can be very dramatic. You can see this by setting up a sail horizontally. As tension is increased on the luff the draft will move forward, but the leech may drop six to eight inches toward the floor as it becomes loose.

Think of the mainsail in two ways. Most people regard it as a driving, motivating force, but few stop to think of it as a way to balance the boat. When it comes to balance, there will be times when, in order to get the most out of the main, it will be necessary to think of trimming it so that it doesn't hurt you.

Under certain conditions, such as beating to windward in a heavy breeze, it is often better to ease the main or even let it partially luff if it is not practical to reef. It's a common mistake in a breeze to overtrim a mainsail when, more often than not, it is better to ease it.

What should a mainsail cross section look like during a beat to windward? It depends a lot on wind speed, but it is virtually impossible to draw the perfect sail shape for every one knot increase in wind speed. The accompanying diagrams, however, do give a good idea of what the conscientious sail trimmer should be trying to achieve.

In light air the sail must be full, with the draft in the middle third of the sail and the forward one third of the sail shaping gradually and smoothly from the mast to the point of maximum draft. (See figure 1.) A common mistake is to have too much fullness too far forward, especially in very light air. The after one third of the sail that includes the leech should shape to weather just enough to induce a slight weather helm in the boat.

For light air sailing, the outhaul should be slackened and the boom positioned close to the centerline of the boat. Set the mainsheet traveller a bit to windward. This permits the mainsheet to hold the boom amidships without tightening down on the leech. Experiment with the mainsheet and the traveller until the boom is on the centerline and the mainsheet is sufficiently trimmed to shape the leech slightly to weather. If the boat is otherwise well balanced, it should be possible to induce weather helm by tightening the mainsheet, and lee helm by slacking it. Try firming the leech until you get the required amount of weather helm. You'll know when it's right. You can let the boat go and she'll just gently eat up to weather.

In medium air ease the leech and get the draft forward in the sail by increasing luff tension. Keeping the main fairly full the increased luff tension will bring the draft forward and will slacken the leech, allowing it to stream out straight aft. Place the traveller amidships while tightening the mainsheet. If there is too much weather helm, ease the mainsheet traveller further to leeward. Put more tension on the outhaul, and have just enough tension on the leech line to minimize any unnecessary fluttering. (See figure 2.)

In heavy going, the sail should be

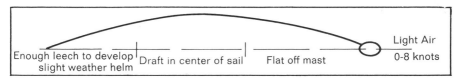

Enough leech to develop
slight weather helm

Draft in center of sail

Flat off mast

Light Air
0-8 knots

Figure 1

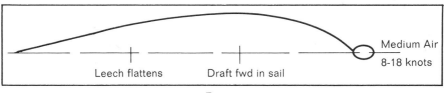

Leech flattens

Draft fwd in sail

Medium Air
8-18 knots

Figure 2

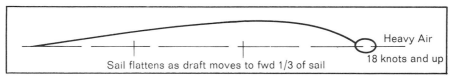

Sail flattens as draft moves to fwd 1/3 of sail

Heavy Air
18 knots and up

Figure 3

very flat with the draft in the middle of the forward third of the sail. Continue to increase luff tension, while also hardening up on the outhaul and mainsheet. As wind strength increases, the traveller should be allowed to go all the way to leeward.

The final step before reefing is to ease the mainsheet and allow the forward portion of the sail to luff. This will keep your boat relatively upright and driving. (See figure 3.)

Shaping Up the Main

Elements of draft and twist   John Marshall

For many of us, having fun in off-shore racing usually means winning. However, the aesthetics of the sport also are just as compelling. So when you get a chance to indulge yourself in the sheer beauty of sailing and come a little closer to winning as well, you're very close to what it is all about.

That's why I love mainsails: tall slender One-Tonner mains, perfectly formed Star-boat sails, the awesome sweep of *Intrepid*'s mainsail.

No matter what the size of your boat, or the proportions of the sail, a well-mannered main is the most responsive, tuneable, and adjustable sail on the boat. The mainsail can assume an endless variety of shapes, each beautiful to eye and soul because each shape suits its function perfectly.

For any given situation there is an ideal shape for a main and in most cases, with a good eye for shape and a little caressing here and there, you can persuade your main into the shape you need.

Some sails are pretty automatic, for the shape is substantially built-in and flows from one setting to the next with hardly any fuss. Others require more coaxing and attention to shape them up. I'll concentrate on mains for masthead-rigged boats; particularly the newer high-aspect-ratio sails. I'll start by describing the available adjustments and what they can do for the sail. Then I'll talk about when to use them.

First, let's consider cross sectional shape in terms of two parameters: (1) the depth (camber to chord ratio); and (2) fore-and-aft draft position.

Depth is controlled in different ways in different parts of the sail.

In the lower third, foot adjustments that change the distance from leech to luff have the greatest effect. Imagine for a moment, a 30-footer with a 10′ boom. With the zipper shelf unzipped and outhaul eased, the sail is effectively loose-footed, and it may be a foot or more deep at the boom.

As the outhaul gradually is tightened and the clew moves aft away from the luff, depth is removed and the lower part of the sail is substantially flattened out. Simply doing up the zipper has no real effect on draft even though it can provide some structural support in the after part of the foot.

To further flatter the sail, an additional clew ring or flattening reef about 10″ up the leech can be pulled down and out. Because the sail is narrower (from luff to leech) at the reef ring than it is at the foot, taking the flattening reef out to the black band has the same effect on the sail as taking the clew several inches beyond the band. It can really flatten it out.

Like the outhaul, the flattening reef must be used as a continuous, rather than all-or-nothing adjustment. Often 1/3 or 2/3 of the total adjustment available with the flattening reef can produce the desired effect. There are three main settings: fullest, with outhaul eased; medium, with outhaul at the black band; and flattest with the flattening reef ring at the black band (Fig. 1).

Draft in the body of the mainsail, particularly near the top, is much less sensitive to outhaul changes. But it is very sensitive to changes in mast bend. With a narrow, high-aspect-ratio main, relatively small

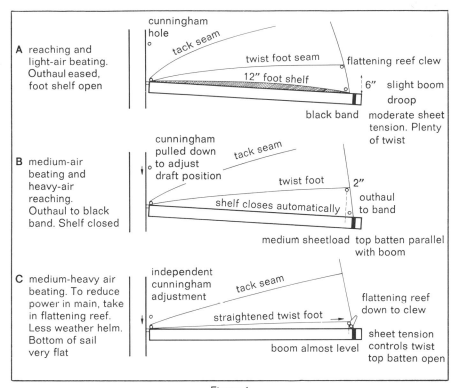

A reaching and light-air beating. Outhaul eased, foot shelf open

cunningham hole

tack seam

twist foot seam

flattening reef clew

12" foot shelf

6" slight boom droop

black band · moderate sheet tension. Plenty of twist

B medium-air beating and heavy-air reaching. Outhaul to black band. Shelf closed

cunningham pulled down to adjust draft position

tack seam

twist foot

2" outhaul to band

shelf closes automatically

medium sheetload · top batten parallel with boom

C medium-heavy air beating. To reduce power in main, take in flattening reef. Less weather helm. Bottom of sail very flat

independent cunningham adjustment

tack seam

straightened twist foot

flattening reef down to clew

boom almost level · sheet tension controls twist top batten open

Figure 1
Effect of Foot Shelf and Flattening Reef on Mainsail Shape

changes in mast bend are dramatic in their effect on the sails. As a result, most of the latest custom boats, One Tonners, Admiral's Cuppers, Canada's Cuppers, as well as many stock boats, are designed with spar-bend control in mind.

Such goodies as adjustable midstays and forestays, movable partner control, movable steps, adjustable permanent backstays and running backstays, enable one to flatten out or deepen the main at will. Virtually, *every* boat can achieve some degree of bend control very easily and sail a little better as a result.

In order to flatten the body of the sail, the mast must take a curve so that the spreader section is forward of both the head and tack. A bend is measured as the forward offset of the mid-point of the luff of the sail from the straight line from head to tack of one-half the fore-and-aft dimension of the mast. This amount

is safe for virtually any offshore boat. For example, if the mast on your boat is eight inches long on its fore-and-aft axis, it is safe to bend it four inches to flatten the sail. You can even reverse the bend four inches (with running backstays) to make the sail fuller.

Newer rigs are being designed to use even more bend. However, always consult your designer before going too far, for spreader failures have occurred where owners did exceed safe bend limits.

The third adjustment that affects the depth of the main is the mainsheet. If mast bend is right and the lower part of the sail already is flattened out, increasing mainsheet tension will, in some particularly versatile mains, actually cause the upper part of the sail to get flatter.

More often however, mains become tight-leeched when trimmed extra hard, and they become deeper.

When you are trimming down, watch the angle of the upper battens carefully. In fresh air, helm balance can be the most important consideration. A tight leech can cause a sudden increase in weather helm if this occurs. And if this occurs it is best to stop trimming the sheet and put up with whatever backwind remains.

Finally, the leech cord can be useful in adding depth in some cases. There are a fair number of mains around with poorly setting leeches that require heavy leech cord tension to keep the battens from tailing off to leeward in light air or on reaches. With such sails it is better to use the leech cord, even to the point of cupping the leech tabling between the battens, in order to increase total camber and continue the body curve of the sail out to the leech.

Fore-and-aft draft position is primarily controlled by luff tension. On high-aspect-ratio sails this adjustment is particularly effective, for the body of the sail lies close to the luff. Increasing luff tension by hauling down the cunningham brings the draft forward rapidly. It is particularly necessary to increase luff tension in windy weather, or when the mast has been bent appreciably.

Bending the mast does reduce draft in the forward part of the sail more than in the after part, but it also tends to leave the sail in a flatter configuration, which is draft aft. Thus increased mast bend, without a cunningham adjustment, produces an excessively draft aft shape. Pulling down on the cunningham restores the configuration to a uniform circular arc (Fig. 2).

For most conditions, the deepest point in the camber of the main should lie about halfway from luff to leech. Getting the camber this far aft in light air or reaching, when a

Figure 2
Effect of Mast Bend on Sail Shape

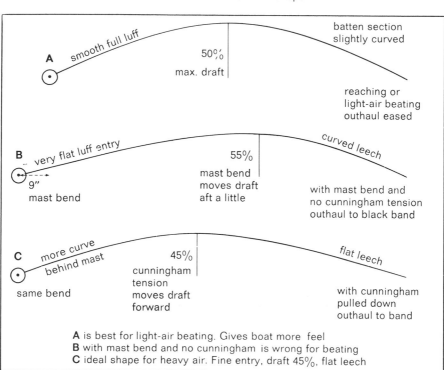

A is best for light-air beating. Gives boat more feel
B with mast bend and no cunningham is wrong for beating
C ideal shape for heavy air. Fine entry, draft 45%, flat leech

straight or reversed mast is feeding cloth into the luff, calls for extremely loose luff tension, even to the point of forming definite wrinkles at the luff.

In moderate to fresh air, more luff tension is required to hold the draft centered as the sail stretches and the mast is bent. Be careful not to overdo cunningham tension, however, since extra fullness forward increases backwind. And flattening out the back of the sail reduces the power produced.

These adjustments to the sectional shapes are always important, but also it is necessary to come back to the basic adjustments; sheet and traveler trim. Any aerodynamicist will tell you that the angle at which you set an air foil to the flow has more to do with the power produced than factors such as depth of draft or draft position. If the sail is lined up too close to the direction of flow (under-trimmed) it backs slightly or even develops a severe luff and produces little power. Too close a trim can lead to a total separation of flow from the sail surface (stalling), with a drastic reduction in lift and increased drag.

So for any sail, not just a main, the ultimate question, when trimming it, is simply, "How hard should I pull it in?" This may seem pretty elementary, but the trouble is that the right answer is so hard to find. The difference between a champion and the runner-up, even at the Olympic level, often is measured in very small changes in the trim angle of the sails.

When we talk about trim angle, it is important to remember that a sail, unlike a rigid foil, is capable of variations in angle (twist) at each height in the sail. Generally, the bottom of the sail is trimmed-in closer to the centerline than the top, so it's the amount and distribution of twist that is vital both to the performance of the boat as well as the basic trim of a given point in the sail such as the boom.

Control of trim and twist is affected

Figure 3
"Frigate," British Admiral's Cup Team Captain, set up for "point high conditions." Main is trimmed down hard with little twist and a well closed leech. A boat which doesn't enjoy as perfect helm balance in these conditions might need to put in some of the flattening reef to open the lower leech

when going to weather by a combination of the mainsheet and traveler; on reaches by the vang and mainsheet. Suppose we're beating with the mainsheet cleated. Traveler adjustments can trim or ease the entire sail in and out, and will vary the trim angle at all heights uniformly and equally (Fig. 3).

Changes in twist, on the other hand, can be made by varying mainsheet tension. With a very tight mainsheet, the leech of the main can be made to be virtually straight. Easing the sheet opens up the top of the sail faster than the bottom, and this adds twist. This is the configuration where the upper sections are set at a more open angle to the

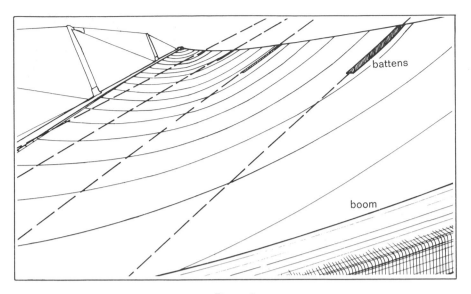

Figure 4
Looking at a sail from directly under the foot gives the mainsail trimmer the best view of the cross-sectional shape and particularly of the batten angles and twist

center line than the middle of the sail or the section at the boom.

When reaching, the boom extends out beyond the end of the traveler and the vang must take over from the mainsheet to provide the downward tension to control twist.

When you are beating, the flow over the main is largely controlled by the genoa, and therefore, logically you should look at mainsail trim as a process of matching the main to the genoa.

First and most important, always set the main with some twist to match the difference in the apparent wind flow at different heights in the rig, caused primarily because the head of the genoa is more open than the foot.

With a masthead rig, the widening of the wind-angle aloft for the main is much less extreme than on a $7/8$ or $3/4$ rig, where the head of the genoa ends well below the head of the main. Stalling the head of the main by over-trimming is less of a problem with a masthead rig. But it does happen, and stalling often gives you an upper limit to the amount of mainsheet tension to apply. Because

of genoa overlap, the bottom of a main is virtually stall-proof on a beat, and it can be moved around a bit to achieve proper helm balance and power requirements without much worry.

There are several ways to check whether the main is trimmed correctly from an aerodynamic point of view. Telltales can help. I use a telltale right at the leech of both the upper two batten-pockets, and sets of streamers about half way from the luff to the leech in the upper half of the sail. These check for stalling caused by overtrim.

If the flow is attached (not stalled), the leech telltales stream straight aft from the sail and the lee side telltales flow smoothly aft as well. The turbulent wake of the mast makes the leeward ones harder to read, but still they are very helpful. Weatherside telltales on high-aspect-ratio mains are relatively poor indicators for undertrim compared to the weather-side telltales on a genoa; again because of mast wake. However, they can help on some boats with particularly clean masts or on boats with wider, low-aspect-ratio mains. It is worth checking to see if the weather telltales behave in any orderly fashion that you can correlate with good trim or speed.

I also look closely at the angle between each batten and the boom when I sight them from below the center of the boom. In conditions requiring the least twist, all the battens may be cocked to weather of the boom. In conditions requiring substantial twist, I use less sheet tension and the upper battens should fall progressively more to leeward compared with the lower ones (Fig. 4).

The top batten, though, is the best indicator. It will need to vary from an average setting that is a few degrees to weather of being parallel with the boom to being somewhat angled to leeward of the boom angle in conditions that require substantial twist.

Study the luff of the sail for the subtle signs that indicate it is just on edge. When the sail is trimmed for the headsail setting and wind conditions, it will go light all the way up to the head when the boat is steered too high and the genoa luffs. By looking up the mainsail luff from the lee side, often it is easier to read a slight softening of the sail that would be hard or impossible to detect from the weather side.

Mainsail trim is particularly critical in several situations because stalling in the upper part of the sail is likely to occur. Light-air beating and close reaching are two of the most important.

In light air upwind, many boats tend to have lee helm. It's tempting to treat the main purely as a balancing vane and trim it to try to balance the boat. The problem here is that several factors combine to make the main very stall-sensitive.

First, stalling is far more likely to occur on any lifting surface at low flow speeds — i.e., light air. Second, the genoa usually is eased out a bit in light air (especially if the boat has lee helm), so the apparent wind angle at the head of the main is very wide

relative to a more normal wind speed. As a result, it is easy to have the main over-trimmed for such conditions. Third, any high aspect ratio mainsail is stall-sensitive to begin with, when compared to lower aspect ratio sails used in the past.

In very light-air conditions you must do everything you can to increase the power produced by the main. You can do this by straightening or even reversing the mastbend to get greater fullness, by slacking up the luff substantially to get the draft aft, and by easing the outhaul

Photo 5
In light air mainsail trim is very important. Note very full main, draft well aft, boom to weather of centerline, and top batten open

a moderate amount. If it is necessary, use some leech cord to keep the leech from dumping off to leeward. Carry the traveler well to weather so the boom is positioned on or near centerline. *But,* be very careful not to oversheet and close the upper part of the leech.

The top batten either should be parallel to the boom or at an open angle of up to 5° or so. The lower two or three battens can be kicked well up to weather without stalling the sail because of the bending of the lower wind flow by the genoa overlap. But the upper part of the sail must be open (Photo 5). Try to keep the main working as a lifting surface. Stalling reduces forward drive dramatically, and does little if anything for balance beyond what careful trimming *to* the stall can accomplish.

Because flow over the main is so strongly dependent on proper genoa trim, the trim situation changes any time the jib is eased a bit; to foot off in sloppy water, for example, or drive for a mark that has been overstood slightly. As the jib is eased, its head tends to twist out, opening the upper slot. The local apparent wind for the main swings rapidly aft and if the upper part of the main isn't twisted out simultaneously, the sail will stall (Photo 6).

When close reaching, the stalling problem is even more severe because the genoa staysail, tallboy or spinnaker staysail have less wind-bending effect up high than they do down low. In some reaching situations I'm sure it is actually necessary to stall the top of the main in order to get the most drive out of the body of the sail. But in general I think most people do overvang their mains, especially in light to moderate air. Try experimenting with a more twisted shape. Allow it to twist to the point where the sail luffs evenly all the way up the mast.

General guidelines for reaching should include having the main extra full. The foot shelf should be eased all the way out and the mast

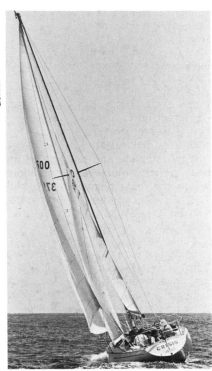

Gordon Menzie

Photo 6
Substantial twist in main is required to match genoa staysail and jib topsail flow patterns created by double head rig

reversed by easing the backstay and setting the running backstay if one is available. Beware, however, of making the sail too full when close reaching with a starcut or a spinnaker and a large inside headsail or staysail.

The apparent wind can be bent so far forward by the other sails that the main will have to be trimmed almost as it is for beating: with the boom near the centerline and only a medium full shape in the sail. Do not bag the sail out fully until the boom can be eased 15° or so to leeward *without* luffing the main. This is particularly true in fresh air when steering becomes a problem. In such conditions keep the main fairly flat and ease the vang in gusts.

I've discussed some situations where insufficient twist can cause stalling problems. But in moderate air beating conditions particularly in smooth water ("point high" conditions) relatively hard sheeting with little twist and a very closed leech can be very fast. The genoa is sheeted the hardest and flattest in these conditions and its wind-bending effect on top of the higher wind speed itself, combines to make the main very stall resistant.

If the stability and balance of the boat permit, these are conditions where the least twist is successful. This is a situation where the battens will be angled to weather of the boom which should be located on centerline, or nearly so.

Outhaul the sail to flatten the lower third, and add mastbend so that you still have plenty of depth and power but backwinding is minimal. Use *only* enough luff tension to hold the draft near the middle of the sail. Unless weather helm is a problem you want the curvature in the sail to extend well back into the batten panels to add power and help your pointing.

A fairly tight-leeched main is close-winded, not only because it keeps the bow up and adds helm, but also because the upwash forward of the main is greater when the main is heavily loaded and gives the jib a bit of a lift in its own apparent wind.

As the air freshens further, weather helm may increase to the point where balancing the boat becomes the major consideration for boat speed. A boat does need some weather helm to "eat" to weather properly. But by far the most common error committed in a breeze is to sail with too much weather helm.

Excessive heel angle is the worst offender in creating a severe helm, but bad mainsail trim often is just as basic. In fresh-air conditions, try for a flat cross-sectional shape and an easy leech. Bend the mast to the maximum amount available and set up a flattening reef in order to open the lower leech and straighten out the bottom of the sail. Set up the cunningham hard and make sure the draft is noticeably forward of center.

Don't twist the sail excessively but just ease the sheet a few inches so that luffing or backwind spreads most of the way up the luff in the hardest gusts. With the sail flattened out a great deal, more traveler can be let out in the gusts without having the backwind get out of control. The traveler should be played in and out constantly to help keep the boat on her feet and balanced.

In any racing situation, coordination between helmsman and sail trimmer is valuable. But in fresh gusty air it is essential. If you're on the traveler, watch the helmsman, anticipate which way he wants to put the bow and use the main to help him get there. And always remember rule #1 for mainsail trimming in heavy air: when in doubt let it luff. Don't be afraid of backwind, just try very hard to keep the boat balanced and "in the groove" (Photo 7).

Mainsail trimming for the most part does boil down to some pretty common sense ideas: the sail should be deeper and more powerful for footing, reaching and rough water; it

Photo 7
Mainsail shown here is nicely under control with about 1/4 to 1/3 of the sail allowed to backwind to maintain balance and keep the boat on her feet

must be flatter and harder-leeched for high pointing and smooth water; and generally it should have more twist in lighter air when the jib is eased a bit, or when the main is overpowered. However, there also are some things that go a bit beyond more adjustment. These are the basics of what you must build into your main if it is to be a really successful sail.

For beating, the deepest point in the sail should lie naturally about 50% of the way from luff to leech. Many mains have the draft much too far forward and are far too flat in the leech area. The result is that they have to be forced into decent shape. A main with a straight entry and smooth arc-shaped sections minimizes backwind and puts the power-producing center of the sail quite far aft of the mast where the turbulence from the rigging and spar is minimal.

The next thing to look for is adequate draft for light-air work to windward, as well as for reaching and running. In high aspect ratio sails a good light-air shape can be remarkably deep but still permit good control in a breeze.

The sail also should be able to be set with plenty of depth, *and twist,* without the leech's tripping or dumping to leeward. Many mains *look* all right with the vang or sheet socked down and the leech cord hanked in tight. But they are slow sails because the whole top is going to stall if it is trimmed in and it can't be eased up without having the roach dumping off.

Finally, a good main has to have the capability of being controlled and flattened adequately for fresh-air beating. It must be able to be sheeted down hard without having the leech close and without generating excessive backwind.

If you have a good mainsail and you learn to work with it, you'll enjoy your sailing more. You'll enjoy it more because you're going to be faster and also because it is a pleasure to have a sail that really looks right.

The Mainsail Leech

Key to shape and power   Bruce Dyson

You **may not be** aware that the leech of your mainsail is perhaps the best indicator to tell you when the shape of the rest of the sail is correct. But the leech area is not an independent part of the sail as many sailors still believe, and when an adjustment is made to the leech, there are other adjustments that usually must be made to keep the proper shape in the rest of the sail.

For example, if the mainsheet is tightened to decrease the amount of twist in the leech, there are at least two or three adjustments that must also be made. The cunningham may have to be tightened or eased, the outhaul may have to be tightened or eased and the traveller may have to be moved up or down.

But the biggest single item affecting the shape of any mainsail leech is the tension applied to the mainsheet. On a high performance dinghy, for instance, the mainsheet entirely controls the amount of twist in the sail. If a sail is cut too full, in most cases the upper part of the sail, and the leech, will luff — even in light air.

For this reason, a mainsail must be cut reasonably flat in the middle and upper sections for top performance. And this includes light air sails! If the sail is cut this way, it can be sheeted lightly without having the forward section of the upper part of the sail break into a luff.

If such a flat or medium cut sail is used in light air, the boat will not only go faster but may, in some cases, point higher because the leech will remain soft i.e. the sail never hooks to windward, remaining either parallel to the centerline of the boat, or dropping to leeward. This means that all the components of force will be directed ahead. (See Figures 1A and 1B.)

As you might have guessed, the top of a mainsail is even more critical in this regard because the total sail area here is pulling forward, even at the trailing edge (see Figures 2A and 2B).

The position of the traveller is a big contributor to proper leech control. Personally, I feel the traveller should never be pulled to windward above centerline on any boat that does not have an overlapping jib, but I realize this is not a hard and fast rule because of the many potentially different cuts of sails.

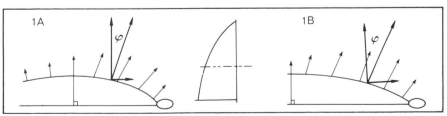

Figure 1
Note the forward components of figure 1A are smaller than those of figure 1B. All components of the section in figure 1B are pulling forward compared to the 1A section where the leech components are pulling aft. Also note the difference in sail fullness in each figure. The flatter section is faster.

Figure 2
A similar situation exists here as in figure 1, but the flatter
camber of figure 2B optimizes total forward drive. Here again,
a flatter section is a faster section.

If the sailmaker has built the main
with a tight leech, it will be necessary
to let more twist into the sail to keep
the leech from hooking to windward.
This is often done by *soft sheeting*,
but using this technique means that
the traveller may have to be pulled
slightly to windward to keep the right
overall position for the leech. A tight
leech can also be helped by pre-
bending the mast which will flatten
out the middle and upper sections of
the sail and loosen the leech.

If the mainsail is cut with a full or
loose leech, take the bend out of the
mast and make sure the traveller
does not go higher than the centerline.

In four to five knots of wind, leech
tension must be changed constantly
because slight changes in wind
strength are very significant. For example, if the wind increases from
four to five knots, it has increased
25%. But the boat will also increase
in speed, which will create an increase of wind speed over the deck
of perhaps 35%! A one knot increase
in wind is a minor change at 20
knots. But as you can see, at four
knots it becomes a major one.

Look at it another way. If, in the
same four knots of wind, two boats
are sailing side by side upwind with
one boat moving at three knots and
the other moving at 3.25 knots, the
apparent wind, or wind over the
deck, of the first boat is six knots.
But the second boat's apparent wind
is 6.25 knots or about 5% more wind
velocity — strictly because of boat
speed.

In light air these differences may
be, in some cases, as great as two
to one; with one boat having twice
the apparent wind of the other. So
you can see how important it is to
get the boat moving. And the best
way is to not oversheet the main or
tighten the leech. Both can create
excessive drag.

In a light to medium breeze (6-10
knots) a sail always looks its best. It
is smooth and the shape will appear
to look right. But very often the leech
may be too tight. The best way to see
this is to get someone else to sail
your boat, and you follow directly
astern in an outboard. From this position it should be easy to see how
tight the leech actually is

If you can see *any* part of the leeward side of the second batten up
from the boom, this is a good indication that the leech is too tight. There
are three ways to correct the problem: (1) ease the mainsheet, (2) ease
the traveller or (3) bend the mast.
Though bending the mast is one
solution most people do not think of,
I feel it is the first thing one should
do; adjusting the mainsheet comes
second, and moving the traveller to
leeward is the final step.

Be aware that it is very easy to
overtrim the mainsail in this 6-10
knot area. Doing so takes much of
the power out of the sail, and in
itself, will create a light leech, even
in the upper sections. Many middle
of the fleet sailors do this because
the sail will appear to be very
smooth and wrinkle-free, giving the
impression of a well set main.

But once again, if you get out of the boat and look at the sail from behind, it should become very obvious what is wrong with the sail trim.

So far I've talked of leech tension in light air and medium air. What happens when the air comes on 10-15 knots? Here again, leech tension is still the largest single factor in optimising boat speed, and it is still the best indicator of when the rest of the sail is set correctly.

In these wind strengths a leech having less twist is the answer. Try to eliminate twist by first tightening the mainsheet. But remember, any time the mainsheet is really sheeted home the traveller must be eased, or the leech, if it is properly cut, will hook to windward in this wind strength.

Here again, if you can look at the leech from a point directly astern you will get a much better idea of what to do about a bad leech. If you can see any leeward part of the second batten, the leech is probably too tight.

Now for my favorite type of sailing — heavy air. First pull the mainsheet in until you think you're going to break something. Then make it even a little tighter. The mast must be restricted from bending too much and the traveller should be *well eased* not only to prevent a tight and hooking leech, but also to minimize heeling moment. In the stronger breezes, the traveller position and amount of mast bend are far more important than mainsheet tension, assuming the sheet is pulled in very tight. In heavy airs, it is the traveller that controls the leech and heeling moment, and mast bend that controls the amount of power in the rig.

In heavy air, the first consideration is the outhaul. Tightening it will flatten the chords of the sail which in turn will flatten the leech (see figure 3). The second thing to change is the cunningham. If the draft is too far back in the sail, the leech will hook naturally to windward. Applying some cunningham will move the draft forward and will flatten the leech, even though the chord depth remains about the same (see figure 4).

The last thing to do to soften the leech in heavy air is to ease the traveller. But don't do it if you can keep the boat sailing flat enough with the traveller on centerline. When you do ease the traveller always be

Figure 3

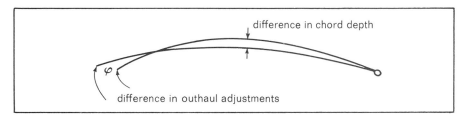

difference in chord depth

difference in outhaul adjustments

Figure 4

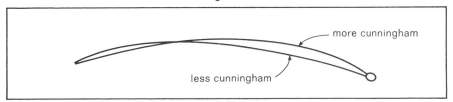

more cunningham

less cunningham

ready to pull it back to centerline if you hit a lull in the breeze.

Most of the time in medium and heavy air the mast must be prevented from bending instead of inducing bend as you might do in light breezes. In these wind strengths the mainsheet is putting enormous bending loads on the rig, and the mast must be correctly made to fit the sail to get maximum power.

In heavy air the depth chord ratios of the middle and upper sections should be reasonably flat. In medium air they can be somewhat fuller. But in very light air they should not be cut much fuller than they are for heavy air. The depth/chord ratios have to be worked out for every boat. But my point is that a flat sail *does work* in light air. A flat cut sail softens the leech which makes the requirement for sheet tension far less critical.

Remember, the leech of the mainsail is the key indicator of sail shape and power. But keeping it properly adjusted is a constant process of adjusting the mainsheet, outhaul, cunningham and mast bend to give it the proper shape for maximum drive and speed. It is not easy to do, but it is the most important thing you can do!

How to Trim a Cat

Tips on the full-batten main   Don McKibbin

Opinions on the proper sail trim for catamarans are as numerous as are classes, so I will confine myself here to some basic guidelines that can be used as a starting point to maximizing sail performance.

In the typical cat-rigged catamaran mainsail with full battens let us assume the sail has a good basic shape with the position of the chord depth, in general, about 14% of the chord length and located 40% to 45% aft of the mast. (See figure 1A.)

Remember that while full batten sails offer definite advantages for achieving proper sail shape a good sail can also be handicapped by poor battens or battens that are either too stiff or too limber for the existing conditions.

Not only stiffness, but also how tightly the battens are loaded into the pockets has a definite effect on the amount of camber in the sail.

Ideally they should be tapered from the leading edge to a point approximately 40% of the batten length and they should be relatively more limber near the head to maintain a constant shape in the sail.

It is unusual to have a single set of battens that can handle all wind conditions. Spend time selecting and working with your battens, whether they are fiberglass or wood. You will be repaid with better boat speed.

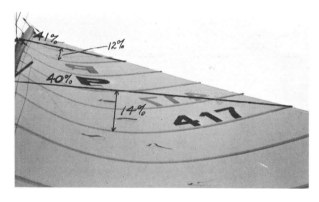

Figure 1a
A full battened
sail showing
proper camber depth
and position from luff

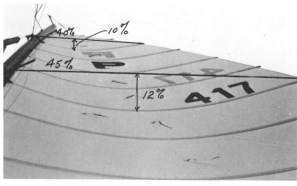

Figure 1b
The same sail with mast
bend and downhaul
tension applied. Note
how draft is reduced but
point of maximum depth
remains about the same

Once you have the proper sail shape it must be trimmed for maximum driving force and minimum heeling force.

When sailing on the wind, the first place to check is the leech area of the sail. It is critical in a large roach full batten sail. Do not trim so that the leech is hooked to weather because it will act as a brake and also create excessive weather helm and heeling force.

The plane of the mainsail can actually be trimmed to the line the boat makes as it moves *through the apparent wind,* not the centerline of the boat. Depending on the amount of leeway, which can vary from 3° to 8° depending on the boat, the leech can be trimmed to this finer angle. (See figure 2.)

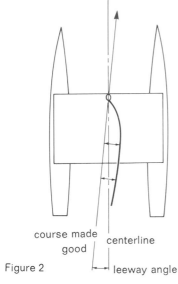

course made good / centerline

Figure 2   leeway angle

Most small catamarans use a bendy mast for draft control. The amount of bend influences the amount of luff roach the sailmaker builds into the sail. When the mast is properly bent, the sail should have the correct amount of camber and it should be located the proper distance aft of the mast.

With the stable sailcloth used today a problem might arise in light to moderate air when the principal means of bending the mast becomes

mainsail tension on the leech: if the sail is oversheeted a tight leech will result. But setting the sheet and then utilizing the traveller to adjust trim will avoid this tight or "hooking" leech.

As the wind increases, compressive loads on the mast will begin bending it and this will result in a looser leech. More sheet trim is necessary. And to keep the draft from moving too far aft in the sail the downhaul also must be used. But this downhaul luff tension must be coordinated with mast bend in order to keep the draft in the proper location.

Figure 1B shows how mast bend can flatten a full batten mainsail. You can see how the increased bend has drawn some of the draft out of the sail; and by increasing downhaul tension the maximum chord depth remains approximately the same distance from the luff.

If hiking cannot hold the boat reasonably level when going to weather, rather than easing the sheet, ease the traveller outboard. The amount of heel is probably as good a guide as anything for proper traveller adjustment.

Off the wind the traveller will be eased even further outboard and, depending on the sail, some bend may have to be kept in the mast to keep the draft from moving too far forward.

If the boat is rigged with a jib there are some additional trim problems. The jib has two purposes. It is a very effective sail itself, but also directs rapidly moving air over the lee side of the mainsail, particularly in the mast area where flow is normally very turbulent. The air coming off the leech of the jib can flow smoothly through this area and greatly improve mainsail efficiency. However, the jib must have the proper shape and be correctly trimmed to do this.

The jib is controlled by luff tension, sheet lead position, sheet tension, and battens if they are present.

One of the main factors in jib shape is luff sag. It is present to some degree on all boats but if it becomes excessive, the result is an overly full sail; particularly near the head where chord lengths are short.

If there is excessive luff sag it becomes very difficult to maintain the proper slot shape between jib and main, for the jib leech is going to be tight and will direct air into the main instead of *along* it. The backwinding that results is quite easy to see, although it may not be quite as obvious with a full batten main.

Luff tension has the same effect on the jib as with the main: increased tension draws the draft forward and eases the leech, and less tension moves the draft back and tends to tighten the leech.

If the sail has an adjustable luff you have considerable adjustment possibilities. But if the jib is secured at the tack, luff tension adjustment becomes limited and you must properly stretch the sail on the luff wire initially.

In light to moderate winds the sheet lead will normally be well inboard to narrow the slot and increase sail camber. As wind velocity increases it should be moved outboard and aft, if possible, to open the slot and ease the leech.

On boats having a fixed fore and aft lead position like the P-Cat and Hobie 16 some adjustment can be made by moving the jib up or down on the headstay. One good starting point is to try and have roughly equal sheet tension on the foot and leech.

The proper amount of sheet will vary with wind velocity, but the tendency is to overtrim. Try to develop an even looking slot, and then check your speed with another boat, using various lead and sheet positions. When you have maximum boat speed for a certain condition, mark the jib as well as the mainsheet so you can come back to the same setting without being off an inch or two one way or the other.

Jib sheet settings can be very critical and should always be matched to the mainsail sheeting to maintain an effective slot. And just as with the mainsail battens, a definite amount of shape control can be affected by carefully selecting and tapering the jib battens.

Figure 3A shows how a tight jib leech backwinds the main. Figure 3B shows the effects of a loose leech, and 3C depicts the correct jib shape and trim for optimum smooth flow over the main.

Remember that even in a one-design boat you must work out the

Figure 3

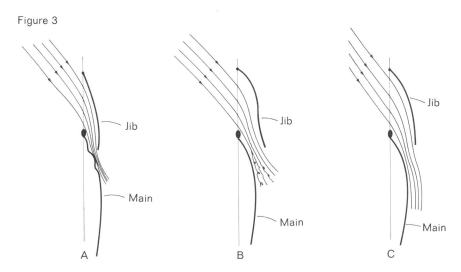

lead and sheet trim for your own boat. There is enough difference in the rig and sails so that what is correct for one boat is not necessarily right for another. You can use the fairlead positions on a boat that is going well, but only as a starting point.

Proper sail trim for reaching and running becomes more a matter of trimming for maximum effectiveness from the individual sail, though the slot must still be considered until you are almost dead downwind.

One approximate trim guide off the wind is to ease sheets until a luff appears and then sheet in just enough to remove the luff. But to get even closer to the optimum angle of incidence try sheeting in roughly 5° from the luffing point.

Any modern, well designed catamaran is capable of high performance, but it is essential to have proper sail trim in order to bring out its full potential. And the best way to learn that is to go out and practice!

Genoa and Jib

Halyard Hoist and Sheet Lead

The basics of genoa set   Norris Strawbridge

The tall masts and high aspect ratio rigs found on most boats today have made the genoa the prime source of power while on the wind.

Wind tunnel tests have shown that a jib in a stable attitude and with a constant air flow will be most efficient if the draft or maximum chord depth is one-third to one-half the distance aft from the headstay. A horizontal section of the sail should appear as a smoothly decelerating curve. (See figure 1.)

Although it is most efficient, this shape is the least forgiving and is easily disturbed by slight changes in air flow caused by pitching or changes in the relative wind. If the draft is moved slightly forward (figure 2), the sail will become much more forgiving and overall efficiency may even improve.

But the draft should never be allowed to move aft of the center of the sail. This shape (figure 3) usually referred to as "blown out," results in excessive backwinding of the main, produces very little forward drive, and distorts the leech causing the slot to close and the whole sailplan to stall.

Sail shape is controlled by three things: sheet tension, lead position and halyard tension. Increasing halyard tension will move the draft forward and flatten the body of the sail. (See figure 4.) Easing the halyard until the luff begins to scallop will allow the sail to bag and this will increase drive in light air or when close reaching.

To get your jib halyard properly adjusted, first run the jib shackle up to the truck on a messenger and allow it to seat in the sheave. Then make the wire halyard just hand

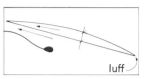

Figure 1

Figure 2

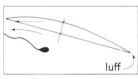

Figure 3

tight and clearly mark it, for this is the point of maximum hoist. The full load of the sail on the wire will stretch it enough to keep the shackle from jamming in the sheave later.

Next, determine the maximum strength of the wire halyard; if it is

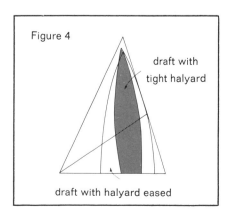

Figure 4

draft with tight halyard

draft with halyard eased

more than 4,000 lbs., it will be stronger than the head on any 5 oz. jib so use this lower figure as your maximum allowable load. Now borrow a dynamometer and you are ready to calibrate your halyard.

First slack the halyard until the luff starts to scallop. This is your lower limit or zero point. Mark the halyard at this point with a small seizing where it comes through the sheave out of the mast.

Next, increase halyard tension marking the mast opposite the halyard seizing for every 500 lbs. of load up to the maximum limit. But increase this halyard tension only when the boat is head to wind and then allow the sail to readjust itself before taking a reading with the dynamometer.

If you try to increase the tension while the sail is full, you will have to overcome the friction of the hanks on the stay as well as the tension in the luff of the sail.

If you reach maximum hoist before you attain the maximum allowable load, slack off on the halyard and take a bite with a cunningham at the jib's tack fitting. If you plan to use a cunningham or several stretchy luff sails, put a mark at one inch intervals on the mast and start a chart showing inches of hoist versus pounds of tension for each sail.

For example, your 5 oz. number one with the cunningham completely taken up might have 3,500 pounds on the luff when the mark on the halyard is eight inches below the spot it leaves the mast. Keep a running record for all your sails and you will get a graph of the best halyard tension for various wind speeds.

Correct sheet lead position is also extremely important. The lead always should be positioned so that the head of the sail luffs at the same time as the foot. If you have tufts of wool in the luff, use them to position the lead for normal sailing. If the top tuft stalls first, move the lead forward until they all stall at the same time.

If the mainsheet traveller is moved to leeward to control weather helm, the jib lead should be brought aft. This will ease the leech and allow it to fall off and open the slot. Also as the halyard is tensioned, the leech will be tightened, and unless a cunningham is used the lead must again be brought aft. In light air with a loose halyard move the lead forward to close the slot. This is also a good time to experiment with inboard tracks and narrower sheeting angles.

A genoa can be efficient for close reaching until the wind reaches about 50° relative if you have a reacher or a spanker, and can be used up to 85° if the only other sail you have is a spinnaker.

When reaching with the jib, ease the halyard as much as possible and start by moving the lead aft. This will open the slot and will, in effect, widen your sheeting base. It is perfectly correct to have the head of the sail luff slightly. In fact if it doesn't the body probably will be overtrimmed. Constant attention to the sheet is very important on this point of sail and tufts on the luff are invaluable.

Finally, when you are satisfied that your sail is properly set never cleat it and relax. Continual evaluation of the sheet, halyard, and lead positions is an absolute requirement for good sail trim.

Adjusting a Genoa

More basics of headsail trim   Peter Schoonmaker

Sailmakers and others often make the setting of a sail look like an art. While there may be some truth to this, the basics are really very simple. Take the genoa jib for example. In Photo 1, we see a jib that is prop-erly set. To obtain this shape we have first taken up the backstay to get a firm headstay. In light air the headstay should be just firm. In medium air, it should be quite tight, and in heavy air, it should be as hard

Photo 1

Marcia Campbell

Marcia Campbell

Backstay tension for:
Light air

Medium air
Photo 2

Heavy air

as you dare to pull the backstay (Photo 2).

I might mention in passing that a jib can be cut to compensate for a sagging headstay simply by putting a hollow in the luff of the sail. This is done all the time with boats that can't get their headstay tight. There may be any number of reasons why the headstay can't be taken up as far as is really necessary. The hull may be too old to stand the strain; the rig may not be designed to take the strain; or it may be simply that a cruising man does not care to go those few higher degrees into the wind and doesn't want to subject his boat to such a tight rig.

But no matter whether the luff of the sail is compensated for by hollowing out the luff, or is achieved by tightening the headstay, the next step is to have the halyard tension at the proper level for the particular wind condition that exists. What you must achieve with halyard tension is to have the draft in the sail in the right place.

Photos 3 and 4 show the genoa with different halyard tensions. You can see the different draft locations. The more strain on the halyard, the tighter the luff and the farther forward the draft will move. In Photo 3, you can see the draft is quite far aft (because of a looser luff). In Photo 4 it is quite far forward because of increased halyard tension.

But in order to keep moving toward a total correct genoa setting, there are some other adjustments that also must take place when the luff is tensioned for light or for heavy weather. First, the fairlead that carries the genoa sheet must be moved each time the wind condition changes. In light air, it should be moved forward a couple of inches from an optimum midpoint. And in heavy air it should be moved aft several inches from the midpoint. If possible, you should also try to move the fairlead inboard in light air for this will often be beneficial (Photo 5).

If sea conditions are smooth, the lead can remain inboard even if the

Photo 3

Photo 4

wind begins to blow harder. But you should move the fairlead aft just as though the lead were on the outboard track. Fairlead tracks will vary with different boats but it is a good idea to have at least two tracks, one outboard and one inboard, on an ocean racer (Photo 6).

Light air conditions may allow you to have the clew of the genoa, the fairlead in other words, as close as seven or eight degrees off the centerline. But, in heavy weather, you probably will have to have the fairlead out at about ten or eleven degrees. A heavy cruising boat usually will not be able to carry close sheeting angles like these, and you probably will create more leeway by trying to bring the lead angles in this close.

Photo 5

 appears with vertical credit text "Marcia Campbell" along the left side.

Photo 6

If you are interested in figuring the fairlead angles on your boat, here is a simple formula to use. Simply measure the distance from the tack of the sail to the clew and divide this distance into the distance from the fairlead to the centerline. For example, if the distance from the tack to the clew is 15′ and the distance from the clew to the center-line is 3′ the answer is .200. Trigonometry tells us this is the sine of the enclosed angle which, in this case, is just under 12°. Using the same foot dimensions, other angles would be 7° = .1212; 9° = .1564; 11° = .1908.

Once you have the draft in the proper location for the wind condi-

tions you are sailing in, move the jib fairlead aft of the point you feel is the proper spot. When you sheet the sail in under this condition, it should have too flat a foot and the leech should sag.

To find the right fairlead position, slowly move the fairlead forward again until the following things occur. First, as you luff into the wind, the backwind in the jib should be even all along the leading edge, but it should start halfway up the luff. Second, the foot of the genoa should be slightly tighter than the leech. It should be just touching the shrouds but the area aloft should be several inches from the spreader: this assumes the spreader tip and the chainplates are about the same distance from the mast. Finally, the middle two thirds of the leech should parallel the curvature of the mainsail.

You must be careful not to stretch the leech of a genoa by moving the clew of the sail too far forward. This often occurs among inexperienced sailors. When they see a flutter along the leech, they attempt to remedy it by moving the fairlead forward to put a downward strain on the leech.

Once a leech has been stretched this way there is only one remedy: to hollow it out by removing the area that has been stretched. This of course means the sail now will have more leech hollow than normal and consequently less sail area.

What should you do to correct a fluttering leech? If there is a leech-line present, tighten it just enough to stop the fluttering. A little quiver doesn't hurt half so much as a cupped or tight leech. In fact, some sailmakers build a little flutter into the leech on the theory that the cloth of the sail panels will stretch more than will the stitched tabling on the leech.

With proper use, the sail should develop into a nice clean leech that neither fades to leeward, flutters, nor hooks to weather.

After you have given the sail some reasonable use, particularly in the

Photo 7

wind conditions the sail was built for, look the sail over again with these points in mind. Look at the luff to see whether the roping has been put on evenly with no excessive puckering when the halyard is firmly set up.

One other thing that might cause you to worry is the flapping of excess foot roach. If you do have a good bit of roach built into the foot, use a leechline to quiet it down. When you are sailing close hauled, it flaps simply because it is unsup-ported cloth (Photo 7). But it does add valuable sail area on a reach. This reminds me to mention that when you are reaching, don't forget to move your fairlead out and forward. Move it far enough forward so that it keeps the upper half of the leech from floating too much from twist. On a 30 footer, you may have to move the lead forward a foot or more.

If your genoa still doesn't behave after you have worked with it for a period of time, and you have used it correctly, do call your sailmaker. He may find you are sheeting the sail the wrong way. Who knows, you might be using the same sheeting as you did on the old genoa you have replaced, and the new sail isn't built quite the same way. Your sailmaker usually can spot this right away and save you many hours of seemingly fruitless adjustments.

Of course, once in a blue moon you may get a lemon, and in that case it may either be a case of minor adjustments done back in the loft, or, in a very few cases, you may be in line for a whole new sail. But always try and work the solution out for yourself first. You'll be surprised how much you'll learn in the process.

Genoa Overlap

Getting the most from LP

John R. Stanton

Headsail sheeting practices assume increasing importance with each incremental amount of overlap. It is essential that the airstream leaving the genoa leech flow parallel to or slightly convergent with the adjacent mainsail section.

A flow that is too strongly convergent will "backwind" the mainsail and reduce its effectiveness while a divergent flow results in a loss of genoa drive and possible stalling along the mainsail's foot, which increases drag.

Genoa trim angle is largely established by the amount of overlap and the location of the trimming point. A beamy boat is better for optimum genoa trim since it allows more settings for the athwartship adjustment of the genoa sheet lead blocks.

A genoa with a large overlap must be sheeted with the clew positioned well aft, which can restrict the trim angle possibilities.

As a general rule, the trim angle for a 150% LP masthead genoa should be at least 7° greater than the trim angle measured between the centerline and the mainsail boom. A 180% genoa should be at least 5° larger than the trim angle of the boom. Anything less reduces boat performance, for sail interaction will become retrogressive as the trim angle of the genoa is decreased to that of the mainsail.

The geometric divergence, or decalage, as it is called in aerodynamics, between the adjacent genoa and mainsail chord lines is necessary because of the downwash streaming

DEFINITION OF TERMS

Figure 1

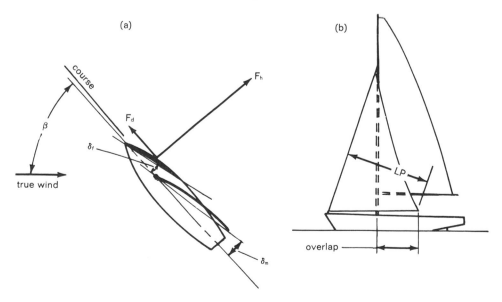

from the leech of the genoa.

It is possible to determine the heel and drive forces for any craft on different headings and sheeting angles. There are three methods available: analytical, wind tunnel tests, and full scale tests. But the last is probably the most difficult because of the problems involved in simultaneously controlling several interrelated parameters.

Let us consider a small fast ⅞ rig sloop in a moderate breeze sailing on a heading of 40° to the true wind. Optimum genoa trim angle is between 15° and 16° (see Figure 2A). If the genoa is overtrimmed to 7½°, the driving force will be reduced by 23%! And from Figure 2B we see the corresponding increase of heeling force will be only about 2%.

These characteristics are typical of most overlapping headsails and help to demonstrate why the genoa is a very effective sail.

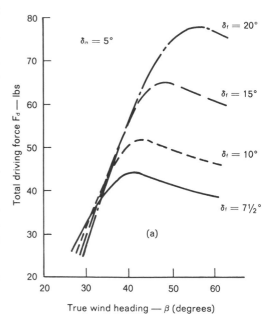

VARIATION OF DRIVE & HEEL FORCES WITH CHANGES
TO GENOA TRIM ANGLE FOR A SMALL SLOOP Figure 2

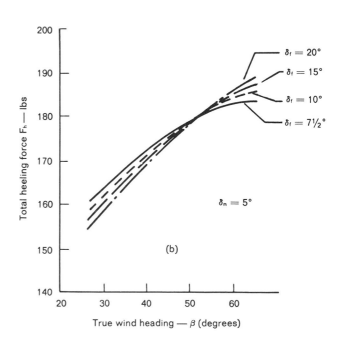

Figures 2A and 2B show that a variation in the trimming angle of the headsail will produce a large change in driving power but a modest change in heeling force.

But the diagrams also point up the constant danger of overtrimming the genoa. Unlike the mainsail, there is almost no increase of heeling force. Moreover, the downwash streaming from the lower leech of a strapped down genoa can give the illusion of increased speed when, in reality, speed has actually been reduced.

The best indicator of optimum trim is your speedometer. Any serious racing boat should be equipped with a sensitive and accurate instrument. This is especially true of larger boats which are not as responsive to "seat of the pants" trimming as are light displacement dinghies.

The genoa sheet leads or turning blocks should be located near the rail at an angle of 8° to 12° from the centerline, depending on the type of boat. It appears, therefore, that a conflict might exist between this comment and the information in Figures 2A and 2B. Let's examine the situation a little more closely.

Sail trim is primarily a function of the heading of the true wind, the true wind velocity and the boat's speed.

Whenever true wind is less than 9 points (about 100°) off the bow, the speed of the relative wind will be *greater* than true wind speed. But the heading of the relative wind will be *less* than the true wind heading. As the true wind velocity increases, boat speed also increases but at a slower rate, and therefore relative wind velocity and relative wind heading *both* increase. See Figure 3.

A sail polar diagram is another very effective means of illustrating the variations in driving force over a range of headings. See Figure 4.

Examination of the polar shows that in light airs (3 to 4 knots) the boat is grossly underpowered, especially when sailing close on the wind. The problem here is to maximize the "speed made good", V_{mg}. The solution is simple. Ease the genoa a bit (of course the mainsail should also be eased) which will increase camber and the drive to heel ratio F_d/F_h. At the same time let the boat fall off about 10° which will increase the angle of attack and, therefore, the force developed by the genoa.

Boat speed should increase markedly on the new heading. Although

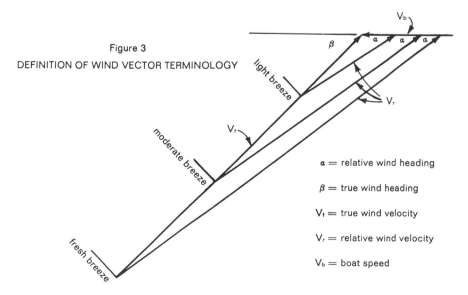

Figure 3

DEFINITION OF WIND VECTOR TERMINOLOGY

α = relative wind heading

β = true wind heading

V_t = true wind velocity

V_r = relative wind velocity

V_b = boat speed

the distance covered is greater, the speed made good to windward, V_{mg}, is greater than on the original heading. See Figure 5.

In a moderate to fresh breeze (12 to 18 knots) a boat is apt to be sailing at her maximum speed. Any further wind increase will probably overpower her or heel her to the point where the added drag from heeling will actually slow her down. Nonetheless, any well designed boat should be capable of carrying her #1 genoa and mainsail in a moderate breeze without reefing. This, then, is another criterion which helps to determine trim angle and overlap.

Figure 4 showed that the maximum speed made good, V_{mg}, in a fresh breeze, is closer to the wind than either of the previous cases. This fact suggests the following course of action: head up until the luff begins to flutter; then winch in the genoa sheet to flatten the sail and trim it closer to the centerline. The optimum trim angles run from 8° to 12° according to the guidelines prescribed in the December issue.

With less camber and a smaller angle of attack, the genoa develops less aerodynamic force. It is, however, the maximum load which can be carried by the boat without reducing sail area.

The amount of genoa overlap on any sail plan is basically determined by three factors:

1. Drive force required.
2. Sheet block location limitations.
3. Rating rule assessments.

We have already discussed the first two in some depth, but should

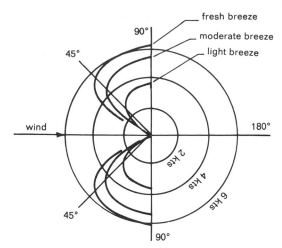

TYPICAL VELOCITY POLAR FOR A SMALL SLOOP "ON THE WIND"

Figure 4

also consider the rating rule assessment to better understand the impact of overlap on performance whether it be real or rated.

The new International Offshore Rule has established a minimum LP of 150%. This is equivalent to an overlap of about 60% as measured along the foot of the genoa (see Figure 1B).

Unlike the Cruising Club of America Rule, where designer and owner had some freedom of choice, the IOR dictates that all genoa LP's shall be at least 150% and may run as large as practical limits will allow, which is about 190%.

In a moderate to fresh breeze a 150% genoa provides ample driving force for most cruiser/racers. However, in average conditions of 7 to

COMPARISON OF "SPEED MADE GOOD" IN A LIGHT BREEZE

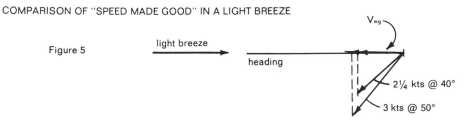

10 knots, most craft can carry genoas with a larger LP.

Although the added driving force may not be very large, it can, and often does, provide the winner with the necessary edge.

This poses a dilemma for anyone who usually sails in average wind conditions. However, before succumbing to the temptation of increasing your LP beyond 150%, make a careful study of the penalties involved, and the possibility of improving performance by using multiple headsails.

In some boats maximum performance in a moderate to fresh breeze can be achieved with a 160% to 170% LP genoa and under these circumstances the half foot, or so, penalty may be a bargain.

Thrust curves are particularly use-ful guidelines to the designer when selecting the design LP for a boat. A plot of the driving force in parametric form C_iA versus heading and LP is laid out. The designer selects a reasonable heading, such as 45° and determines which curve will maximize the driving force with a minimum increase in rating. See Figure 6.

Occasionally the thrust curves display very flat characteristics or are otherwise inconclusive. The designer then must make an educated guess or calculate and plot the locus of maximum speed versus rated overlap at a given wind condition. The curve should display a peak which will be the location of the optimum LP.

In the next article we shall discuss some other factors that influence headsail performance and selection.

TYPICAL PERFORMANCE OF A SMALL SLOOP WITH A VARIETY OF GENOAS.
IN THIS CASE OPTIMUM PERFORMANCE IS ACHIEVED WITH A 160% LP GENOA.

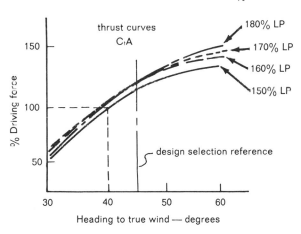

Figure 6

Jib Adjustment

Clew position on small boats

Steve Colgate

Mainsail twist is the falling off to leeward of the top part of the sail from inadequate leech tension. The same problem exists with the jib, but it is the fore and aft placement of the jib lead (the block that the jib sheets run through) that determines how much twist a jib will have.

If the lead is too far aft, the jib sheet will pull along the foot of the sail, but there won't be enough downward tension on the leech. The result is that the top part of the sail will tend to luff first.

However, other things can have the same effect as moving the jib lead block forward or aft. For instance, if the mast is raked (leaned) aft by lengthening the jibstay (see figures 1 and 2), it effectively moves the sail aft and the clew is lowered.

If the jib lead remains in the same place, this frees the leech of the jib. Flying Dutchman sailors often use this to free their leech in heavy weather, for their jib leads are placed a maximum distance aft and it is illegal for them to move them further back.

A good thing to remember is that the opening or *slot* between the jib leech and the body of the mainsail should remain parallel. This means that if we induce twist in the mainsail in heavy weather to reduce drive in the upper part of the main and thereby reduce heeling, we also must do the same thing to the jib.

Conversely, in light air, any fullness should be down low in the jib. You can accomplish this by easing the jib sheet, which has the same

Figure 1

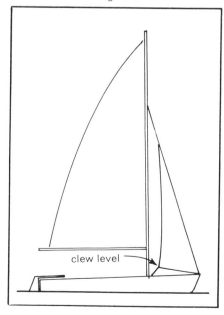

clew level

Figure 2

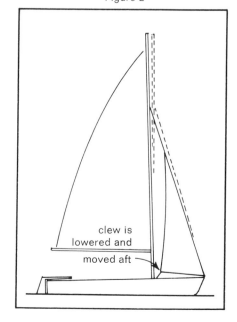

clew is lowered and moved aft

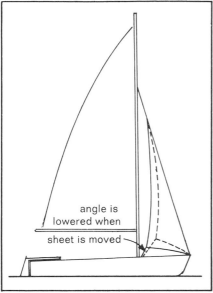

angle is
lowered when
sheet is moved

Figure 3

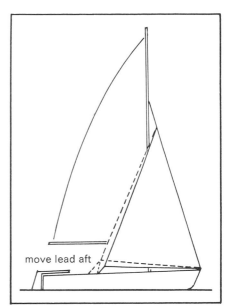

move lead aft

Figure 4

effect as easing the outhaul on the main along the boom. Easing the jib sheet increases draft by shortening the distance between the tack and the clew, and this gives you greater drive in light airs and lumpy seas. However, there is one detrimental side effect to freeing the leech. As the clew goes out, the angle of the jib sheet is lowered. (See figure 3.) Therefore, to regain the proper leech tension using *less* jib sheet tension, you must move the jib lead forward.

The jib tack, jib halyard tension, and jib downhaul, or Cunningham, also affect the location of the clew and the jib lead.

One usually increases the tension on the luff of the sail to control the jib's shape as the wind increases. As the jib stretches under the force of the increased wind velocity the draft tends to move aft in the sail, and more luff tension is required to keep the draft in the same location.

But if luff tension is increased by tightening the jib halyard, the clew rises in the air as a result, and the lead will need to be placed further aft. (See figure 4.) In heavy air you may even want a little twist in the

sail, and the lead may need to come back a bit further.

However, if you get your luff tension by pulling down the luff downhaul or jib Cunningham, the clew will be lowered and the lead will *appear* to be aft of its previous location. (See figure 5.) Since it is blowing relatively hard when this is done, you may want to change the jib lead position, for it is now effectively aft of where it had been. This may produce the desired twist.

As a boat falls off onto a reach, the jib sheet is eased and a great deal of twist can develop. In order to correct this, the lead must go forward again. In the old days sailboats did not have effective boom vangs for their mains and the top part of the mainsail twisted off to leeward when reaching. In order to make the jib leech match the curve of the main, sailors would move the jib lead aft.

Not so, today. Effective boom vangs keep twist in the main to a minimum and, therefore, little twist is needed in the jib. So in most cases the lead, when on a reach, should go *forward* not aft, to pull down on the leech and reduce twist.

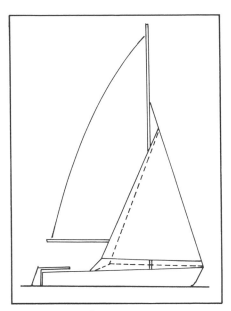

Figure 5

A narrow keelboat will get away with having the jib lead fairly well inboard and still maintain speed while pointing high. A beamy center-boarder though, would have her jib leads further outboard in order to obtain enough drive to get through the seas.

Think of the lateral placement of the jib lead in the same terms as the mainsheet traveller. If the traveller needs to be eased, the jib lead should probably be eased outboard too. The best way to tell whether your jib lead angle is correct is to test your boat against another. Sail closehauled alongside another boat of the same class and vary the lateral position in or out. The correct location will show up in increased speed.

You can measure the angle by using the table and diagram in figure 6. To do so, first measure along the centerline from the tack fitting to a point just forward of the mast (distance A-B on the diagram). From B measure at right angles to the point that intersects a straight line running from the tack fitting to the jib lead (distance B-C). Divide B-C into A-B and carry it to four places. Then consult the table below for the jib lead angle in degrees. Example: A-B is 59″ and B-C is 11″. 11 ÷ 59 is .1864

One other sensitive adjustment for the jib lead is its correct distance outboard from the centerline of the boat. To find this point first draw a line from the tack of the jib to the jib lead and measure the angle it makes with the centerline of the boat. This is called the *jib lead angle* and it will vary greatly from boat to boat.

Figure 6

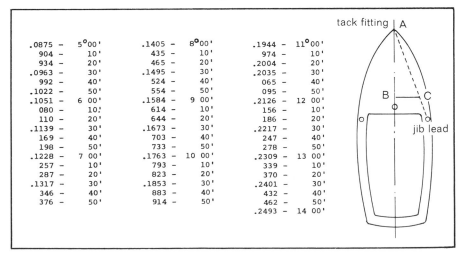

.0875 –	5°00'	.1405 –	8°00'	.1944 –	11°00'
904 –	10'	435 –	10'	974 –	10'
934 –	20'	465 –	20'	.2004 –	20'
.0963 –	30'	.1495 –	30'	.2035 –	30'
992 –	40'	524 –	40'	065 –	40'
.1022 –	50'	554 –	50'	095 –	50'
.1051 –	6 00'	.1584 –	9 00'	.2126 –	12 00'
080 –	10'	614 –	10'	156 –	10'
110 –	20'	644 –	20'	186 –	20'
.1139 –	30'	.1673 –	30'	.2217 –	30'
169 –	40'	703 –	40'	247 –	40'
198 –	50'	733 –	50'	278 –	50'
.1228 –	7 00'	.1763 –	10 00'	.2309 –	13 00'
257 –	10'	793 –	10'	339 –	10'
287 –	20'	823 –	20'	370 –	20'
.1317 –	30'	.1853 –	30'	.2401 –	30'
346 –	40'	883 –	40'	432 –	40'
376 –	50'	914 –	50'	462 –	50'
				.2493 –	14 00'

which is a hair over 10½° in the table.

Start at about 9° on your boat and in light air come inboard with light jib sheet tension to about 8°. In heavy air you may be able to go outboard to 11° or even 12° with success. But remember these adjustments always vary with boat type and the wind and sea conditions.

Jib Sheeting Angles

Considerations of the fairlead   Bruce Dyson

The **tendency** in recent years for every size of boat has been to narrow the jib lead angle. Star or 5.5 sailors can use as little as a 7° lead in a steady light breeze with a flat sea. Lightnings, Solings, and some others have been using an 8° lead with equal success.

When the Tempest was first introduced, the standard lead was 13°-14°. But it didn't take long for the top sailors to narrow this to 10°, and there is still room for improvement.

Still it is worth remembering that when someone says he is using an 8° lead, he is probably talking about the angle off centerline of the actual sheeting point and *not necessarily* the angle of the chord of the sail.

The two angles can differ by many degrees depending on the length of the jib sheet between fairlead block and clew (see figure 1). Only on boats where the clew of the sail leads right to the block when going to windward (in all conditions except in very light air) will the sheeting angle and the chord, for all practical purposes, be the same.

Andy Kostanecki, 1969 National Tempest Champion, has devised an interesting system for the Tempests that gives total fore and aft jib lead adjustment as well as in and out adjustment, from approximately an 8° to a 15° angle of lead. Both adjustments can be changed by remote control from the windward side of the boat (see figure 2).

Figure 2

Unusual jib lead setting on Tempest. Forward end is hinged, allowing track to move in or out. Jib car on track provides fore and aft movement.

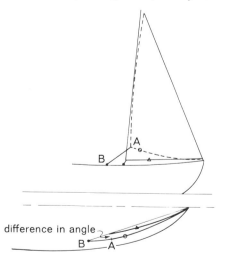

Figure 1

Because this system is very easy to adjust, many Tempest sailors have been guilty of over adjustment, including myself.

I remember one race where I adjusted myself right out of first place. I continually narrowed the lead in an attempt to point just a little higher than a boat to windward of me.

Eventually I choked the slot and my boat stopped. I finally realized the windward boat had a slightly different slant of air than I had. But by this time it was too late.

The point is that while there are many different settings for the jib, only one is right at any given instant.

There is no magic setting for any jib lead: there are just too many variables. A boat with a high-wetted-surface-to-sail-area ratio should normally have a wider jib lead angle than a boat with equal sail area and less wetted surface, particularly if the lines of the hull with the higher wetted surface are not fine.

Hull drag will be much higher and the boat will require more power to move it through the water. This means the jib lead has to be set wider and the sail not sheeted as tight to get this maximum power. Pointing is sacrificed for the extra speed.

There is one notable exception to the sail area/wetted surface rule. A Soling has 10 sq. ft. less sail area than the Tempest, but its jib can be sheeted at a slightly narrower angle.

This is primarily due first to the lack of overlap of a Soling jib, and second the Soling's lateral plane. I would estimate a Soling keel has twice the lateral plane of a Tempest and this helps its pointing ability and greatly decreases the side slipping tendency.

But back to setting the lead. The more twist that's allowed higher up on a jib, the narrower the lead can

be. But the fullness cut into a sail must be taken into consideration.

If a sail is cut full, the amount of twist must be precisely controlled or the luff angle of attack at the top will become too great and it will break far before the middle and bottom sections. A flatter sail can be allowed to twist more without this premature luffing.

The position of the maximum depth of draft can also affect the sheeting angle (see figure 3). A jib cut in the old style with maximum draft at 35% of chord length is sheeted slightly differently than that of a more modern 45% to 50% sail.

To get equal angles of attack, the 35% sail must have a narrower lead than a 50% semi-circular cut jib (see figure 4). Here you can see that when both are sheeted at the same angle, the angle of attack is higher on a 50% sail. This higher angle of attack translates into higher pointing ability.

There are, however, three important points to remember when using a 50% draft jib. First, take extreme care not to get a tight leech by placing the sheeting fairlead too far forward.

Second, a certain amount of twist must be allowed to prevent having an overly tight leech. And finally, the relationship of the main to the jib is very critical. If the draft is too far forward in the main the 50% jib can cause excess backwinding and choke the slot — even if the lead is set slightly wider.

Figure 3

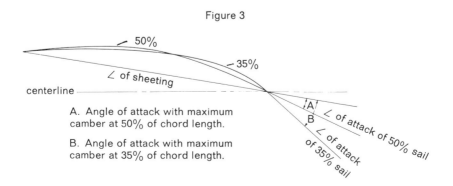

A. Angle of attack with maximum camber at 50% of chord length.

B. Angle of attack with maximum camber at 35% of chord length.

In fact, it is almost essential to have a semi-circular cut main if you are going to use a semi-circular cut jib. The 50% main — 50% jib combination is in widespread use in the Tempest class now and is proving to be the fastest all-round combination for them.

Sea conditions create another variable for the proper lead setting. In general, a lead should be set wider to provide the extra power needed to get through a chop.

If the conditions are not the same on both tacks, i.e., the sea is not running in the same direction as the wind, set the leads accordingly. Use a wider setting on the tack where the boat is sailing into the waves, and a narrower setting on the tack where the boat is sailing broadside to sea.

Once you really learn how to adjust your jib leads and become completely familiar with your boat, it is possible to effectively use just one suit of sails in all conditions!

This has been proved many times over. But the right jib lead adjustment for the right conditions is always going to be the critical factor.

Just to review, jib lead angles depend on:

1. The strength of the wind.
   a. Light air — narrower lead
   b. Heavy air — wide lead
2. Amount of jib overlap on mainsail.
   a. More overlap — wider lead
   b. Less overlap — narrower lead
3. Shape of jib.
   a. Flat jib — narrow lead, more twist to create fullness.
   b. Full jib — average lead, less twist.
4. Position of draft.
   a. If minimum draft is forward — slightly narrower lead
   b. If maximum draft is 50% back — slightly wider lead
5. Shape of main.
   a. If draft is forward — wide lead
   b. If draft is aft — narrower lead

Always bear in mind that these solutions are relative, and that every lead adjustment should be small. But there is one rule that nearly always works, even though it usually takes too many years to learn:

"When in doubt — let it out!!"

3

Spinnakers

Fundamentals of Spinnaker Handling

Set, trim, and takedown   Steve Colgate

To most novices the spinnaker appears to be a frightening thing. It adds a great deal of sail area and power to almost any sized boat and an inexperienced skipper and crew inevitably get it all tangled and fouled up at first. For that very reason it's a challenge to achieve smooth, trouble-free spinnaker work, and there is great satisfaction when the challenge is met.

First, you must always make a decision whether or not to fly the spinnaker at all. Is the wind too heavy or light? Is the wind too far forward or aft? Is the crew experienced enough? Usually these questions are interrelated. For instance, some spinnakers can be carried to advantage when the apparent wind is well forward on light to medium days (as close as 55°-60° relative from the bow), but they would cause broaching and weather helm at the same apparent wind angle on heavy days.

The wind strength and direction weigh heavily on the choice of types of *chutes*, as they are often called (short for "parachute" spinnaker). There are close reaching, reaching and running chutes. The former are flatter in cut and made of heavier cloth, while the latter are fuller and lighter.

In 5.5-meter sailboats I've set a running chute in light air with the wind well aft only to find that the increased boat speed brought the apparent wind so far forward that a reaching chute was called for. Not long after, I set a reaching spinnaker anticipating the same true wind angle after rounding the weather mark. But I found that, since the wind now was heavier, even the

increased boat speed failed to bring the apparent wind forward much. That day we should have set the running spinnaker.

Another factor in deciding whether to fly the spinnaker or not is its sail area relative to the jib. On some boats the jib is quite large, and if you find the wind too far forward or heavy enough to cause broaching, you may find the boat will go faster without the spinnaker. On others, the spinnaker has so much more area than the jib that even if you are broaching with it up you will probably net out with a faster speed through the water. If you are racing, go by the old axiom, "When in doubt, set."

On very heavy days it almost always pays to carry a spinnaker if you're racing. I've heard the argument on cruising boats many times that if the boat is already at hull speed, setting a spinnaker won't improve her speed. That's fallacious reasoning because in a trough of a wave and up the other side the boat is rarely going near hull speed, and it needs the extra power of a spinnaker. And under surfing conditions, there is no such thing as hull speed, for all sailboats can surpass it. The spinnaker will give just enough more power to start the surf earlier and make it last longer.

On very light days a chute can be set, and will fill well if the spinnaker cloth is light enough and the apparent wind relatively far forward. But with the wind aft, particularly with left over slop rolling the boat around, a jib may do just as well. The spinnaker will just flop back and forth wrapping around the jibstay and

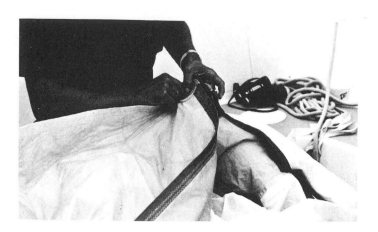

Figure 1

catching on the spreaders. You're often better off without it in such conditions.

Now, how to "get the damn thing up." Ever heard those words before? Let's assume we're sailing a small one-design keelboat with a three-man crew. Pretty much the same procedures are involved in both larger and smaller boats, they just have more or fewer people.

A spinnaker is a triangular sail made of nylon. The two vertical edges are called *luffs* when the sail isn't set because the spinnaker is symmetrical and both edges are identical. When the spinnaker is set, the edge leading up from the pole is the *luff* and other edge is the *leech*. The edge along the bottom is called the *foot*.

Some potential problems can develop before the boat even leaves the mooring. If the spinnaker is improperly packed, it can get twisted as it is hoisted. Most spinnakers are packed in sailbags, buckets, deck depressions or other containers. All are commonly called spinnaker *turtles* because the container originally used was a piece of plywood covered by an old inner tube, secured along three edges, under which the spinnaker was stuffed. Placed in the bow, this object looked like a turtle

and the name stuck.

To properly *turtle* a spinnaker, find the head of the sail. Usually it is the only corner of the sail with a swivel. Grab one luff near the head and follow down the edge of the sail flaking it back and forth.

After you have followed down one side of the sail, change hands and follow down the other side to the other clew flaking in the same manner. (See figure 1.) Mark the location of the head with a finger lest it get lost in the folds of the sail. Then, still holding on to both edges, stuff the spinnaker into the turtle.

The three corners of the sail should be on top of the bag or container, and should be separated. (See figure 2.) If a sailbag is used, the three corners are usually tied together with the head between the tack and clew. This will work 99% of the time, but sometimes the three corners get a 180° twist so that the tack and clew are reversed in relation to the body of the sail. The spinnaker might rotate itself out of such a potential wrap, but if the wrap tightens up, it will be the devil to get out.

One of the best ways to picture how you set up for a spinnaker is to imagine a slow-motion movie of a spinnaker being hoisted, run back-

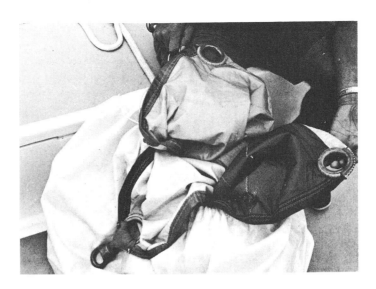

Figure 2

wards: in other words, from out and drawing, the spinnaker will collapse and slowly fold itself back into the turtle.

Watching this will show you that all sheets and halyards *must* be outside all shrouds, jibsheets, barber haulers, etc., in preparation for the set.

Study figure 3 and learn the various lines involved in spinnaker work. The *after guy* or more commonly, "guy" runs through the pole which is always set out to windward opposite the main boom. The free corner of the spinnaker has a *sheet* attached to it like any other sail. The only tricky thing about the foregoing terminology is that during a jibe, the pole is switched over to the new windward side and the *old* guy becomes the *new* sheet (attached to the free corner of the sail) and the old sheet becomes the new guy (running through the jaws in the end of the pole).

There are two lines to hold the pole in position: the *topping lift* to keep it from falling when the spinnaker isn't full of wind, and the *foreguy* (some people call it the spinnaker pole downhaul) to keep the pole from *skying* (pointing way up in the air) when the spinnaker is full.

The most common error I've run

across is the failure to make a last minute check to see that the spinnaker halyard is clear. Discovering that the halyard is inside the topping-lift, fouled around an upper shroud or was led between the jib halyard and jibstay when the jib was raised, once the spinnaker is halfway up and filling is too late. (See figure 4.)

Another common error on a set is not separating the corners fast

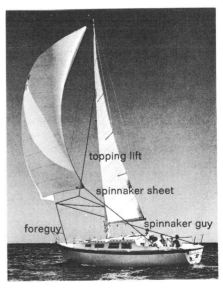

topping lift

spinnaker sheet

foreguy

spinnaker guy

Figure 3

Figure 4. Last minute check would have shown #470's halyard to be inside and on wrong side of topping lift.

Figure 5. Failure to separate tack and clew promptly can result in spinnaker wrap.

enough when the sail is hoisted. This allows the spinnaker to rotate with tack and clew close together; a wrap can develop. (See figure 5.) The skipper often suspects the spinnaker was bagged improperly when this happens. Actually, either the sheetman failed to pull on the sheet, or the tack of the spinnaker wasn't pulled up to the pole fast enough, or both.

Once a wrap exists there are various ways to get it out, but corrective action must be fast and positive before the situation deteriorates. First, head down and blanket the spinnaker behind the mainsail. It's amazing how many skippers do the opposite, feeling that if they fill the chute the wrap will spin out. Second, get a crew member up on the foredeck to pull down along the leech, shaking all the while.

If this fails, try lowering the halyard a few feet. This allows the swivel to work in case it was jammed in the block and the halyard line to rotate in the event that the lay of the line twisted on the way up.

If all else fails, lower the spinnaker to the point where the foredeck man can reach the twist and work it out.

There is no mystery about what makes a crew member into a good spinnaker trimmer: it takes experience and concentration. Neither of these can be taught. One is developed and one is innate. We can teach the basic rules of spinnaker trimming and, depending on the person, he may eventually become good at it.

But even the basic rules can be misleading. Nothing is hard and fast in sailing and for every rule there's an exception or two. First, let's examine the general principles behind spinnaker trimming. When running, the spinnaker is fairly well stalled. It is dragging the boat downwind. True, there's a little flow around the backside of the luff (from a crew member's vantage point), but that doesn't result in much drive. Therefore, we want the greatest projected area possible.

Just as a large parachute will let a man down more slowly than a small one, the more area of spinnaker exposed to the wind, the greater its effectiveness. This is done by keeping the pole well squared (aft) and the sheet well-trimmed. The dotted line in figure 6 shows the amount of area exposed to the wind with the pole forward. The dotted line in figure 7 is much longer with the pole aft indicating a greater "projected area" (pole exaggerated for effect).

If there weren't a price to pay for having the pole well aft, that's where we'd set it, but there is. As we square the pole aft, and also trim the sheet to keep the spinnaker from collapsing, it is drawn in closer and closer to the mainsail. This means the spinnaker is in the bad air of the main and loses efficiency. So we ease the pole forward and ease the sheet to get the chute away from the sail plan. Somewhere there is a happy medium between starving the spinnaker behind the main and losing projected area through too much ease. This is where experience comes in.

The next general aspect of spinnaker trimming to remember is that a spinnaker is a symmetrical sail and should look symmetrical when flown. There are a few exceptions to this such as when close reaching or in light air, but it's generally true. If the spinnaker is misshapen because the pole is too high or too low, it will lose much of its effectiveness.

Keeping the above two general aspects of spinnaker trimming in mind, all the rest of the basic rules fall in place. Following are some of the requirements for pole position. A good starting point is to set the pole square to the apparent wind. The masthead fly is in undisturbed air and is a good guide. Set the pole at right angles to it.

As the boat sails further downwind, however, air over the main tends to flow forward and around the mast making the spinnaker practically by-the-lee. This means the pole will need to be squared back past perpendicular to the masthead fly. Actually it will be perpendicular to the shroud telltales. I would use the masthead fly until the wind is well aft and then switch to shroud telltales.

There are some unusual cases where the masthead fly isn't very accurate for spinnaker trimming, such as on a 12-meter yacht. Being a $\frac{3}{4}$ rig, the head of the spinnaker is considerably lower than the masthead fly and the apparent wind at the top of the mast is noticeably farther aft than that at pole height due to increased wind velocity aloft. Another exception to setting the pole perpendicular to the apparent wind is when you are using a very short-foot spinnaker. In that case, squaring the pole brings the clew near the jibstay and much of the projected area is lost.

The pole should generally be level. Not parallel to the water, as I continually hear people saying, but per-

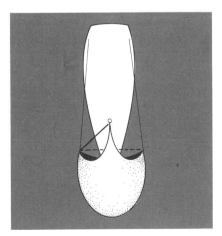

Figure 6
Pole forward,
sheet eased.

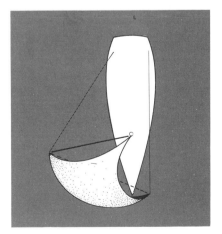

Figure 7
Pole aft,
sheet tight.

pendicular to the mast. This means that if you raise or lower the outboard end of the pole, you should raise or lower the inboard end (the end attached to the mast) a corresponding amount. The idea is to get the spinnaker as far away from the sail plan as possible, but I think keeping the pole level to achieve it is overemphasized.

The pole would have to be cocked 25° from level to decrease its effective length 10% and yet it takes almost 20° of cocking to lose 5% of its effective length — so the first few degrees off of level really don't make much difference. Probably more speed is lost by fussing around with the inboard pole height than is gained by having the pole exactly level. Also, a slight cock upwards will put the pole in line with the guy and reduce the bending strain on the pole.

More important is the height at which the whole pole is set. The general rule is to keep the tack and clew of the spinnaker level with the plane of the deck (not with the water). But this really goes back to keeping the spinnaker symmetrical. When the two corners are level, the spinnaker will be symmetrical, will look good and fly well.

The exceptions to this are mainly while reaching and in either high or low wind velocities (which we will go into in a later article). While reaching, particularly when flying the spinnaker with the jib set, the tack of a normal reaching spinnaker on a class boat is usually set higher than the clew. This opens the slot between the spinnaker and jib. It also eases the luff of the spinnaker and flattens in the chute. A cross-section through the middle of the spinnaker with the pole down might look like figure 8, whereas with the pole end higher, it would look somewhat like figure 9.

Once the pole is set correctly, it's a fairly simple thing to play the spinnaker. The sheet should be eased until one sees a slight curl along the luff and then trimmed to make the curl disappear. This must be done

constantly and is where concentration plays its biggest part.

The spinnaker guy should also be played if the boat is small or if you are running in a slop. As the boat rolls to windward the pole must be squared and the sheet eased. As it rolls to leeward, the pole should be eased forward and the sheet trimmed.

All changes in apparent wind direction necessitate a change in pole position and sheet trim. If the boat starts surfing, if it falls off a plane, or if the wind velocity changes, the apparent wind direction will be affected and the spinnaker trimmer will have to make adjustments. Moreover, he must learn to anticipate these changes ahead of time.

Now let's look at some special cases. For example, one hears a lot about easing the spinnaker halyard. But when is it a good time to ease it off — and how much?

The next time you are on a reach with the spinnaker set, look up behind the mainsail on the lee side. Then ease the spinnaker halyard six inches or so while looking at the *leech* of the sail, not the head. It will become obvious how much the slot between the spinnaker and the main will open up to allow free air passage.

When running downwind in a breeze, easing the halyard has two effects. First, it gets the spinnaker away from the disturbed air of the mainsail and second, it allows the spinnaker to be more vertical than when it is fully hoisted.

In light air, however, the halyard can't be eased, for the spinnaker will just come straight down. Nor can it be eased on a reach in heavy air because the sail's center of effort will go further out over the water and possibly cause a broach. And on a run in heavy air an eased spinnaker will be more apt to roll from one side of the boat to the other (oscillate) than one fully hoisted. In short, easing the halyard is rarely done on a run and is really only beneficial on a medium air reach.

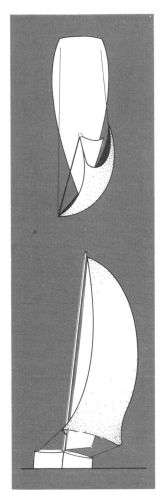

Figure 8
Pole low.

Figure 9
Pole high.

As the wind increases, there's a point where a spinnaker can overpower the boat if it's used at its maximum effectiveness. The choice then is to either reduce the effectiveness of the spinnaker or change to a jib. Doing the former is often the best choice. In some boats you can broach along an entire reaching leg and still beat a boat that does not have a spinnaker.

To reduce a chute's effectiveness, ease the pole forward and down, and overtrim the sheet. But make sure the spinnaker halyard is two-blocked. Then lead both the guy and sheet fur-

ther forward to pull the sail down and keep it in tight behind the sailplan. Trouble usually results when the spinnaker gets out too far into fresh undisturbed air.

When reaching, the sheet lead should also be forward of the transom if the spinnaker is short along the foot. With the lead aft at the stern, trimming the sheet to stop a curl just stretches the foot. If the lead is brought forward, a pull on the sheet will uncurl the luff and, if the spinnaker is designed well, it won't tighten the leech. A tight leech must be avoided on a reach because it creates a drag to leeward and backwards.

Spinnaker trimming in light air takes a great deal of patience. Lower the pole way down, but always keep the outboard end a little higher than the clew. Then when a puff of air comes and fills the spinnaker, the pole will be at the proper height. In other words, keep the pole at the right height for the 10% of the time that the spinnaker is filled; not the 90% of the time when it is drooping.

Another reason to keep the pole a little higher than the clew in light air is that a low pole can stretch the luff and fold it over. (See figures 10 and 11) When a puff arrives, the spinnaker is unable to fill because of the shape of the luff.

This same thing can happen in some very full shouldered running spinnakers. The luff can collapse from a "starve," and though you know you must pull the pole aft, you have to first overtrim the sheet to unfold the luff. Only then can you pull the pole back.

Be careful in light air not to have the pole too high for this causes the spinnaker to droop to leeward and it will need a stronger puff to fill it.

Another light air problem is caused by the jib. Air flowing past the lee side of the jib causes a suction on a reach and if the spinnaker collapses, it sucks into the jib and it is very difficult to fill it again. The natural tendency is to trim the jib to get it away from the spinnaker, but actually the opposite should be done. The first time it happens, free the jib sheet to break down the flow over the jib. If it happens a few more times, take the jib down.

A few words on jibing the spinnaker. The key man (or men) should handle the guy and sheet, and he (they) must keep the spinnaker downwind at all times. A masthead fly is very helpful at this time. As the boat turns downwind square the pole back and ease the sheet. For reach to reach jibes mark the sheet so that it's eased quickly to the mark.

On a small boat, the foredeck man

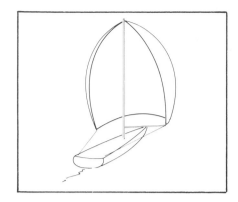

Figure 10
Pole level.

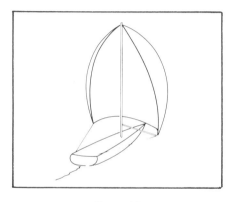

Figure 11
Pole carried too low.

should always be facing the spinnaker and have his back against the mast for leverage. On reach to reach jibes he should take the pole completely off; first off the mast, and then the old guy. The spinnaker is then freewheeled through the jibe and the pole connected up to the guy on the new windward side. If he has trouble getting the pole onto the mast, the man on the sheet should collapse the spinnaker momentarily by easing the sheet.

On a run he should take the pole off the mast, but should not disconnect the old guy. Don't pull the pole across the boat to the sheet but rather, hold the pole out (with the old guy still in it) and reach for the sheet. This maneuver will keep the spinnaker full throughout the jibe.

Taking a spinnaker down to leeward is quite simple; the only major problem is letting the chute get out from behind the mainsail. The person gathering in the chute must have control of the sail by bringing the sheet forward to a spot just behind the shrouds.

The guy is then eased and the halyard lowered as the sail is gathered in behind the mainsail. On a small boat if someone lets the guy go before the sheet is under control, the chute will go flying aft to the stern and be the devil to gather in. About the only thing to do if this happens in a blow is to head the boat dead downwind.

There may be times when a windward douse is in order. If you are racing and are coming into a mark on the wrong jibe, a takedown to windward will be the new leeward side after the douse. Or if you know you must set the spinnaker again and the next set is on the other tack, a windward takedown will prepare you properly for the next set.

Take the pole down before you intend to douse and then just pull the spinnaker around to windward with the new guy. In some larger class boats it's hard to do on a reach, but it can be done quite easily on a run. Many smaller boats set and douse the spinnaker to windward as a matter of course.

Fouls and Their Prevention

Some twists on spinnaker tangles   Bruce Cameron

Flying a spinnaker can be one of sailing's great pleasures. This extraordinary sail can add the extra knots that make off wind sailing exciting. And almost nothing beats the thrill of surfing downhill behind a spinnaker, sheets and guys taut and the boat vibrating like a planing dinghy.

For the passagemaker, a spinnaker provides drive forward where it is needed for easy downwind steering, and gives you a great improvement in speed over the normal fore and aft sail combinations.

But spinnakers do require a talent in setting, holding and striking, and lack of such talent can result in the sail going overboard or fouling and becoming damaged. A more frequent problem is an hourglass tangle with mid-section of the sail wrapped around itself or the headstay, its upper and lower sections still drawing admirably. Such a tangle may be very hard to undo. How does one prevent these problems and reduce the possibility of their happening?

Always remember a "chute" requires several pairs of hands to set. The actual number will depend on their individual abilities, the size of the boat and the weather conditions. If you are shorthanded it may be best to leave the chute in the bag, or at least strike it early when trouble or tricky maneuvering approach or darkness nears.

A friend of mine tried to set a spinnaker motorsailing across the Bahama banks with one inexperienced crew. The sail fell under the bows, and was run over and chewed up by the propellor until it looked like a truck had driven through it. It was an expensive mistake.

Let's examine ways to get the sail up and drawing properly. Then we'll discuss some ways to prevent fouls, and finally some solutions for a fouled spinnaker.

Most problems involving the spinnaker (including tangling) seem to occur when it is being set. This is a tricky and at times strenuous process, particularly if the sail begins to fill before the halyard is fully secured. To get the chute up and drawing quickly, it should be hoisted in the lee of a jib. To make it even easier, a turtle can be used, and sail may be raised in "stops."

By hoisting the chute in the lee of a set jib, the sail will go up easily with no pressure on it and adjustments or corrections can be done before the sail is full and drawing. When all looks right, the jib may be lowered or the spinnaker trimmed to weather so that it fills.

To stop a spinnaker, spread the sail out with head and clews secured, then gather it together from leech to leech and, working down from the head, stop it with light cotton line that can be easily broken by hand. Locate the stops every few feet except near the head where they tend not to break. (See figure 1.) It is critical that the two leeches be free and parallel. If they are not and the sail is hoisted, the chute will fill with a twist in it, and you will have an hourglass tangle.

A turtle requires similar preparation, but it eliminates the possibility of stops not breaking. The turtle itself is normally a turtle-shaped can-

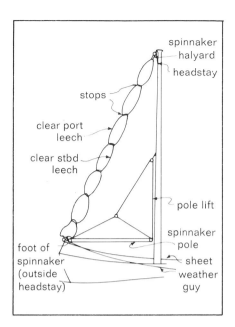

Figure 1
Stopped Spinnaker

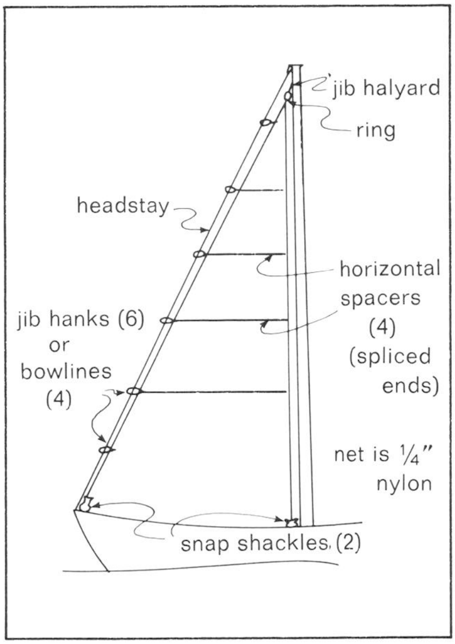

Figure 2
Removable Spinnaker Net

vas container into which the sail is packed and then fastened near the base of the headstay. It can be as simple as a plastic bucket or a sail bag.

The packing process is much like packing a parachute in that the sail is stretched out and then stuffed into the turtle with each leech free and clear of the other. The final product will have the clews and head protruding out of the turtle on the sides. They must be separated from each other and easily located.

After the spinnaker is set and drawing well, several things can be done to prevent a foul or tangle that might occur from a poor jibe, variable winds, or bad helmsmanship.

Obviously, good helmsmanship helps to keep the chute full and prevent fouls. And carrying a reaching sail on the headstay can prevent it from wrapping around the stay.

But a more positive measure is to use a spinnaker net; it attaches to the headstay and if properly set will prevent the chute from wrapping around the stay.

There are two basic types of spinnaker nets. The first (see figure 2) is a removable affair and is set like a jib. Its head is attached to a jib halyard, the track is secured at the headstay base, and its clew attaches to the mast base. Several hanks or bowlines hold it to the headstay. Build it with ¼" line.

A second type of net consists of several shock cord *preventers* that run from the mast to the headstay. This type is permanently attached. While the first type must be removed to raise a jib, the second type will ride up the headstay above the jib as it is hoisted. (See figure 3.)

No matter how many precautions are used it seems that eventually everyone experiences tangles and fouls. If the chute is free of the headstay and merely twisted in itself, the foul may be cleared quickly. The first thing to do is to stretch out the foot of the sail by hauling in on the sheets. This may untwist it.

Short jerks on the halyard may also help, though it may be necessary to grab the leeches by hand to

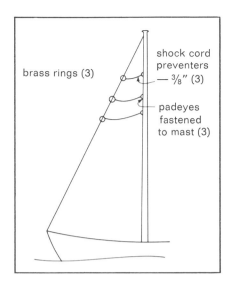

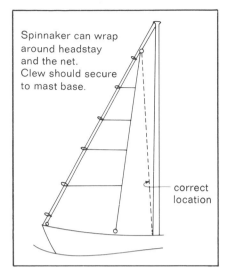

Figure 3
Shock Cord Net

Figure 4
Improper Net

straighten and, hopefully, untwist them. Be careful not to tear the light cloth with your fingernails.

As a last resort, the spinnaker can be dropped to the deck and freed. But this can be a long process, particularly if the sail should surround the headstay in the foul and can't be lowered. Of course, the sail also can be cut down.

However, the two times I have seen really bad tangles the sails were recovered undamaged, and the solutions were largely trial and error. One occurred when a yawl anchored near me with a badly hourglassed spinnaker still flying.

I joined the small crew to try to pass the sail around the headstay, but it was blowing fairly briskly and the mess would not *budge*. Additionally, the boat was head to wind with the flogging sail preventing anything productive. The halyard had been eased off, and yet the head of the sail was so tightly tangled it remained at the top of the stay with two ballooning sections below and a huge tangle between them.

Working in a bo'sun's chair was difficult because of the flogging sail, and it was impossible to pass the

sail around the stay from the swinging chair. Finally we took a length of small line and stopped the top half of the hourglass from top to bottom, slowly lowering the man in the bo'-sun's chair as he did it. The sail stopped flogging then and it was passed around the headstay and lowered undamaged. I later learned they had not used a net.

More recently, I was sailing a 40′ sloop from Connecticut to Rio de Janeiro and I used a spinnaker occasionally. When the permanent shock cord disintegrated from long use, we fashioned another with several lengths of line that ran from the forestay to the halyard. The bottom end of the halyard was attached to the tallboy track about midpoint between the base of the headstay and the mast. (See figure 4.)

When we jibed, the spinnaker became hourglassed completely around *both* the forestay and the net. Obviously, I should have tacked the halyard to the mast base not just to the tallboy track. If I had done so, the sail could not have gone completely around the net as it ultimately did.

First we tried to shake the net.

Then the halyard was slacked but the sail still would not come down. Then we discovered that all the halyards except the main were also caught in the mess: if we wanted to use the bo'sun's chair we would have to use the main halyard. This was not very encouraging, for a healthy sea was running and if the main were lowered, we would roll violently — an extremely uncomfortable situation for someone in a bo'sun's chair.

Our plan was to lower the main, go quickly up in the chair and take a look. If the problem could not be resolved quickly we would reeve another halyard to raise the main and thereby steady the boat while the problem was being worked on.

But fortunately the head was not wrapped tightly around the stay and the unshackled spinnaker head could be pushed down the headstay.

The main went back up and we were again on our way. But we still had a huge mess of spinnaker amassed around the base of the stay. Our final step was to rehoist the sail, stopping it with ties as it cleared the deck. The fouled chute was soon working again.

There is a thrill sailing with a spinnaker and the threat of a fouled chute should not prevent you from using it. However, do take all precautions. And always be prepared for the hourglass, for someday it is going to occur.

Spinnaker and Mainsail Interaction

Downwind components of air flow   John R. Stanton

Sail interaction occurs whenever two or more sails are flown in close proximity to one another. Spinnaker and mainsail interaction is no exception.

Wind flowing past an isolated spinnaker when running adheres to classical concepts of fluid mechanics and can be determined with considerable accuracy. A similar situation also exists with each of the headsails flown from time to time in combination with the spinnaker. (See figure 1.)

But as soon as the mainsail is hoisted, the spinnaker operates within what is often called the "shadow" of the main. It is a very descriptive adjective but it is an oversimplification and a bit misleading.

When a sloop is sailing downwind, the entire spinnaker operates in an air mass that has been modified by the mainsail. The velocity, velocity gradient, and direction all vary from the original free stream values, and usually in a non-uniform way.

As you may recall from previous

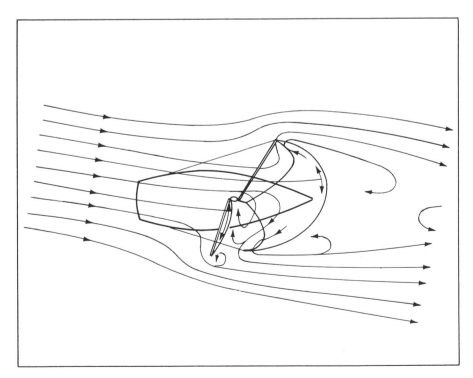

Figure 1
Flow pattern for spinnaker and mainsail.

articles, the streamlines approaching a sail "dead on" are decelerated which builds up pressure on the windward surface. The pressure gradient distends the flow lines around the luff and leech, and those streamlines nearest the sail's edges roll up into vortices because of the separated flow.

The flow lines approaching the mainsail to windward of the boat's center line accelerate as much as 20% as they pass the luff and move downstream. Because the luff of a spinnaker extends well beyond the mainsail luff, it lies in the path of this accelerated flow and thereby receives a dividend in a localized increase in dynamic pressure.

However, the leech area of the spinnaker is another matter. It lies directly in the wake of the mainsail and in close proximity to it and this effectively blocks the free stream flow. As a consequence, the leeward sections of the spinnaker are dependent for flow on the higher pressure air near the luff.

The center of pressure of a spinnaker on a run is located in a vertical line about 1/3 the projected width to leeward of the luff. The exact location is influenced by several factors, but it is largely a function of the spinnaker's aspect ratio and the mainsail area/spinnaker projected area ratio.

The wind streamlines that lie to windward of the spinnaker's center of pressure distend around the luff of the spinnaker in a classic manner. The only noteworthy difference is the small velocity gradient increase near the luff that occurs as the direct result of the mainsail interaction I described in an earlier paragraph.

The flow to leeward of the center of pressure can be more accurately compared to the flow that exists between a mainsail and the overlapping portion of a genoa, often referred to as the "slot effect."

Under normal circumstances, the pressure recovery in the lee of an isolated sail is only about 30% of the dynamic pressure developed on the windward surface. The pressure differential that exists between the two surfaces provides the useful drag, or driving force.

The passage of air to leeward between the mainsail and the spinnaker has an equalizing effect on both sails that tends to degrade their performances. The air pressure on the lee of the main is *higher* than desired, while the pressure on the windward surface of the spinnaker is *less* than desired. As a result, the pressure differential across both sails is less than their full *individual* potential.

And since driving force is a direct function of both pressure differential and sail area, the net thrust of the combined sails is less than the sum of the individual sails. In fact, it is likely that a few of the modern ocean racers with extremely large foretriangles and small mainsails would sail as fast downwind under spinnaker alone where the rules permit it.

Interaction between the two sails decreases as the gap increases. It is rapid at first, then drops at a sharply decreased rate as the gap begins to exceed about $1\frac{1}{2}$ the mainsail chord length. Therefore there is some merit in the practice of easing the spinnaker halyard and allowing the head to fly some distance to leeward of the halyard block, for this opens up the gap between the mainsail and spinnaker.

A more powerful influence on the gap can be exerted by the spinnaker pole. Of course the pole should always be horizontal in order to produce the maximum projected exposed width. However, the pole should be eased slightly forward of the imaginary line made by the extension of the boom to increase the gap between the mainsail and spinnaker at the foot. The projected length is shortened as the pole end moves forward; very slowly at first, in accordance with the cosine of the angle.

For example by easing the pole forward 10°, the projected length is shortened by only 1.5% but the gap is increased by 17.4% of the pole length. (See figure 2.)

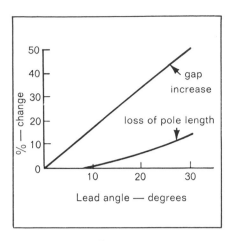

Figure 2
Effect of pole lead on spinnaker
width and gap.

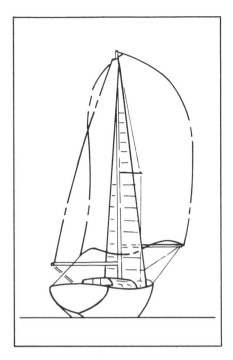

Figure 3
A Tallboy (shaded) with spinnaker and
mainsail on a run.

There is an optimum angle, usually between 10 to 20° at which point the advantages of the increased gap are offset by the reduced projected area. The precise value of the best "pole lead angle" varies from rig to rig, but it is generally related to the ratio of the mainsail chord length to spinnaker width.

In other words, a boat built with a small, high aspect ratio mainsail and a large, broad-footed spinnaker should carry the pole at a smaller angle than an equivalent craft equipped with a larger mainsail and smaller spinnaker.

The recent trend to very tall rigs has produced some large spinnakers with high aerodynamic aspect ratios, some of which have approached 2.0. This is desirable in theory and if the craft could fly a spinnaker alone, it would be a very efficient running sail. But in practice the high aspect ratio spinnaker has a larger portion of its sail area blanketed by the mainsail, and as a consequence, the average aerodynamic load per square foot is slightly reduced.

Some designers have countered the trend to high aspect ratio spinnakers by placing the mast farther aft, occasionally as much as 45% of the LOA. A number have recommended extending spinnaker poles

10 to 15% beyond the foretriangle foot length. The effect has been to increase the size of the spinnaker, slightly reducing the aspect ratio, and to place a larger portion of the projected area to windward of the mainsail luff.

The total power developed by the spinnaker is much greater, and the average load per square foot, or the efficiency, is higher. On balance, the advantages appear to outweigh the disadvantages of a higher rating, or "pole penalty."

Secondary headsails, broadly categorized as staysails, also can be flown with a spinnaker on a run. It is not unusual to see staysails of all shapes and sizes flying simultaneously in a fleet of boats on the same course. One of the most popular and most effective staysails is generically known as the Tallboy, also referred to (with minor modifications) as a slatsail or splint. (See figure 3.)

The Tallboy does increase sail area

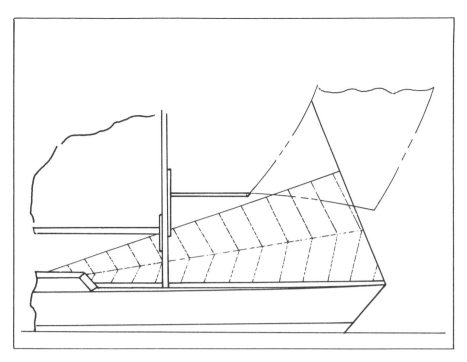

Figure 4
A typical low aspect ratio spinnaker
staysail (also called a "half bra"
or cheater).

slightly, but its primary function is to act as a slat at the luff of the mainsail. In this capacity it induces the streamlines to turn around the mast and accelerates the flow to leeward. The velocity and pressure gradients in the gap between the mainsail and spinnaker are intensified slightly, developing small but tangible increases in pressure differential across the mainsail and the leeward portion of the spinnaker.

On a dead run, the Tallboy's tack should be fixed to the deck near the windward rail abreast the mast, or as close to that position as the spinnaker pole will allow. The clew should be sheeted slightly forward and to leeward of the mast. The leech must be taut to minimize sag and twist, while the foot tension should be low so that the sail will develop proper camber in the lower panels.

The interposition of another sail to windward and between mainsail and spinnaker does interfere with the flow on the spinnaker. But in the case of the Tallboy type of sail, the benefits outweigh the disadvantages and the drive of the entire rig *is* slightly increased.

With the true wind well aft, that is more than 160°, there is nothing to be gained by flying a spinnaker staysail larger than a Tallboy. Whatever gain in area is achieved is usually offset by reduced overall efficiency.

Most rating or racing rules limit "ancillary" sails to some form of staysail set to fly within the established limits of the deck and rig. If we accept the hypothesis "Staysails larger than a Tallboy are a hindrance on a run" as correct, we are left with the question of what additional sails, if any, can be flown on this point of sailing? The answer is found under the spinnaker.

When properly set, the spinnaker flies several feet above the deck, with tack and clew in the same horizontal plane. The opening between the foot of the spinnaker and the deck provides an excellent opportunity for the imaginative skipper and sailmaker to add effective sail area without incurring any penalty.

Staysails set beneath the foot of the spinnaker should be very low aspect ratio sails that not only add area in their own right but further impede the limited "leakage" flow under the foot.

Few seem to attain their full potential because of the difficulties involved in trying to keep them full and drawing. There is much that can be done to improve them but it requires an enterprising sailmaker to bring it to fruition. (See figure 4.)

Sensing the Wind

The Effects of Apparent Wind

Velocity and direction in points of sail   Steve Colgate

Apparent wind is a very simple concept but it continues to mystify many people, some of whom have been sailing for years.

Apparent wind is a combination of the wind produced by a boat's movement through the air, and the wind produced by nature, the "true wind." It is the wind you "feel" when aboard a boat. Cigarette smoke, telltales, electronic wind direction indicators on cruising boats all show apparent wind direction.

I often hear the comment from new students "You said we sail within 45° of the wind when closehauled, but the wool on the shrouds indicates that we're sailing almost into the wind." This of course is their first experience with apparent wind.

Imagine yourself standing up in a convertible. It is a calm day, so there's no true wind. As the convertible starts forward, you will begin to feel a breeze on your face that will increase as the speed of the car increases. At 10 mph you will feel 10 mph of apparent wind on your face.

Now put yourself in the same car facing north. There's an easterly wind of 10 mph blowing and it is hitting the right side of your face. As the car starts forward you don't feel two different winds, one on your right side and one on the front of your face, but rather a combination of the two that comes from an angle that is forward of the true wind.

By taking boat speed and true wind speed and drawing to a consistent scale you can determine the force and direction of the apparent wind.

For example, if your boat speed is six knots and the true wind is twelve knots, measure off the units to scale

and draw a parallelogram. Its diagonal will be the apparent wind as shown in figure 1. By measuring the length of the diagonal using the same unit scale you can determine the speed (in knots) of the apparent wind.

In this case the diagonal or apparent wind measures 17 knots, and bears 27° from your heading. True wind is 40°. But notice how the direction of the apparent wind changes with the true wind in the following three diagrams. (For illustrative purposes we'll keep true wind speed and boat speed constant, though this would only be the case in actual practice if the boats were different sizes. (See figures 2-5.)

Four points should become obvious. First, the apparent wind is always forward of the true wind unless

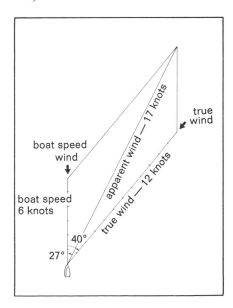

Figure 1
Apparent Wind — Closehauled

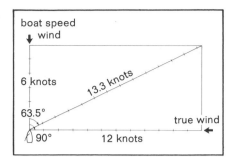

Figure 2
Apparent Wind — Beam Reach

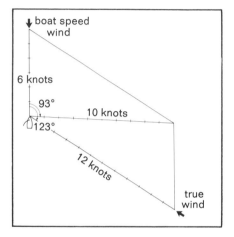

Figure 3
Apparent Wind — Broad Reach

important, therefore, to determine the actual direction of the true wind, and the angle your present heading is to it.

If you know you are steering 20° from dead downwind on one tack, then you will be on the same point of sailing when you are 20° from dead downwind on the other tack. The time to jibe should be when your destination bears 40° off your bow from your present heading.

The key, of course, is to determine the direction of the true wind. By glancing at your telltales and at the wind signs on the water (streaks and ripples), you can judge about how far forward of the true wind the apparent wind is.

A more positive way of determining true wind direction is to head off momentarily until the apparent wind and the true wind line up, i.e., dead downwind. The difference between the new heading and your former heading, 20° in this case, when doubled to 40°, is the number of degrees you will jibe in.

The second point, as the true wind comes aft apparent wind speed lessens, is obvious if you have ever seen a powerboat head downwind. Sometimes they cruise along at the same speed and in the same direction as the true wind. Their exhaust hangs around the boat like an enveloping cloud. Apparent wind is just about zero.

Novice sailing students rarely correlate wind velocity with boat direction and often comment that it's a shame the wind has died. They invariably make this comment on a run.

This lessening of the wind speed and thereby the force of the wind on the sails can lull you into forgetting the difference when you round a mark and start on a beat. You might start sailing on a run, and have no idea of the apparent wind strength on a beat. The wind may even have increased during the run. But either way you should think about shortening sail (on a cruising boat) before you come around onto a beat.

the true wind is dead ahead or dead astern. Second, as the true wind comes aft, apparent wind decreases in velocity. Third, when the true wind is well aft, a small change in true wind direction makes a *large* change in apparent wind direction. And fourth, when the boat is on a beam reach or closehauled, apparent wind has a higher velocity than the true wind.

The first point is important when considering when to jibe. Because it is desirable to sail at a slight angle to the wind rather than dead downwind, you may not be heading directly to your desired destination and will have to jibe to reach it. It's

It is much easier to do this while still on the run. Let's say a boat is going nine knots in a sixteen knot breeze. Going dead downwind, apparent wind is true wind minus boat speed, or just seven knots. This doesn't feel like much and the force on the sails is also relatively light. When the boat starts beating she may slow down to six knots, but apparent wind will increase to almost 21 knots!

You would assume that since the apparent wind is now three times greater than it was on the downwind leg, it will exert three times the force against the sails. Wrong.

The force of the wind quadruples as the velocity doubles and in this case the wind force is nine times greater on the close hauled course than it was was on the run. Couple this with the increased heeling moment of the close hauled course and the boat may very well be overpowered. You should always consider this during the run.

The third point I made about apparent wind is that when the true wind is well aft, a small change in true wind direction makes a large change in apparent wind direction. Compare figure 3 with figure 4. A 30° change in true wind direction makes a 38° change in apparent wind. And in comparing figure 4 with figure 5, we find a 16° change in true wind makes a 28° change in apparent wind.

This, among other things, is what makes steering dead downwind so difficult. For a small swing "by the lee" actually results in an exaggerated swing (by the lee) of the apparent wind. This can cause the boat to oscillate as the apparent wind swings madly back and forth from one side to the other on relatively minor changes in heading. And at the worst, it could force a flying jibe on the inexperienced helmsman.

My fourth point is that when a boat

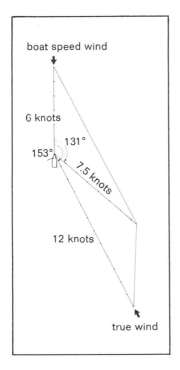

Figure 4
Apparent Wind — Running

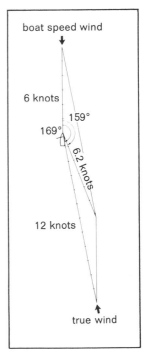

Figure 5
Apparent Wind — Running

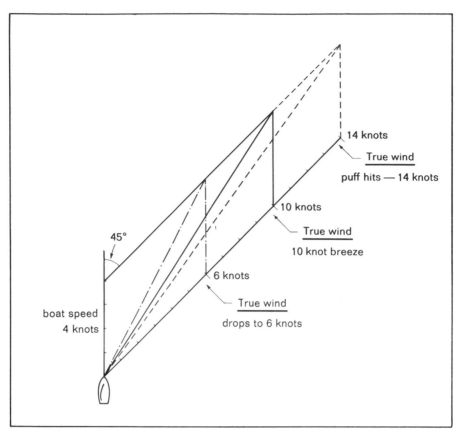

14 knots

True wind

puff hits — 14 knots

10 knots

True wind

10 knot breeze

45°

6 knots

True wind

boat speed
4 knots

drops to 6 knots

Figure 6

is either reaching or beating, the apparent wind has a greater velocity than the true wind. You are, in effect, "Making your own wind." In iceboating for example, this is an important part of the resulting high speeds: the speed record on iceboats is over 140 mph and the wind was probably only around 50 mph. Obviously the wind was created, and the faster the boat went, the higher the apparent wind velocity.

But these high speeds can be attained only because of a lack of friction. A normal sailboat's speed is limited by hull resistance, skin friction and wave making drag, so it cannot take full advantage of this increased apparent wind. A planing sailboat is more apt to get up on a high speed plane on a reach than a run just because of this increase in

apparent wind.

Some sailors don't seem to care about apparent wind and its effects. They say that it's the wind you've got and who cares where the *true* wind is.

It is helpful but perhaps not essential to know where the true wind is. But you definitely should develop an awareness of wind direction and the changes in *apparent* wind strength you can expect when your boat's heading changes.

We have seen what happens to apparent wind when the true wind direction changes, but boat speed and wind velocity remain constant. Now we'll change boat speed and wind velocity but keep true wind direction as a constant. Figure 6 shows a boat sailing closehauled on starboard tack with the true wind 45° off the bow. Boat speed is four knots and the true wind speed is ten knots. Let's see what happens when a puff hits.

The extension of the true wind line to 14 knots indicates a four knot increase in wind velocity. When we work the solution out graphically we learn a basic axiom: "In a puff the apparent wind will come aft."

To be absolutely correct, this would apply only if there were constant boat speed throughout. However, if the increase is just a puff, by the time the boat picks up speed the puff will have passed; so the axiom is essentially true.

We already know that we should point higher in a gust in order to reduce heeling. Now we have another reason to do the same thing. As the gust hits, apparent wind will go aft causing more heel, less drive and a changing angle of incidence (the angle the apparent wind makes with the sails). The net result is that the sails are now improperly trimmed unless you head up or ease the sheet or traveller.

This particular change in apparent wind direction is very important, especially on light days. If you have a three knot breeze, the wind velocity in a puff is apt to *more than double* the regular breeze. If it is blowing 15 knots, a gust may get to only 20-22 knots — only a third higher. Therefore, the movement aft in apparent wind direction is often greater on *light* days than it is on heavy ones.

The dot-dash line shows the resulting change in apparent wind if it suddenly dies. With boat speed remaining constant and the wind velocity lowering to six knots, the apparent wind will go forward. One way for the novice to remember this is to imagine the wind dying completely just as though someone had switched off a giant fan. Obviously, in the absence of any wind, the only breeze you would feel would be that produced by the forward motion of the boat and would come from dead ahead. So any reduction in true wind velocity must bring the apparent wind forward.

This happens quite often on light days, particularly to large cruising boats that have a great deal of momentum. The sails will start luffing and give the appearance of sailing too high or too close on the wind. Actually the boat is only travelling through a light spot or "hole" in the wind. The helmsman must make an immediate decision: Is it a valid wind shift, called a header, or is it just a hole? If it is the former, he must head off to fill the sails. If it is the latter, he could kill what little speed he has by heading off instead of shooting through the light spot with momentum and picking up the breeze on the other side.

It's always a difficult decision to make unless you can see a puff ahead. Usually the wisest course is to head off very slowly and evenly. If you're still luffing after turning 20° away from the wind it's probably a flat spot.

One warning. A skipper who reacts precipitously and turns the boat quickly downwind actually aggravates the situation if it's just a hole in the wind. The turn itself forces air against the lee side of the jib causing it to luff or back. In a short time he will find himself 30° below his previous course, but the jib is still luffing because of the turning movement of the boat.

Of course it may not be a hole, but rather a true header (the wind shifts towards the bow). The boat is sailing a straight course in a light, steady breeze and suddenly, because of the wind shift toward the bow of the boat, the jib starts to luff.

The skipper decides that instead of heading off to fill the sails, he will tack. As he turns the bow into the wind, the jib will fill as the apparent wind comes aft, due to the turning of the boat.

Because the jib has stopped luffing, it can appear that the wind has shifted back to its original direction. The skipper can have the impression that he has been lifted (the wind direction has changed more toward the stern of the boat) when actually it is only the pivoting of the boat that has caused the change.

An inexperienced or indecisive skipper will stop his tack in the middle and return to his original course. At first it will appear that he has made the correct decision because, by making the incomplete tack, he has slowed the boat which puts the apparent wind fairly well aft.

As the boat picks up speed the apparent wind will again come forward and he will find himself still sailing in the same header he had before.

Now let's consider cases where windspeed remains constant but boat speed varies. For instance, if the boat starts surfing down the face of a wave (much as the surfboarder would use a wave) the apparent wind goes forward. Sometimes it goes forward to the point where it will flatten the spinnaker back against the mast and rigging!

At other times the boat may slow down for some reason. The apparent wind comes aft and its velocity will increase. Last month I mentioned that as the wind velocity doubles, the pressure on the sails and rigging quadruples.

When a boat runs hard aground at high speed it is often dismasted be-

cause the rig and sails have a tendency to keep on going even though the hull has stopped. But another important reason is that the apparent wind pressure on the sails has increased suddenly.

A good example of this happened to *Mare Nostrum*, a 72′ yawl, on the 1955 Transatlantic Race from Cuba to Spain. We had a spinnaker, mainsail, mizzen (the small sail on a yawl's after mast) and a mizzen staysail (sort of a jib for the mizzen mast) set in fairly fresh winds of about 20-23 knots.

The swivel on the spinnaker halyard broke and the chute went streaming out ahead of the boat. Before we could get it aboard, it filled with water, went underneath the bow, and hooked on the keel. This slowed the boat down so suddenly that the top half of the mizzen mast toppled forward under the increased load on the mizzen staysail.

So always remember that whenever there is a change in either *boat speed* or *direction* or *wind velocity* or its *direction*, there must also be a change in the apparent wind. A helmsman must be alert to it and either change his course accordingly or the crew must trim or ease the sails.

Steering and Sail Trim

Gaining a feel for "the groove"   Bruce Goldsmith

The skipper winning the most races inevitably is going to be the one with the best *touch*. I call *touch* the simultaneous coordination of steering and sail trim with wind and sea conditions.

Tactics and wind patterns can be reduced to a matter of odds; they tend to be spread out over a group of equal sailing minds over a given period of time. But the guy who wins most is the one who can squirt out on two out of five starts, or squirt out of a pack after rounding a leeward mark.

This same fellow doesn't even seem to be pointing particularly high,

but he always winds up to windward.

This guy has a great touch. A few people seem to be born with it. Most aren't. But studying how to coordinate steering and sail trim to the wind and sea conditions, all at the same time, should help you develop your own touch.

First, a little bit about your mainsail. It's the key driving force in most small boats. In general, a full sail with its maximum draft well forward has what I call an accelerating shape (Figure 1a). This shape has power but doesn't really produce top speed and pointing ability.

Now a sail that is very flat with

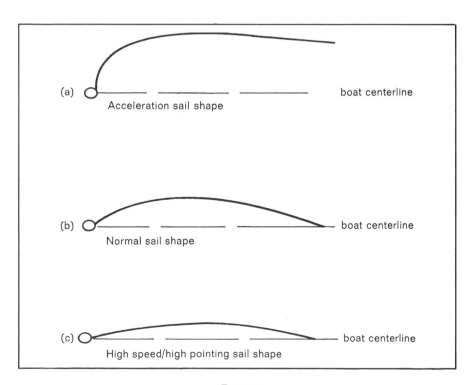

Figure 1

its maximum draft aft has a shape that can give you the potential for high speed and high pointing ability (Figure 1c). But it cannot provide the top acceleration and power you can get from the accelerating shape.

You can achieve this complete range of shapes on most boats simply by changing the sail's luff tension and by adjusting the trim of the mainsheet. The greater the luff tension on the sail the further forward the draft will be pulled.

If the mainsheet is also trimmed down, the mast (on a small boat) will deflect, which removes the draft from the front of the sail.

This downward trim also tightens the leech, actually adding a small amount of draft in the after part of the sail. The total effect of all these adjustments is that the entire draft will be reduced and moved aft in the sail.

Sailing upwind is really a never ending series of accelerations; the shifting to higher speeds and higher pointing angles and then a slowing down again as the wind comes and goes.

The smaller and lighter the boat and the more erratic the wind velocity, the more pronounced the acceleration and course headings are going to be.

The guy with the great touch can first trim loosely for acceleration; but he is also able to change to a high speed, high pointing sail shape just as he reaches the end of his maximum acceleration.

Simultaneously, he will alter course from what has been almost a close reach to a high pointing angle. And, as the inevitable slowdown comes once again from a drop in wind velocity, he gradually eases the sheet and makes the boat drop off to an angle that is again a close reach in time for the next puff.

If this lull is going to last more than a few seconds, it is important in small boats to use the speed you have built up to help get your boat to windward.

The best way to do this is to hold the sail trim, steer a little higher, and simultaneously roll the boat to windward in a slow manner.

In extreme lulls this tactic can land you a couple of boat lengths to windward without losing much potential speed. The theory here is that the sail is going to luff no matter what direction you point the boat, for the only wind left now is caused by boat speed, and the relative wind is going to be directly on the nose no matter where you are headed.

But this condition will abruptly change again as the next puff hits. It is essential that you be set up to accelerate again as the puff comes by easing the sheet, heading off slightly, and letting the boat heel.

This maneuver sets the boat up for the "squirt" that everyone cherishes and it is especially noticeable in small centerboarders.

Ideally, you should always trim the sails and position the boat with gentle sheeting changes and smooth steering — all done just an instant before the puff hits.

If you do it too soon you will waste precious distance sailing to leeward. If you do it too late you will waste the first part of the puff and must use some of it to get the right trim and angle for acceleration. This delays the *squirt* and, with boats around you, can be the difference in having clear air or not.

When you are sailing in steadier winds it's more important to maintain maximum boat speed, and individual spurts have less significance.

In this case you must search for an upwind *groove*. When you have found it the boat will nearly sail itself. It should have a very slight weather helm, and be sailing nearly flat.

Small changes in wind velocity and heeling moment will hardly change this feel at all. But remember this steering groove is only made possible by the shape and position of the sails. You must continually try to flatten your sails more to the high speed, high pointing sail shape.

And if you start to sail too far off

the wind, the boat will gyrate quickly from the weather helm to a lee helm as the boat becomes level again from its former heeling angle.

But if you try to sail to windward this way you will be sailing more by observing the leading edge of the sails than by really feeling the groove.

If the sails are set too flat the boat will tend to have a constant *lee* helm, for the same forces that created a weather helm with a full draft sail now cannot deflect the wind enough to get a bite to windward with the excessively flat sail.

Heeling the boat slightly will decrease the lee helm a little bit, but it will also reduce the drive. You will notice the boat never squirts on a puff.

The feeling is one of constant *blah* when a sail has been set too flat.

When you are sailing "in high point conditions", namely, steady medium force air of 5 to 15 mph with no waves, the groove will be very close to a point at which the sails are set too flat. In these conditions make sure you get the boat moving properly again after each tack, and closely watch for the occasional lull.

Steering the boat now becomes the critical factor, for the boat must be kept at just the right pointing angle. Many times the sail will be so flat forward that you can be too high on the wind and pinching, and it still won't luff.

And by the time you feel the boat slowing, it is already too late and falling off won't help much. The reason: your sails are not set to give you that fast acceleration again.

If there is someone alongside who seems to be able to steer his boat a little higher, and can sail faster with sails set flatter, eat your pride and set your own sails a little fuller. And steer the boat at a little less critical angle.

So far I've tried to show the sail setting/steering relationships which can run from one extreme of acceleration to the other, which features super high speed and high pointing.

My discussion assumes a moderate sailing breeze of about 5 to 15 mph. But sailing in winds on either side of this range should merely narrow your thinking toward the sail shape that applies.

For instance, if you're in a drifter, steering and sail set will remain in the acceleration stage longer. Even after the boat gets moving, the sail shape and steering won't change much toward the high speed/high point range.

However, in winds over 15 mph acceleration isn't the problem; you are now sailing almost entirely in the high speed/high point end of the range.

Closely note, though, that waves can really play havoc with your touch in these heavy air conditions. You'll also find you have a tendency to underreact to the changing situation when the really big breeze comes in.

Strong wind and relatively small waves are typical of a rapidly increasing breeze and it is necessary to get to the flat end of the sail set range very quickly.

The tipoff here is that weather helm increases and the boat feels glued into the water and bound up. It happens because the mainsail has not been flattened enough for the wind. In other words, you never shifted out of second gear! You have power but no boat speed.

Now as the waves build up you might tend to keep flattening your sails even more to make the boat free up and get into high gear. This is a fatal mistake, for at this point you will be pointing too high and waves will be giving you trouble, forcing you to make leeway.

In short, when you finally get around to flattening way in for the breeze, you really should be moving back to a slightly fuller sail set and driving off a little bit more to compensate for the waves. This is a time when that groove can really be elusive.

Coordinating your steering and sail set with the wind and sea conditions is a subtle matter. Changes must be smooth and simultaneously coordinated. If you are not moving your boat as fast as some of your competitors you've got to react immediately with a course change and a different sail set.

Believe me, it's a constantly changing situation. Running from acceleration bursts to the high speed range is always an exhilarating experience, and you can't learn how to do it overnight.

But once you get it you can lock in the groove and really perfect that bit of expertise every great sailor carries around with him — that little technique called *touch*.

Sail Balance on the Wind

Coordination of main and headsail trim   Arvel Gentry

Sailing **fast to windward** involves a complex interaction of sail shape and trim, boat balance and helm, and how the tiller is moved in response to each wave or cross-chop. There are optimum trade-offs for all these sail trim factors and they must become almost an automatic reflex.

Making a boat go fast usually comes with experience, but this learning process can be shortened by developing a sound approach to trimming the sails and for steering the boat. This month I will describe my own personal approach to making a boat go fast to windward by discussing the basic sail trim settings for the genoa and mainsail.

Obviously, no single article can possibly cover every aspect of sailing to windward, and I'll just try to touch on a few aspects of the problem that I think are particularly important. I will assume we are sailing a keel boat of MORC size or larger with a masthead rig and overlapping genoa.

As I proceed with the various steps in trimming the genoa and mainsail, keep in mind the following basic interaction effects that occur between the two sails.

First, the genoa causes a *slowing down* of the slot air flow over the forward lee-side of the mainsail. Just the right amount of slowing down of the slot air will be beneficial for it permits the mainsail to be sheeted in at a tight angle without stalling. Thus, the genoa helps keep the mainsail lee-side from separating.

However, if the genoa is sheeted too close (or the main let out too far), the pressures will become the same on both sides of the mainsail. It will then start to shake (commonly called backwinding) and its contribution to

the total driving force will be reduced.

A properly trimmed mainsail creates an upwash flow field in front of the genoa (a wind shift corresponding to a lift) which allows the boat to be sailed closer to the wind without the genoa's luffing.

The high velocities created by the mainsail in the region of the genoa leech cause increased velocities and reduced pressures all along the lee side of the genoa. This gives the genoa its great drive and also helps keep the lee-side genoa flow from separating. Proper mainsail trim is very important in getting the most out of the genoa.

As we search for proper sail trim, we attempt to find the best compromise between all these effects. We want the genoa to help the mainsail without pushing it to the point where the mainsail's contribution to the total driving force is reduced. And we want the mainsail to be trimmed tightly enough so that it gives the maximum help to the genoa leech velocities without reducing its drive.

In practice I find that flow separation on the leeward side of the sails is the key factor that controls what we do in trimming them. Separation on the windward side is not nearly so important. While we can't see air, we can see what it does to our sails and to pieces of yarn or ribbon telltales that we attach to them. But where to put these telltales and how to use them are questions that are worth studying in detail.

I'd like to do two things in the following discussion. First, help you establish your own systematic approach to trimming the sails. Second, help you learn what the different sail

Photo 1
Telltale and tuft arrangement

adjustments actually are doing to your sails.

Photo 1 shows the telltale system I use. I've numbered each telltale on the photo for easy reference. The telltales are made from ½" by 6" strips of 0.5 oz. spinnaker cloth. The strips are cut with a pointed soldering iron using a metal straight edge; plastic tape is used to attach them to the sail. I find these ribbons more responsive in light winds than telltales made from yarn (although they do tend to stick to the sail when wet). Each of the numbered telltales has its own purpose in achieving the proper sail trim.

To aid in steering the boat, I've developed a system of short (4") ribbons that are placed near the luff of the genoa. This system is marked with the letter T in Photo 1. I refer to these as "tufts" and to all of the other ribbons on the sails as "telltales." The tuft system consists of one short ribbon right on the rope luff, two more in a plastic window, and one just aft of the window. The port-side tufts are red and the starboard ones green.

The plastic window is put as close to the luff tape as is possible, for it is important to be able to see the first two tufts. The tufts are attached to the window with transparent tape. The same tuft arrangement can be used without the window but it may be difficult to see them under certain lighting conditions.

The lee-side telltales tell when the air has separated from the surface of the sail. The air in these separated regions is rather mixed-up and unsteady and causes the telltales to twirl wildly. When the air is completely separated from the lee side of a sail, it is stalled and its forward driving force is greatly reduced. However, separated flow on only a portion of a sail can be almost as bad and will put you out of contention quickly.

This partial separation occurs most frequently on the after-half of a sail and is particularly important on the mainsail and on the genoa under certain conditions. When a sail is not generating lift because it has too low an angle to the wind, it will shake or luff. However, when it has too high an angle you can't tell from the sail shape; you must look at the lee-side telltales.

When I start sailing on a new boat I first install the telltales and tuft system shown in Photos 1 and 2. Next, with a label maker, I put numbers by each genoa track screw, on the traveler, outhaul, and on the mast for halyard tension. I also wrap a piece of tape around the spreader six inches in from the end, and another twelve inches in. These help me judge the distance the genoa is lying off the spreader.

Next I begin to check sail trim while beating (I'll assume about 8 to 10 knots of wind). To begin, I guess at genoa halyard tension and fairlead position. The genoa is trimmed so that it lies three to four inches from the spreader, and the mainsail is set so that it is not luffing. All are just approximate positions.

The first task is to check the genoa car location. The usual way to determine this is to sail close hauled, luff the boat up, then adjust the genoa car so the genoa luffs evenly all along the luff.

However, I have a different approach that I believe is a bit more precise. First, sail the boat precisely on the wind by making all the lee-side tufts at T lie down. The part of the genoa at T is then just on the verge of luffing. Now look at telltale 7 (Photo 1) at the top of the genoa luff. If it is twirling, the sail needs to twist off more so move the jib fairlead aft a bit. If the sail is luffing at 7, it has too much twist up high, so move the fairlead forward. Again sail precisely on the wind with all the tufts at T lying down.

Now have the helmsman start to bear off slowly and, from the pulpit, watch both the first leading-edge tuft at T-1 and telltale 7. As you start to bear off, both these ribbons will suddenly twirl as a small separation bubble forms all along the luff. The sail is not stalled, it only has this small separation bubble all along the luff (SAIL, May 1973).

If the twirling starts at 7 and T-1 at the same time, the wind is coming into the sail at about the same angle all along the luff. Again, this use of telltale 7 and tuft T-1 at this time only gives the approximate genoa car location, for overall sail shape is frequently even more important.

Write down the genoa car location number; then observe telltale 7 as the car is moved way forward, and again when it is moved too far aft. Always sail with tuft T-1 just lying down smoothly but the sail at T not luffing. From this exercise you will see how different amounts of twist affect the flow over the luff of the sail.

Now return the genoa car to the location you have marked. Sail with the first tuft at T-1 showing just a

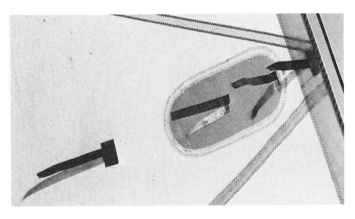

Photo 2
Tuft system
Headstay and
jib luff are
at far right

slight amount of agitation. Check all the lee-side telltales on the genoa. If any of the leech telltales, (3, 4, 6, and 8) are twirling, then try increasing the halyard tension and letting the sheet out a bit to maintain the same distance off the spreader. At this point we still may not have exactly the correct genoa car location or halyard tension. But before we spend more time on the genoa, let's switch our attention to the mainsail.

The mainsail has a strong influence on the flow over the genoa and we should be sure it is trimmed properly before we worry further about the genoa. The mainsail is controlled by the mainsheet, traveler, outhaul, cunningham, vang, leech chord, batten stiffness, and mast bend. The mainsheet and traveler, however, are the key adjustments for they affect mainsail position and twist.

To start, set the traveler on the centerline. Let way out on the mainsheet and then pull it in as you watch the top lee-side telltale, 13. Stop when 13 twirls, and let the sheet back out until it lies down.

Now check the lower part of the main near the mast to see if it is being *backwinded* by the genoa. Personally, I don't like the term "backwinding" for it seems to imply that the genoa is throwing air against the lee side of the main, and this is not what is happening at all. The mainsail is just reacting to an increase in lee-side pressure resulting from the genoa's slowing down of the air in the slot. However, everyone does seem to use the term and therefore I will, too.

If the main is being backwinded, move the traveler to windward until the backwinding stops. Now readjust the mainsheet again until the top telltale 13 twirls, then just lies down again. Repeat these traveler-mainsheet adjustments until the sail is not being backwinded and the top telltale is just lying down.

If the genoa has a large amount of overlap, a 180% genoa, for example, it may be difficult to stop the back-

winding without pulling the mainsail so tight and so far to windward that the mainsail leech hooks sharply to windward. To fight this problem, first try tightening the outhaul. If this doesn't work, try increasing by an inch or so the genoa's distance off the spreader.

Now check the mainsail leech telltales, 10, 12, and 14. If any of them is twirling, and 9, 11, and 13 are not, you have a leech flow separation problem because the leech is hooking too far to windward. First tighten the outhaul and then the cunningham to let the leech fall off some. Remember, when you apply tension to one edge of a sail, the other edge will fall off some. You also may have to move the traveler down a bit.

If the bottom row of telltales (9 and 10) are twirling, the lower part of the mainsail is either in too tight or the genoa is not trimmed in enough. Move the traveler to leeward until they settle down and adjust the mainsheet until the top row of telltales again are lying down. Your main purpose in all this is to learn how to coordinate the traveler and mainsheet tension to get the proper twist in the sail.

After a few repeated cycles of these adjustments, write down or mark the traveler position so that you can return to it. Now observe the mainsail lee-side telltales as the traveler is moved further to windward. The leech telltales, (10, 12, and 14) will twirl about the same time followed quickly by 9, 11, and 13 as the complete sail stalls. This tells you that all parts of the mainsail are working equally hard in generating lift *and in helping the genoa.* Now return the traveler to its proper best position.

Sight up along the mainsail and see if the top batten is hooking to windward of the centerline of the boat. If it is, then you may not be getting maximum forward drive out of the upper part of the sail, even though telltales 13 and 14 are lying down. Let the leech fall off, so that it does not hook to windward, by letting out the mainsheet a bit and moving the traveler slightly to windward. If this causes telltales 10 or 12 to twirl, then increase the cunningham tension and again adjust the mainsheet and traveler to get all of them to lie down.

Whatever you do, always trim the sail so that telltales 13 and 14 are lying down; sometimes if you trim the main so that the top battens are pointing straight aft, telltales 13 and 14 will be twirling and the upper part of the sail will be stalled; so using just the batten alignment procedure may lead to bad mainsail trim.

After the mainsail is trimmed, turn again to the genoa. Watch the genoa tuft system at T and telltale 7 first as the boat is sailed precisely on the wind, and then as you bear off slightly to see if the mainsail adjustments have had any effect on proper genoa settings. If they have, then repeat the genoa trim procedure.

As an experiment, try sailing only with the T-1 tuft twirling in steady wind and smooth water. Then let the traveler way out and move it all the way windward to stall the sail and watch what happens to the T-1 tuft each time. In this way, you will see how mainsail trim does affect the air flow over the genoa.

You should have the two sails trimmed pretty well by this time. However, a number of questions are yet to be resolved. How good is the boat's balance? Is there too much lee or weather helm? How is the shape of the genoa? Should we barber haul it, and how much? What about sail trim in very low or very high wind conditions? And finally, how is the tuft system used in steering the boat to windward? Next month's article will pursue these questions.

But good windward performance depends not only upon basic sail trim, but also on boat balance: having just the right amount of weather helm.

We have now seen how to use the telltales and tufts to achieve the basic sail trim settings. Once you

have these settings, sail to windward with the first lee side tuft, T-1 in Photo 2, showing just a slight amount of agitation. Let the tiller go and watch the boat's movement. If the boat starts to head up slowly into the wind, the boat's balance probably is good.

If it heads off instead, you have what is called *lee helm* and it should be corrected before going farther. First try moving crew weight forward and to leeward in light air. If possible, lean the mast farther aft.

If the boat turns sharply to windward when you release the tiller, then you have too much *weather helm*. Try moving the crew aft and to the weather side, and ease the mainsail traveler down until only a moderate amount of tiller pressure is required to keep the boat going straight. If you still have too much weather helm, try leaning the mast forward.

Once you have the boat in reasonable balance, turn your attention to the genoa. The trim of both sails might look about as they do in Photo 3. Examine the leech of the genoa and the curve of the mainsail in this picture. You will see that the distance between the genoa and the main increases from the spreader down to the boom, and the shape of the genoa leech does not follow the mainsail shape (as it should). With smooth water conditions, this is a good time for a barber haul.

To rig a barber haul, hook a line to the jib clew with a shackle, run it across to the windward winch, and pull the clew "into" the boat. As you do this, ease off on the genoa sheet to maintain the same distance off at the spreader. This easing will create more twist and camber in the sail but the fixed distance off the spreader can be maintained. The boat now should not only point closer to the wind, it also should keep up its speed. What we have done with the barber haul is to get a better method of controlling the *total shape* of the genoa.

With a barber haul, you may have

| Photo 3 | Photo 4 |
| Without barber haul | With barber haul |

to move the jib fairlead a bit forward to get the desired leech shape in the genoa. After all this is completed, check genoa telltale #3 (Photo 1). If you barber haul too much, this telltale will twirl.

As you barber haul the genoa in, you also may have to move the mainsheet traveler to windward more, and ease the mainsheet at the same time to maintain proper attached flow all up and down the mainsail. If the genoa hooks in sharply at the leech, first check the leechline. Let it out until the leech shakes, then tighten it just until the flutter stops. Also increase the jib halyard tension. This will ease the leech so that the air gets a straighter run from the sail's mid-point to the leech. Photo 4 shows the sail with the barber haul set.

When to barber haul and how much are difficult questions to answer. Basically, the barber haul should be adjusted so the leech of the genoa follows the curve of the mainsail. But there will be times when the genoa should be trimmed tighter and other times when it must

be moved farther outboard. But when and how much?

One useful approach lies in the axiom "know thy boat." By this, I mean you should have a very good idea of what boat speed you should be able to achieve at different velocities of apparent wind. I call this *maximum windward speed* and it is obtained by recording apparent wind speed and boat speed readings when beating in smooth water conditions. A large collection of these data points can be plotted (boat speed versus apparent wind speed) and a smooth line drawn through the highest points. However, it is important that each point be an honest data point; that is, that the boat be sailed at the apparent wind angle and with sail trim settings that you feel give the best speed-made-good to windward. As you learn more about your boat and how to trim its sails, this maximum windward speed curve should, of course, be revised.

When the water is smooth and the boat has reached its maximum windward speed in moderate (10-12 knots) try the barber haul. But first, sail close hauled without a barber haul for a few minutes and observe the average speed. Write both the boat's speed and the average wind speed down. Now barber haul the genoa in and watch boat speed.

If boat speed does not drop, then obviously you should be barber hauled for this wind and sea condition. If the boat speed does drop, you must now determine if the closer pointing angle achieved is offsetting the speed reduction. More testing is required.

When the wind and chop increase and the boat cannot reach maximum beating speed, the barber haul will have to be eased off to get speed back up.

In light winds you need more camber in the genoa and you should ease the sheet. This, however, moves the sail farther from the spreader and the ability to point goes down. Check boat speed and slowly barber haul the clew back in to see if you can get back some pointing ability without losing too much speed. Maintaining unseparated flow on telltale #3 is going to be particularly difficult under these conditions.

At this point you should have both sails trimmed fairly well. Now check both the knotmeter and the apparent wind speed and write down the values. All further sail adjustments should be made carefully with a close watch on the knotmeter. Try changing the genoa distance off the spreader and watch boat speed and pointing ability. This is a very important parameter and careful testing is required to find the optimum distance for each wind and sea condition.

Always record exactly how the sails are set after each adjustment to sail trim. Numbering each genoa and traveler screw, marking every inch along the outhaul and similarly marking the mast for halyard tension, (the backstay as well) makes this job much easier. By using these sail trim numbers, you have a sure way of repeating your trim under similar wind and sea conditions.

After a number of practice ses-

sions you will be able to construct a complete table of the sail settings for the complete range of windspeeds. This table should include the distance the sail should be off the spreader, the genoa track number, barber haul position, genoa halyard, outhaul, main traveler, backstay tension, mast lean position, crew weight position, tacking angle, and best boat speed. Tabulate these trim numbers for each three-to-five-knot change in apparent wind speed.

When race time comes, such a table can be taped to the bulkhead and used as a reference by the crew. Every time the apparent wind speed indicator changes, they should consult the sail trim table and make the necessary adjustments. While this relieves the helmsman from constantly worrying about sail trim, he should, however, check the sail trim himself occasionally and suggest any necessary changes.

Never feel bound to a sail-trim chart if you think a trim change might improve speed under new sailing conditions. If you do make a change, though, have the crew make a note of it so that the trim chart can be revised. In this way, your learning from past experience will be preserved.

All this sail-trim discussion has been for moderate winds of 10 to 12 knots. In light airs you need every bit of sail drive you can get. Slack off the halyard, and the backstay if you think you need more sail camber. Also keep the genoa farther off the spreader. Exaggerate the forward location of the genoa car in light airs. Barber haul with care and watch telltale #3. If it twirls, barber haul it *only* if it definitely gives increased speed or pointing ability.

Never try to point too high, and always keep the boat moving. Frequently check for lee helm, and if it occurs in light winds, shift crew weight forward and to leeward. Lee helm in light airs can be very bad for you will generate excessive leeway.

Too much sail camber can be a

bad thing in very light air. The reasons revolve around the way sail pressures change with camber, and the way boundary layer reacts to pressure and low air speeds.

In general, increased sail camber means there will be a decrease in the suction pressure from the forward part of the lee side of the sail as one moves aft (increasing pressure). In addition, the boundary layer is more prone to separation as air speed gets lower. This means that increased camber at low wind speed may give you a difficult leech separation problem. When this happens, the leech telltales on the main (10, 12, and 14 in Photo 1) and the genoa (3, 4, 6, and 8) will start to twirl.

If the telltales do twirl, the sails have too much camber. On the mainsail, tighten the outhaul, ease the sheet off a bit, and move the traveler to leeward to see if you can get the leech telltales to lie down. On the genoa, tighten up on the backstay and halyard, and move the clew outboard. Remember, a flat sail without separation usually is better than a fuller sail that has leech separation.

When the wind gets high you do have to start compromising. A tight backstay and genoa halyard are very important. Move the genoa car aft and barber haul it if maximum beating speed still can be maintained when it is hauled in. Mainsail trim in heavy winds is primarily a matter of controlling weather helm and heel angle.

First of all, trim the main very flat with the outhaul. Then let the traveler down to leeward and tighten the mainsheet. Be careful to control the leech so that it doesn't hook to windward. Take up on the cunningham tension even to the point of creating vertical folds along the luff. This tension helps keep the sail camber forward and makes the leech fall off to leeward which will ease both the weather helm and the heeling force.

Above all, have everyone, including the helmsman, to windward to keep the boat as flat as possible. If you still can't keep the boat flat it's time to reef the main. If that won't do it, reduce the size of the headsail.

Of course if you can't get either sail to trim the way you think it should, consult your sailmaker. He may be able to tell you what you are doing wrong, or he may need to rework the sail slightly to correct the problem. For example, the leech of the mainsail in Photo 3 was too tight. The sail was considerably improved by letting out two seams by $\frac{1}{4}''$ (after these photos were taken).

Sailing a boat to windward requires, above all else, concentration. And this concentration, by the best helmsmen, is more intense than a beginner can even hope to comprehend. A great helmsman can "feel" the boat. And he reacts instinctively with the proper twitch of the wheel or tiller, always keeping the boat "in the groove" and moving at its best. But what can you do to improve your windward steering?

First, you must know your boat. How does the boat react to varying wind and sea conditions? Is it sluggish and slow to respond, or is it quick to accelerate? How does this responsiveness change with wind speed? Does the boat tend to pound in short chop or does it cut right through it? Can the tiller be moved quickly in choppy conditions without slowing the boat, or must you move the helm slowly? How does boat speed change with varying wind speeds?

The first task when steering to windward is to keep the sails at the proper angle to the wind; and a helmsman usually has two visual clues to help him. If he sails too close on the wind, his sails will luff. If he sails too far off, the sails will stall. A stall usually is detected by watching yarn or ribbon telltales placed about one foot behind the genoa luff. When the lee telltale twirls, the sail is stalled.

While both conditions, the luff and the stall, cause a reduction in the driving force out of the sails, there are usually several degrees of heading angle between the two conditions. If the helmsman wanders back and forth between the two extremes, he soon will be left far behind the other boats. Even if he always sails right on the edge of the luffing condition his boat performance still will be bad. The boat may hit a wave or some chop. Then, after it has slowed, it will be too slow in accelerating back up to speed.

A good helmsman must know when it is best to let the sails luff momentarily or when to bear off slightly for quick acceleration. He must know just where between these two conditions he will get the best steady state of windward performance. And equally important, he must know how to change his steering techniques with differing speeds and sea conditions.

A good helmsman always *knows* how close he is to luffing or stalling, and how rapidly he is approaching one of these conditions. While this does come with much practice and experience, I've developed a special tuft system that replaces the conventional single luff telltale to help shortcut this learning process.

On my boat, the crew uses a complete set of telltales on both the genoa and the mainsail to achieve total sail trim. But the helmsman steers watching only the tuft system shown in Photo 1. This system consists of a line of four short tufts placed end to end with the first one right up against the luff rope.

This tuft system (Photo 2) is based on the fact that the lee-side flow will separate in the form of a small bubble right at the luff of a sail when the boat is headed slightly below the luffing condition. Behind this bubble, flow remains attached and the sail is not stalled. The row of short tufts simply shows the size of the bubble (Fig. 6). Please note that these drawings only show the first 18" of the genoa, and the sail angle difference in the drawings is exaggerated to illustrate the effects of the bubble.

When the sail is precisely on the verge of luffing, the stagnation streamline (the streamline that divides the windward and the lee-side air streams) curves right into the luff rope, and the lee-side separation bubble does not exist. All the lee-side tufts, even the one right on the luff rope, will lie down smoothly (Fig. 6A). The windward side frequently will be separated but this is not so important as the tuft activity, or lack of it, on the lee side.

As the boat heads off a bit, the stagnation streamline moves slightly around to the windward side of the luff rope. This causes high, leading-edge velocities and low pressures as the air makes the sharp turn around the luff. After the air gets around to the lee side, it immediately starts to slow down and its pressure starts increasing. The boundary layer does not like this increase in pressure, and it separates. If the turn around the leading edge has not been too sharp, the flow soon will reattach itself to the sail and continue aft to the leech (Fig. 6-B).

The farther off the wind the boat is heading, the larger the separation bubble gets. Finally it bursts and the entire lee side of the sail separates and the sail becomes stalled (Figs. 6-C and D). The number of twirling tufts tells you the size of the bubble. They also tell you how close you are to the luffing condition (no bubble at all), and how close you are to the stall point. By watching the changes in the tufts you also can tell *how rapidly* you may be moving toward one of these unwanted conditions.

When you first start sailing with this tuft system, don't try to use it to steer the boat. Sail the boat as you usually do, and then after you think you have the boat in the groove, see just what the lee-side tufts are doing. Are they all lying down smoothly, or is the first one slightly agitated? The reaction of the tufts to different conditions does vary slightly with different boats or sails, so I'll just show how they work on my own boat.

On my genoa, the three tufts can swirl before the sail stalls completely. In medium winds, the best

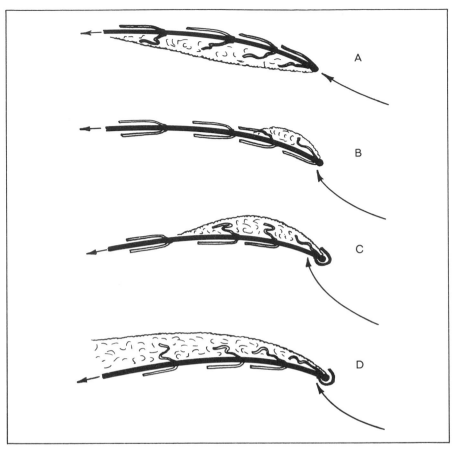

Figure 6

windward performance occurs when only the first lee tuft is slightly agitated.

In heavier air, over 15 knots, the genoa is kept on the verge of luffing a good deal of the time and all the lee-side tufts are lying down.

When boat speed is lost because of wave action or lack of concentration, head the boat off slightly until the first two tufts twirl. Quickly glance at the knotmeter and as soon as speed is back up, bring the boat back onto the wind until the tufts either lie down again, or the first one is slightly agitated.

The basic concept in high winds is to keep the boat upright and to control exactly how the bow strikes each wave or chop. By watching the wave

and chop patterns you will start to see situations where the proper changes in the boat's heading will improve windward performance.

There are several ways to handle waves and chop. At times you may have to bring the bow up to meet a short wave that might stop the boat. The sail may luff momentarily and the speed might drop slightly. You then must head the boat off to accelerate back up to speed. Watch the tufts when you do this so you don't stall the sail. Also keep an eye on the next wave so that it doesn't hit you while you are heading too far off the wind. In fact, it might be necessary to stay high for a second short wave before you bear off to accelerate.

Often you will find that only small changes in the bow position allow you to pass over the edge of a new wave without slowing the boat, and this maneuver actually helps you get to windward.

If you see a smooth spot of water just ahead of a wave, you might bear off slightly to gain extra speed just before you head up sharply to slice through the water.

Steering through waves and chop is complicated by the pitching motion of the boat. This gets particularly bad when the wind begins to drop off, leaving behind a sloppy sea. Here you must search for the best compromise between having the genoa luff (or float) as the bow goes down, and having the sail stall when the bow comes back up.

You should try to avoid being too far off the wind for you will find that if you are, you will spend too much time with the sails stalled. In other words, if necessary, let the sail luff briefly. Then when the pitching stops, bear off slightly to accelerate back up to top speed.

In moderate winds and smooth water most steering problems involve finding the angle that is the best trade-off between boat speed and pointing ability. This, incidentally, is where the tuft system works best. Once you find out just how much agitation (if any) should show on the first lee side tuft to get the boat in the *groove*, it should be a simple matter to keep it there.

Remember though, that pointing ability is determined by the actual path of the boat through the water and not the angle of the boat relative to other boats around. If you pinch too close to the wind you may *seem* to be pointing high, but slower speeds and excessive leeway may produce poor windward performance.

Beating in light air presents a whole new set of problems, and concentration and a light tiller touch both are essential. Avoid rapid tiller movements, for this creates both increased rudder drag and higher hull drag; the boat now is being rotated by the rudder. When possible, let the boat do the work for you.

For example, if the wind shifts and the first two or three lee-side tufts twirl, don't head the boat up by pushing the tiller over. Instead, gently release the finger pressure that has been holding back the slight weather helm, and let the boat head up by itself. Then when the lee side tufts start to lie back down, gently restrain the tiller again to stop the boat's rotation.

If weather helm is not enough to do this and you must move the tiller yourself to get the right angle to the wind, then do it smoothly and gently and give the boat plenty of time to respond. Be patient.

Good windward performance, of course, depends on more than just the helmsman. The crew can help too. If it is at all possible, the genoa should *never* be cleated on a windward leg. A crew member should be on the winch at all times watching the sail distance off the spreader, the knotmeter, and the apparent windspeed indicator.

If he sees the boat is losing speed because of chop, he should let the genoa out so that it is several more inches off the spreader. As boat speed comes back up, he should bring the sail back in again. If the wind drops again, the sail should go back out. If the sea gets smooth and the helmsman starts to point up to take advantage of it, then the genoa should come in.

In some cases, this constant in-and-out genoa adjustment is best accomplished with the barber haul instead of the genoa sheet. In other cases the two should be moved together. It even may help to move the main traveler or mainsheet to coincide with genoa movements. All these sail adjustments should be made smoothly and none should interfere with or counteract the actions of the helmsman.

It does help, when first practising, to have the helmsman and sheet tender constantly talk to each other. But after a while, each one should be able to anticipate the actions of the other without any verbal communication.

Throughout all these maneuvers, the helmsman can use the lee-side tufts to tell just where he lies between the luffing and the stalled condition, and how rapidly he may be changing from one phase to another. However, for top performance, he should keep an eye on the tufts, on the water just ahead of the boat, and on the knotmeter.

Never look only at the tufts. Keep looking around so you can learn to anticipate what oncoming waves or chop will do to the boat. And curiously enough, the sensitivity of this tuft system actually may give you more time to spend looking forward and around rather than just staring at the sail luff all the time. However, even with this new sailing aid, long hours of practice and great concentration still are the keys to good windward sailing.

Of course you must remember that good boat speed is never going to be much help if you are not sailing in the right direction. The helmsman always must keep his brain in gear and constantly at work on developing situations.

Better yet, he should have someone else worry about the tactics. That way he can concentrate only on how to steer to make the boat go fast.

Sail Trim When Beating

Influences of the jib on the main   Peter Sutcliffe

It has been long recognized that the main is heavily influenced by the jib, but what doesn't seem to have been discussed is that the main also affects the jib in a beneficial fashion by lifting it and allowing the boat to point higher.

The classic approach when going to windward is to consider the jib as a contracting slot that increases the velocity over the leeward side of the main and, by Bernoulli's equation, the suction forces. An alternate theory is that the increased velocity over the lee side of the main postpones flow separation providing greater driving force for the main.

But look at the flow pattern around a thin, curved airfoil at an angle of attack to the free airflow. (See figure 1.) It shows the usual streamline pattern on both the windward and leeward sides, with the flow from the trailing edge, the leech, diverted downward from the free stream

angle due to the turning action of the airfoil.

However, the streamlines *ahead* of the airfoil are diverted upward by the turning action of the airfoil that transmits outwards a series of pressure differences to the adjacent air molecules. These travel at the speed of sound, and since the speed of a sailboat is strictly subsonic, such pressure differences are transmitted *forward* as well as to the side and back.

In effect, air molecules ahead of the foil are warned that they will be affected by it, and they start to react before they reach the leading edge. This upward deviation is called, in aerodynamic terms, *upwash;* the downward deviation aft of the leech is called *downwash.* The upwash and downwash angles are proportional to the lift force on the main at a constant windspeed.

Imagine a jib superimposed in front of the main airfoil as shown by

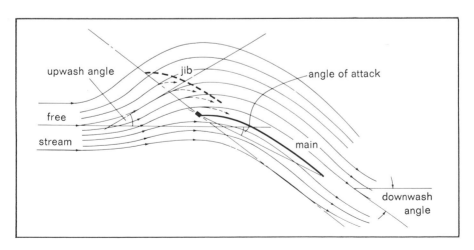

Figure 1
Flow around main.

the broken lines in figure 1. The jib's airflow field is now influenced by the main and the local angle of attack of the jib is increased, in effect the jib is "lifted" by the main. This means that the jib, and therefore the boat, can be sailed closer to the wind because of the main's beneficial effect on the jib.

However, flow is deviated down by the jib, "heading" the main, and it must be trimmed further in than if there were no jib.

I have recently been experimenting with tufts of yarn or wool on the jib of my Town Class sloop and have found that trimming the main in further to the centerline caused the leeward jib tuft to flutter, indicating that the boat could be headed up higher. Similar experiments and conclusions by Bruce Goldsmith have been reported by Robert Smithers in the June 1971 issue of *One-Design & Offshore Yachtsman*.

As previously noted, the upwash provided by the main increases with lift on the main up to the stalling angle of attack. In general, the main should be trimmed at or near maxi-

Sailplan of Town Class sloop

mum lift conditions when beating. Therefore it appears that the optimum setting of the main behind the jib is when further inward movement of the boom (or increase in angle of attack of the main) produces no further lift on the jib (assuming a constant heading). Naturally this would only apply to wind conditions where the maximum sail force creates a heeling moment that can be handled without easing the main.

The interaction between main and jib just described is fairly straightforward for a masthead rig where the entire main is influenced by the jib. However, on working jibs with $\frac{1}{2}$ or $\frac{3}{4}$ masthead geometries, there is a difference.

Here the main divides into two areas: below the top of the jib and above the jib. Obviously the main-jib interaction applies to the mainsail area behind the jib but not to that above the jib. The lower part of the main operates at a higher angle of attack than the jib because the jib *heads* it, and the upper part of the main will be at a smaller angle of attack because it is not *headed*.

The working jib's influence on any main is progressively reduced from the boom up. Hence the angle of attack of the main should gradually reduce from the boom to the point at the top of the jib. It should remain about constant for the rest of the distance to the masthead (ignoring the change in apparent angle of the local wind because of the vertical wind gradient).

How does one determine that the various parts of the main are at the correct angle to the wind?

Tufts again seemed to be the simple solution and I put two sets on my main. The lower ones were about two feet above the boom and about one-third of the way back from the mast toward the leech. The upper ones on the main were just above the top of the jib and about half way back from the mast toward the leech.

After some experimenting, I could trim the lower part of the main in until it no longer lifted the jib which was set to keep the leeward lower main tuft smooth. By pulling the traveller toward the centerline of the boat but keeping the boom at the same athwartships position, i.e., by letting the sheet out and allowing the boom to lift, I was able to induce enough twist to keep the upper leeward tuft smooth as well.

These tests were conducted in relatively light airs, about ten knots, and although I have not yet been able to experiment over a wide range of wind speeds, I believe the same boom setting would hold good until the traveller had to be moved outboard to reduce heeling moment.

I have also found the upper main tufts beneficial in determining proper vang tension for reaching. I had been setting the vang as tight as possible, but I found that if I trimmed normally and let the sail out until it just luffed behind the mast, the upper leeward wool tuft indicated a stalled condition proving that the angle to the wind was too great.

By *reducing* the vang tension and increasing the twist in the sail the upper leeward tuft was made to stream smoothly again, indicating that the flow was attached and the upper part of the sail was operating efficiently.

There may be nothing new here; expert sailors have probably been doing all this for years. But at least I think that now I understand, from a technical viewpoint, why they do it.

Light Air Adjustments

The delicate art of zephyr sailing   Steve Colgate

All skippers and crews can look good in winds from 8-15 knots. It's the heavy and light air conditions that really test you. Let's take a look at light air conditions.

On light, "flukey," drifting days, often you hear how "lucky" some guy was in a race for he got the wind first when it filled in. If you look at the record, though, you'll probably find that the same guy is "lucky" most of the time. Probably he has a little more patience and concentration than the others; he has studied the weather and currents better. And he may be more observant, noticing smoke, darkness on the water or sails on other boats that might indicate a new breeze.

There are some things you can do to make your own boat sail faster in very light air. One of the most important techniques is to heel the boat slightly. At slow speeds, the friction of the water running past the hull is a greater drag factor than it is at higher speeds where wave-making drag becomes more important. Obviously, a clean, smooth bottom on the boat reduces friction, and that's a matter of hull preparation.

But reducing the amount of hull surface in contact with the water (the wetted surface) also reduces friction. Heeling the boat lifts more hull surface out on the windward side than is submerged on the leeward side of most hull shapes. This net reduction in wetted surface reduces friction.

Heeling the boat has the added effect of allowing the sails to fall into their *designed shape*. For example, if three persons pick up a sail by the head, tack and clew, it will take the shape designed into it. But hang the sail vertically and it's a mess of wrinkles. Of course, when a puff does come, it will fill the sail which then will start to pull for you. But if the boat already is heeled, the sail will start to pull immediately as the puff hits. And it will work with the slightest zephyr.

Another advantage to heeling the boat is the slight weather helm it will create. This gives lift to the rudder, helps reduce leeway, and makes it much easier for the helmsman to steer well.

To heel a boat, simply put the crew on the leeward side. This can be done in everything from dinghies to 12-meter boats. In other words, it's worth trying on *any* boat. Make sure the crew stays low and doesn't disturb the existing airflows.

Remember too that any crew movement in light air must be made as though one were walking on eggs. Any thump or sudden movement can kill any forward momentum the boat has built up.

Sails must be adjusted extremely slowly and carefully. A jerk on the jib sheet can separate the airflow over the lee side, and it will take a second or two for it to attach itself again. On a small boat the winch handle often is used more in light air than in heavy to trim the jib just a "click" or two. Both the jib and main sheets must be constantly adjusted in light air, because the skipper can't turn the boat fast enough to follow the changes in wind direction. And if he did try to follow them, it would kill his speed.

In heavy air the reverse is usually the case. The sheets remain trimmed pretty much to one location and the boat's course is adjusted to accommodate the change in wind direction.

In light air, station the crew a little

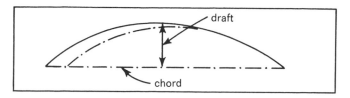

Figure 1

forward of their normal position on boats with a flat run aft, for this too can help reduce wetted surface. Shifting the weight this way lifts the wide transom out of the water, and submerges part of the narrow boat. It also helps create weather helm and if there is a "bobble," increases the drive of the boat through the waves.

Another technique that can help drive a boat into a slop when there's no wind to speak of is to keep the crew low in the boat. This also helps reduce the up-and-down pitching of the bow. And the energy lost in this up-and-down movement can be translated into forward drive.

It's long been thought that one should have flat sails in heavy air, and full sails in light air. However most top sailors in the country have come to recognize that a full sail is needed only when power is required; in heavy sea conditions for example, no matter whether the wind is light or heavy. Even in drifting conditions it is conceded by most that one needs a flat sail.

If there is very little wind, sails have to be set to maximize fully any puff that comes along. If there is a deep curvature in the sail, a puff is unable to attach itself readily to the lee side of the sail, for the airflow has to make too large a turn. A flat sail is, therefore, desirable in such conditions for it doesn't require the air to deflect far from its normal direction to attach to the sail.

Mainsail fullness, or *draft*, is a relationship that exists between the *chord* of the sail (the straight line distance from luff to leech) and the sail's maximum depth. Any adjustment that increases this ratio makes the sail fuller, and vice versa. In other words, if you shorten the chord of the sail, the sail will be fuller than it was even if you haven't changed the depth (Fig. 1).

Easing the outhaul a substantial distance, as in Figure 2, also will have the effect of shortening the chord, which slightly increases the actual draft. But it greatly increases the camber/chord ratio, which is the ratio of the draft, or curvature, to the chord. Therefore, in drifting conditions keep the outhaul out tight.

If you have an adjustable backstay, tightening it will flatten the sail. This flattening happens in two ways. When the backstay is tightened and the mast bent, as in Figure 3, the mast tip is pulled backwards and is closer to the end of the boom. The distance A to B_1 now is shorter than

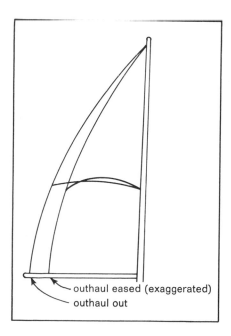

outhaul eased (exaggerated)
outhaul out

Figure 2

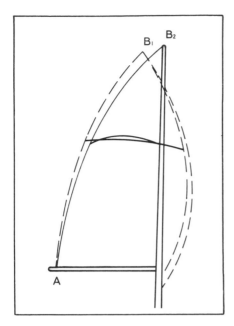

Figure 3

A to B_2, and this frees the leech of the sail.

Figure 4 shows a cross-section of a sail before and after applying backstay tension. Before tension is applied, the leech is tight and the draft considerably greater than after the leech has been freed by backstay tension, shown by the dot-dash lines.

Backstay tension flattens the main a second way by bowing the mast forward in the middle. This lengthens the chord distance (Fig. 5) which is the same cross-section shown in Figure 3. The result is slightly less depth, but a large reduction in the camber/chord ratio. In effect, the excess material built by the sailmaker into the sail along the luff is stretched out, and the sail flattened.

In light air conditions be careful not to overbend the mast or you will "turn the sail inside out." This occurs when the mast is bent *more* than the amount of luff roach that has been built into the sail. The visual result will be obvious by the wrinkles emanating from the clew (Fig. 6).

The Cunningham, the tackle that pulls down on the luff of the sail, and the main boom downhaul should not be tensioned in light air. Both tend to pull the position of maximum draft forward, but neither one will flatten the sail. If you pull down on the Cunningham in light air, the draft will go all the way forward and form a cup along the mast. Any puff hitting it will be unable to make such a sharp bend, and it will fail to produce adequate airflow to produce lift.

The only other adjustment that can change mainsail draft is the mainsheet. If you start with a sail shape like the dot-dash lines in Figure 4 and then pull or *horse* down hard on the mainsheet, the leech will harden up, the battens will cock to windward, and the sail will look

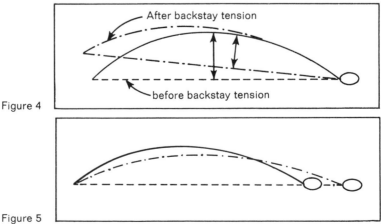

After backstay tension

before backstay tension

Figure 4

Figure 5

much like the solid line in Figure 4. Because this is a fuller shape, we can say that mainsheet tension does make a sail full whereas an eased mainsheet and the corresponding twist of the sail, as the boom rises, make the sail flat.

Therefore, in light air, you should pull the traveler to windward and trim the main using very little force to keep the sail flat. In fact, on a cruising boat, the weight of the boom might be enough to cock the battens to windward, and, in drifting conditions, it often helps to use the topping-lift to take this weight and free the leech of the sail. This will keep the battens from hooking to windward.

In drifting conditions, in addition to having flat sails and light trim, you also must trim the sails as if you were reaching. The boom, for example, never should be over the centerline of the boat. The reason is that if a zephyr does hit the sail, the force is translated into leeway rather than forward motion.

In light air, the jib is played in much the same way as the main. A jib should have very light halyard and sheet tension, and little-to-no luff tension, the equivalent to the Cunningham on the main. In some cases, the jibsheet is best hand-held so its weight doesn't tighten or collapse the jib leech. In addition, it is particularly important that the clew of the sail doesn't fall from gravity toward the bow of the boat. If it does, it will cup the foot and tighten the leech. The effect is similar to releasing the outhaul on the main boom (Fig. 2).

Just as with mainsail trim, the jib should be led further outboard than when there is a breeze. The reason is that in light air you always must trim a sail as though you are close reaching. In light air you cannot "strap" the sails in. Doing so does little more than slow the boat down.

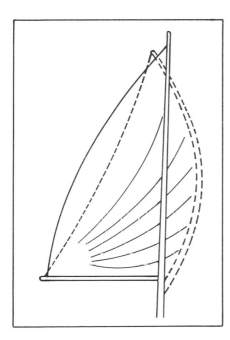

Figure 6

Close Reaching with Multiple Headsails

Aerodynamic effects of auxiliary sails　　　John R. Stanton

The next time you see a fleet of boats sailing on a beam reach, carefully scan their headsails. Unless they are all a particular type of one-design boat, you should be witness to a veritable panoply of headsail arrangements and colors. This often breathtaking phenomenon is particularly prevalent on this point of sailing.

Perhaps you have already asked yourself why a fleet of boats, all sailing a common course, should fly such a potpourri of headsails. There are several reasons, but let us consider just two.

First, the theoretical aerodynamics of reaching have not been as well defined as with close-hauled sailing and running. Very little wind tunnel testing and other analytical work has been done. Most of the testing has been on the race course; hardly what one considers to be controlled conditions.

This data is incomplete and the interpretation highly subjective. Consequently, every skipper must experiment and attempt, through his own trial and error, to select the optimum headsail combination for his boat under these conditions.

The second reason for such a diversity of headsails is that not all boats are equipped with the same suits of sails, even on boats that are otherwise identical. An owner's budget, preferences, and/or prejudices may either limit or expand his headsail selection.

The spinnaker, in particular, can be combined with a host of secondary headsails: genoas, staysails, tallboys, and cheaters are just a few.

Call them whatever you want, they all have but one purpose and that is to improve reaching performance.

They achieve this goal by increasing sail area, sail efficiency and, on occasion, both.

Let us first consider the effect of a tallboy on performance. If it is flown with a spanker, it functions very much as it would with a slightly eased genoa or reacher. The spanker, like a jib, is sufficiently close winded to provide a tallboy with a moderate header to work in.

There will be some slight interference due to pressure equalization between the low pressure area on the tallboy's leeward surface and the adjacent high pressure on the spanker's windward surface, but this is negligible, and presents no practical problem. (See figure 1.)

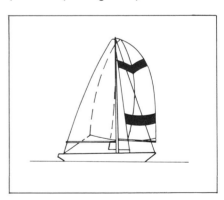

Figure 1
Spanker and tallboy
on a close reach.

A tallboy also makes an effective mainsail leading edge slat.

Just to review the reasoning — airflow over a mast separates and creates a highly turbulent vortex motion along the entire luff of the mainsail. This vortex strength is much more intense on the leeward surface, an unfortunate thing for 75-80% of

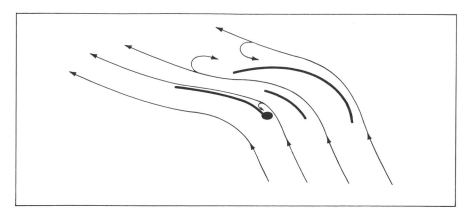

Figure 2
Flow of relative wind over spanker, tallboy and mainsail while on a close reach.

the useful aerodynamic force is developed there.

The point at which this flow re-attaches itself to the sail is a function of the wake width, the mast diameter/sail chord ratio, the amount of camber in the sail and the location of the maximum camber.

Almost any headsail will reduce the effect of mast wake by slightly turning and accelerating air flow, thereby encouraging reattachment to the mainsail's leeward surface. However, most headsails are led too far outboard and have too large an overlap, except near the head, to be really effective as leading edge slats.

A properly designed (and trimmed) tallboy can reduce the mast wake effect by as much as 50%. By introducing a flow of air that is parallel or slightly convergent with the mainsail just aft of the mast, the sluggish wake is accelerated and the vortex action quickly damped. At this point the air stream enters a transition phase to become attached turbulent flow. (See figure 2.)

To be effective as a slat, the tallboy should be tacked not more than 40% of J forward of the mast with an overlap of about 10% of J. This is equivalent to an LPIS (IOR terminology) of approximately 115%.

With the true wind on or slightly forward of the beam, the tack should be on center or slightly to windward depending upon the aerodynamic characteristics of the boat's headsail configuration.

The clew should be sheeted well inboard just short of backwinding the mainsail luff. Proper sheeting may cause interference with the forward lower shrouds in which case you may want to consider something less than the optimum tallboy sail configuration or possibly reposition the lower shrouds.

The spinnaker staysail is, like the tallboy, often misused. This is complicated by the fact that there are no specific design rules to follow to guarantee a successfully cut sail. Each is unique and must be tailored to the particular boat. (See figure 3.)

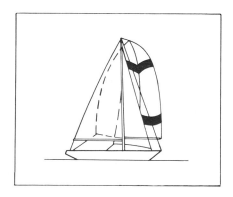

Figure 3
Spanker and spinnaker staysail
on a close reach.

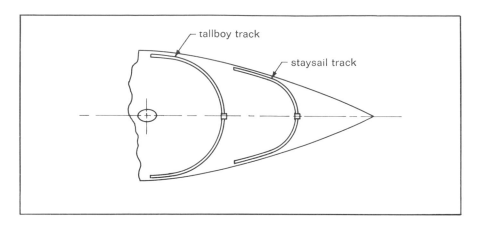

Figure 4
Suggested installation of tallboy and spinnaker staysail
variable tack tracks.

As a rule of thumb I suggest the staysail be tacked between 65-70% of J forward of the mast. The tack location may be varied by using a curved track and car running from rail to rail.

The precise location of the track will vary from boat to boat and the car position will depend on the point of sailing. But in any event, its maximum windward position will be governed by the angle of the spinnaker pole. (See figure 4.)

The staysail should be set flying on a spare halyard located at the masthead.

Overlap may vary from 110-130% LPIS depending upon the width of the sheeting base. A beamy boat, or even a moderate boat with the spinnaker sheeted via the boom bale, should be able to accept the 130% staysail.

There are two aspects of spinnaker staysail design and trim that are often overlooked. First and most important, the sail will always operate in a strong header, and therefore must be cut fairly flat to be effective.

Second, it should be cut to fly with a moderate amount of leeward sag, similar to a balloon jib. This will open up the gap between the main and staysail. And, as I have pointed out in previous articles, the degrad-

ing effects of sail interference are greatly meliorated as the gap/chord ratio increases.

A flat cut staysail with leeward sag has a favorable influence on the mainsail. The downwash from the full hoist staysail inhibits flow separation well aft, almost to the leech of the mainsail. Lateral force is increased and drag is reduced which, of course, produces more thrust.

With an apparent wind angle of 60-70°, a #3 genoa or, in the case of a double head rig, an equivalent topsail can be flown effectively with a spinnaker or spanker.

There is gross interference between the foot of the spinnaker and the genoa about 1/3 of the way up the genoa hoist, but the massive addition to total sail area more than offsets the reduced headsail efficiencies so that, on balance, there is a noticeable increase in driving force.

A qualitative comparison for each of these sails in a moderate breeze (11-16 knots) produces the following:

Tallboy — increases sail area by 40-45% of foretriangle; little interference with spinnaker; mainsail performance improved; total drive increased by about 10%.

Spinnaker staysail — increases sail area by 80-90% of foretriangle; modest mutual interference with spinnaker; total drive increased by almost 20%.

#3 genoa, low LP topsail, low LP reacher — sail area increased by 120-140% of foretriangle; considerable interference with spinnaker; backwinding may limit mainsail trim base; spinnaker trim requires constant attention in light and/or variable winds; total drive increased by about 25%.

The question now becomes simply just what sails does one use on a beam-reach? The answer depends upon several things, not the least of which is your pocketbook. But if money is not your problem, I would recommend using the following headsail combinations:

Light breeze (4-6 knots) — a lightweight general purpose spinnaker, tallboy, and spinnaker staysail, all flying together.

Moderate breeze (11-16 knots) — a spanker, tallboy, and spinnaker staysail for close reaching flown simultaneously. This combination should develop about 28% more drive.

Fresh breeze (17-21 knots) — a reacher and a genoa staysail or reaching staysail, however, if this combination overpowers the craft, I would substitute a tallboy for the staysail.

If you aren't of a mind to buy all those sails here's another set of alternatives. If we assume a #1 genoa and a high clewed low overlap working jib are already on board, I suggest adding a medium weight general purpose spinnaker, a reacher and a tallboy to the inventory to be flown as follows:

Light breeze — spinnaker and tallboy (this selection may seem contrary to what you'd expect, but it is necessary to provide maximum air flow to support the extra weight of a general purpose spinnaker).

Moderate breeze — spinnaker, tallboy, and working jib.

Fresh breeze — a reacher and tallboy if the boat will carry the load. If it can't, experiment to see whether the reacher alone or the working jib and tallboy can produce the best performance.

Maximum Thrust on a Broad Reach

Factors that contribute to speed made good　　　John R. Stanton

It is generally agreed that the fastest point of sailing occurs when the true wind is somewhat abaft the beam; that is when a boat is on a broad reach. The precise angle varies from boat to boat and is influenced by the sea and wind conditions prevailing at any given time. (See figure 1.)

For this discussion, a broad reach occurs when the true wind is 120°-150° relative to the course, although this definition is by no means universally accepted.

The apparent wind is going to be slightly less than the true wind velocity on this point of sail so that the total aerodynamic load is less than the maximum value a boat can experience in these conditions.

However, an increased drive to heel ratio, C_t/C_h, combined with reduced heeling and leeway resistances, permit greater hull speeds before equilibrium occurs between the propulsion force and the drag force. In effect we maximize the propulsion/drag ratio which, for lack of a better name, I shall call *propulsion efficiency*. (See figure 2.)

First let's consider a cat-rigged boat with a Marconi mainsail. When it's sailing with the true wind at 130° the relative wind, measured at the center of effort, is going to be about 100°. Even allowing for twist, it is immediately apparent that the entire sail should be operating at a high angle of attack.

It is essential that sail shape (and trim) should maximize thrust, with only passing consideration given to heeling force. Though there is obviously a limit to this. For as the wind picks up or starts gusting, heel *can* become the major factor.

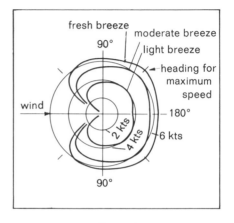

Figure 1
Typical velocity polar for
a small sloop.

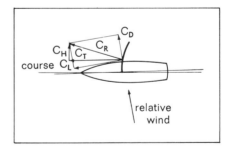

Figure 2
A comparison of force components
on a broad reach.

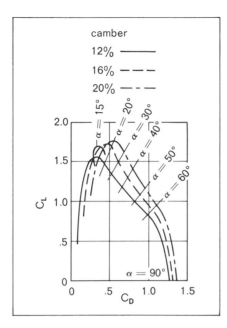

Figure 3
Sail sectional characteristics.

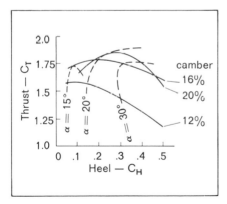

Figure 4
Thrust & heel force coefficients on a
broad reach (130° to true wind)
measured at the center of effort on
a cat rigged boat *(no mast effect).*

Using typical sail sectional characteristics (see figure 3) we can develop a performance chart (see figure 4) that illustrates the effect of variations in trim and camber.

The most obvious point made in figure 4 is that the large increase in drive potential on this point of sail comes with an increase in camber. Extrapolating from the values shown, one can anticipate that absolute maximum thrust should occur with a camber at 22-23%. This corroborates what most experienced sailors have already learned in practice.

Another feature demonstrated by figure 4 is the marked sensitivity to trim that exists when the sail is "full." With a moderate 16% camber, for example, the thrust characteristic is quite flat, making it tolerant of casual helmsmanship and imprecise trimming. This would be a good camber value for carefree cruising as a good turn of speed is possible without constant attention to trim.

Maximum thrust is obtained with larger values of camber, but it only happens over a very narrow trim range. According to figure 4, maximum C_t occurs at trim angles of 20°-22°.

It becomes apparent, therefore, that a racing boat must be steered precisely and sail trim must receive constant attention, if she is to sail at her best. While this may be an anathema to relaxed cruising, it is the very essence of successful racing.

A sail with 20% camber should be trimmed to the apparent wind at an angle of attack of 20-22°. If the sail is sheeted in too high, to about 30° (a very common practice), the driving force is reduced by about 6% while heel is increased approximately 60%!

Too often inexperienced sailors equate increased heel with increased speed. What actually happens is that thrust is decreased, hull drag is increased and the speed made good (V_{mg}) deteriorates. While these novices may revel in the euphoria of sharp heel and a broad wake, their competition will soon pass them by.

At small angles of attack a sail

101

does not develop its full potential. This is particularly important in light airs where a small change in thrust means a perceptible change in speed.

As the wind pipes up, the "hull speed" usually becomes the limiting factor long before heeling becomes excessive. Even though this is peculiar to broad reaching, one must be on the alert for excessive heeling or even a knock-down, in gusty conditions. Under such a situation a smaller angle of attack becomes essential.

Sail twist on a broad reach is also an important factor. A small amount of twist between the foot and head is desirable, particularly if it varies more or less proportionately with the change in apparent wind along the mast.

However, the boom does have a tendency to lift on this point of sailing which creates excessive twist. This can be minimized by sheeting the boom well outboard on a wide traveler or by installing a boom vang. Any excess twist invariably results in loss of thrust; the problem is always to minimize it.

Since some twist is inevitable it is better to have the head function at a lower angle of attack rather than having the foot overtrimmed. For

once the stall angle has been exceeded, and separation has occurred over the lower leeward surface, the lateral force, C_l, is sharply reduced and drag, C_d is greatly increased. This loss of thrust and increased heel is going to be far more detrimental to boat performance than having a "lower than optimum" angle of attack at the head.

But one cannot afford to neglect the effect of mast wake upon thrust. Figure 5 repeats the sail performance shown in figure 4 but also includes the effect of mast wake.

The basic characteristics don't change much but the *absolute values* are sufficiently altered so that they must be accounted for in anything other than a rough approximation of sail performance.

The most significant change shown by figure 5 is the reduced value of thrust (and increased heel) at all trim angles and variations in camber. Maximum driving force is 12-13% less than a "clean" sail (see figure 4) while heel is greater by some 45-50%!

Surface roughness and its effect on airfoils has been recognized for more than 30 years. But complexities of the phenomenon have defied rigorous mathematical techniques, and practical engineers have had to rely on empirical formulations and test data for guidance.

Experiments have shown that surface irregularities and projections definitely reduce maximum lateral force and increase drag, especially when they are located either at the leading edge or on the leeward surface of the foil near its leading edge.

The situation becomes even more aggravated with a sail on a broad reach, for the projected mast protuberance is greatest on this point of sail. (See figure 6.)

Total drag is usually greater than that created by either the mast or the sail alone, but less than the sum of the two elements. The interaction between mast and sail tends to elongate and streamline the apparent mast profile and thereby reduce mast

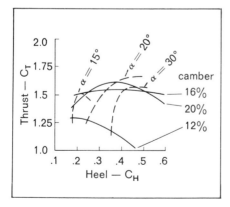

Figure 5
Thrust & heel force coefficients on a broad reach (130° to true wind) measured at the center of effort on a cat rigged boat *(with mast effect)*.

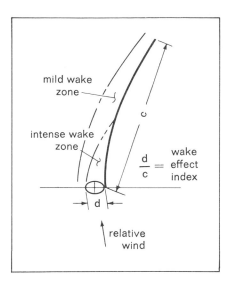

mild wake zone

intense wake zone

$\dfrac{d}{c}$ = wake effect index

d

relative wind

Figure 6
Mast wake boundaries on a broad reach.

drag. On the other hand, the mainsail luff lies within the low velocity region of the mast wake, and this reduces pressure drag on the sail.

Variations in mast and sail drag are principally a function of the mast diameter/sail chord ratio: sail camber and mast shape are secondary factors. At low mast/chord ratios (10% or less), the mast drag is rather low while the sail drag is 75%, or more of its free value, and vice versa.

The sharp increase in heel shown in figure 5 is the direct result of the added mast drag which, on a broad reach, is applied almost entirely in an athwartships plane.

I might also point out that these values do not include the small additional drag effect caused by the supporting shrouds and stays.

The Spinnaker on a Broad Reach

Angle of attack and pole trim   John R. Stanton

Headsail selection and trim, when broad reaching, have a great impact on boat speed, heel and stability.

Compared to the variety of headsails commonly seen flying in a fleet of boats on a close reach, the combinations used on a broad reach are somewhat more restrictive and uniform.

There is almost universal acceptance by the racing fraternity of the general purpose spinnaker as the principal headsail. However, where secondary headsails are concerned, there is still room for individual preference and innnovation.

Cruising sailors, as a group, are less inclined to seek the "ultimate" in speed from their boats. They are more concerned with a combination that provides a fair turn of speed over a broad range of trim, sea, and wind conditions and they prefer sails requiring a mimimum amount of attention.

Refer to figure 1 where we see typical moderate wind polars for a small MORC type sloop equipped alternately with a spinnaker, a reacher and a working jib. Note particularly the increasing divergence between the boat's speed while carrying the spinnaker, and its speeds with the reacher and working jib.

Whether you are on a cruiser or racer, you should recognize that the flow conditions for different sails are similar though not identical.

Both the racer's spinnaker and the cruiser's reaching jib operate at high angles of attack in windward to leeward flow with separation prevalent along the leeches of the principal headsails and mainsails.

Let us consider the spinnaker. With the true wind about 130°, the relative wind at the foot is slightly more than 90°. Near the head it is about 101-102°.

This occurs because the movement of air over the surface of the sea closely resembles the classical concept of boundary layer flow.

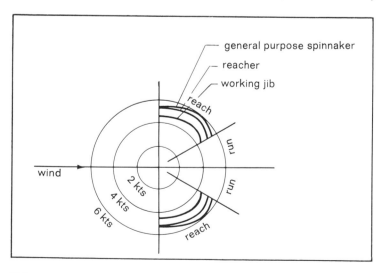

general purpose spinnaker

reacher

working jib

wind

reach

run

run

reach

2 kts

4 kts

6 kts

Figure 1
Comparative reaching velocity polars for a small sloop in a moderate breeze with various headsails.

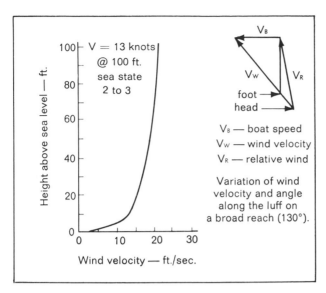

100 ⊢ V = 13 knots @ 100 ft. sea state 2 to 3

Height above sea level — ft.

V_B — boat speed
V_W — wind velocity
V_R — relative wind

Variation of wind velocity and angle along the luff on a broad reach (130°).

Wind velocity — ft./sec.

Figure 1a
Typical Wind Profile.

Typically, the velocity of a moderate breeze at 10 feet is only 65% of its velocity at 100 feet. Therefore, the wind will vary along the height of the luff. (See figure 1A.)

Near the foot, it is necessary to give the luff a slightly positive entrance angle to insure a full and pulling spinnaker. An angle of 2-3° to the relative wind is about right, although it may go as high as 5° without any measurable effect.

The profile of the spinnaker cross section near the foot tends to be parabolic, and contrasts with the more ellipsoidal shape near the head. This is the result of the balance struck between the aerodynamic load and the strain characteristics of the cloth. (See figure 2.)

Leakage around the foot of the spinnaker does not permit a high pressure gradient to be built up. Consequently, the aerodynamic loads along the lower chords peak out at smaller values near the center of the section. The ideal structural shape for this load is a fourth or fifth order equation, although a parabola provides a good approximation for analytical work.

Moving up the luff stay or leech towards the head, sections become more elliptical as the pressure gra-

dient at the luff increases and the leeches, under load, are drawn toward the center of the sail. Thus, camber gradually increases from about 25% at the foot to around 30% just below the head.

Concomitant with the increasing camber we find the relative wind velocity increases by 25% or more while the relative wind direction

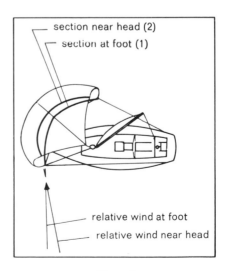

section near head (2)
section at foot (1)

relative wind at foot
relative wind near head

Figure 2
Comparison of spinnaker sections and relative winds at foot and head on a broad reach (true wind — 130°).

105

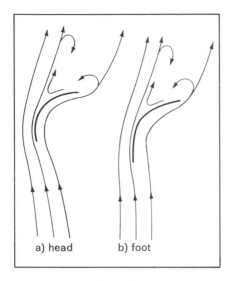

a) head   b) foot

Figure 3
Airflow pattern over a spinnaker while on a "broad" reach.

moves further aft by about 10°.

As a result, the thrust and heel coefficients, C_t and C_h, respectively, increase, and the dynamic pressure increases in accordance with V^2. The resultant drive and heel forces developed at the head, therefore, are considerable, and well out of proportion to the sail area in the region.

Referring again to figure 2, two factors become apparent: (1) the angle of attack at the shoulders (section 2) is very large; (2) the apparent entrance angle, or leading edge angle of attack, is negative. The effect of the high angle of attack is found in the large heel coefficient, C_h. However, the significance of item 2 might not be so obvious.

Note that the lines of flow, shown in figure 3, are induced into an arc as they approach the leading edge, or luff, of the spinnaker. What you see is the coercive influence of the pressure differential, that exists between the windward and leeward surfaces, on the streamlines as the air mass surrounding the spinnaker seeks to regain pressure equilibrium.

Although the apparent entrance angle near the head is negative by as much as 10°, it can be as much

as minus 20° at the shoulders of a "full cut" broad reaching and running spinnaker. Under such circumstances, the angle of attack at the luff more than likely is slightly negative to the induced flow lines as well.

In a fair breeze, the pressure differential across the sail is sufficient to hold the luff firm against the low positive pressure on the leeward luff. However, this is a marginal condition that is sensitive to small changes in trim.

It is my contention that the optimum trim for a full cut spinnaker on a broad reach is achieved when the shoulders are on the verge of breaking. I have come to this conclusion from observing boat performance and sail trim during races.

Unfortunately, there are no valid wind tunnel test data available that I'm aware of, and very little analytical work has been accomplished to corroborate or modify this observation.

The optimum trim is a rather narrow band which may be as small as 1-2°, depending upon the particular chute and prevailing conditions.

Moreover, once the luff breaks, the angle of attack must be increased, initially, two or three times the optimum trim range because of aerodynamic *hysteresis*.* After the fluttering has stopped, the sail can be retrimmed to the optimum condition.

Hysteresis is the alteration of physical characteristics, usually in the form of a loss of energy internal to a dynamic process, which prevents repeatability when the process is reversed.

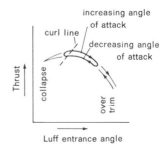

Effect of spinnaker luff hysteresis on drive.

Optimum spinnaker performance requires expert handling and close coordination between the helmsman and the spinnaker trimmer. But the latter may find the job easier by making his fine trim adjustments with the spinnaker pole position rather than the sheet.

Most skippers have adopted the practice of positioning their spinnaker poles semi-rigidly by means of an afterguy trimmed to the windward quarter and a foreguy led to the stem. Obviously, this setup is not well suited to the pole trim technique since constant trim adjustment is required in racing.

A better arrangement is to lead the afterguy through a snatch block on a track on, or inside the rail. The car is positioned well forward so that the downward pull of the guy provides sufficient luff stay tension. A "tweaker" made of light line

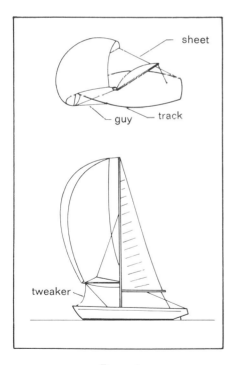

Figure 4
Installation of sheets & guys for pole trim technique on a broad reach (130°).

should be attached to the outboard end of the pole and led to the foredeck to assist with pole handling during a jibe.

The spinnaker sheet may also be passed through a lead block located on the leeward rail and well aft. As the boat falls off the wind onto a broad reach, or dead run, the car should be led forward more or less proportionately to the aftward movement of the afterguy lead block on the windward rail.

The advantage of this technique is to be found in the precise control the trimmer maintains over the luff at shoulder height. For example, when the luff begins to curl inward, a slight relaxation of pole guy tension simultaneously moves the pole forward and upward.

The angle of attack at the foot is increased *slightly;* but, most important, the areas around the shoulders and head are flattened, increasing their angles of attack, which immediately fills out the sail and prevents collapse.

Like everything else in life, there are some limitations to the pole trim technique. On narrow beam boats with large J dimensions, the guy lead angles are not as favorable, resulting in afterguy tension loads twice those found on the average boat. Even on craft with more "normal" dimensions, guy tensions are apt to be as much as 50% greater.

This presents no problem in light or moderate winds, but could become either a structural or handling problem, or both, in a fresh breeze with strong gusts.

In summary, the spinnaker can increase speed substantially provided the crew can give constant attention to the trim. Moreover, fine control of the angle of attack, from head to foot, can best be controlled, on many boats, by applying the pole trim technique rather than by using the sheeting method.

For anyone contemplating using the pole trim technique, here are three points to think about.

1. Experiment with the technique to determine the optimum lead block locations for your boat on a number of points of reaching in light and moderate conditions.
2. Proceed with caution in fresh breezes or gusty conditions, especially with a large boat.
3. If you plan to use the pole trim technique as standard all-weather spinnaker practice, I recommend installation of spinnaker winches one size larger than average for boats of that size and the use of the next larger size rope for the afterguy.

Downwind in Heavy Air

Pushing a boat in wind and waves   Richard duMoulin

Picture a broach and knockdown aboard a distance racing yacht. The crew, clutching the weather lifelines, is staring at the helmsman; the helmsman, clinging to the vessel, helplessly watches the leeward side of the cabin trunk submerge; the fish, peering through the cabin ports, are amazed by the flying debris inside the boat. What could the crew have done to have enabled the yacht to carry its spinnaker effectively in broach conditions?

Before discussing what the crew might have done to gain control, it is important to understand the dynamics of an ocean wave, one of the major causes of broaching. Imagine yourself sailing downwind under spinnaker at eight knots on a 40′ sloop in the open ocean. The wind has been blowing a steady 20 knots, puffing to 25 and 30 knots for 15 hours. The average wave, as determined by oceanographic data, is about eight feet in height (trough to crest), 120′ long (crest to crest), and is travelling at about 14 knots. What is the general nature of these waves and what is their makeup?

First, you should know that, although a wave travels across the ocean's surface, the water through which the wave passes remains in the same general area. Imagine a piece of driftwood rising and falling

as a wave passes by. However, there is a flow of surface water on a wave. Water on the crest of the wave is sliding forward toward the trough, and water in the trough is sliding backward toward the next crest. Our piece of driftwood, even though it does return to its original position has, in fact, been pushed forward by the crest, and then has slid backward in the trough.

This flow of water on the surface acts in two ways to cause broaching. First, it decreases the effectiveness of the rudder. As the crest passes under the stern, the water on the crest, which is moving in the same direction as the boat, effectively reduces the flow of water past the rudder. With an average 8′ wave, the speed of this surface flow is about three knots. So the steering force exerted by the rudder on a boat sailing at eight knots at this critical time is equivalent to a boatspeed of only five knots $(8 - 3 = 5)$.

The second detrimental effect of surface flow is the twisting effect it has on a yacht whose bow is in the trough while its stern is on the crest. This condition is most common when the wind is blowing against the cur-

1) Hoist the spinnaker all the way up.
2) Shift crew weight aft.
3) Vang mainsail.
4) Lower outboard end of pole.
5) Double sheet spinnaker.
6) Overtrim spinnaker sheet.

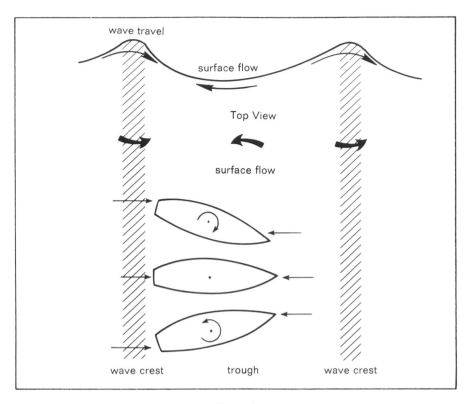

wave travel

surface flow

Top View

surface flow

wave crest   trough   wave crest

Figure 1

rent: the Gulf Stream in a north-easter, for example. Figure 1 illustrates how the stern is pushed forward by the crest while the bow is pushed back by the trough. This situation is made more difficult by the tendency of the bow to dig in and plow under — to trip. The result is a torque that tries to twist the boat around.

Beam and broad reaching are particularly difficult. Running is safer since the two forces meet head-to-head and this is why it helps to *move the crew weight aft* — way aft — and attempt to *run off in front of the crest* rather than to allow the wave crest to hit the yacht's quarter. Modern racing boats are quite buoyant aft and still lift well when the weight is brought back. It often helps to have one of the crew watch the waves and tell the helmsman what's coming, and when to bear off.

In the wind and wave conditions I

have described, the boat that wins will be the one where crew and helmsman can meet the combined challenge of wave action and sail control. Flying the spinnaker will enable a boat to average knots faster than can a boat that is without a spinnaker. Not only will it surf at speeds in excess of so-called hull speed, but it will maintain a higher speed in the troughs and lulls.

In order to push a boat in these conditions, the serious racing skipper must have sturdy standing rigging, well-maintained and designed spinnaker gear, a sharp crew, experienced downwind helmsman, strong steering gear, and a flat, heavy spinnaker. (See Figure 2.)

A large ocean racer should have a narrow-shouldered, flat storm chute, but a smaller boat would be wise to have a starcut reaching chute of medium-heavy weight; it can double as an effective running spinnaker

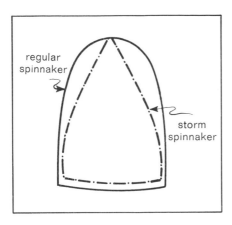

Figure 2

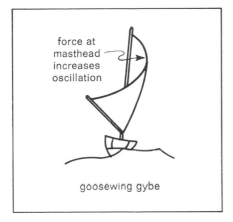

Figure 3

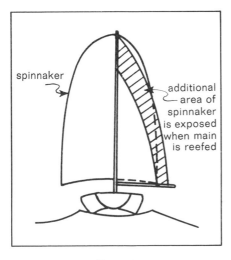

Figure 4

in a breeze. One should be wary of the so-called "storm spinnakers" that some sailmakers manufacture. In my experience, many of the sails are just heavyweight versions of light air spinnakers.

The spinnaker is a well-known heavy air demon, but the mainsail cannot be neglected either. Vanging is necessary to keep the boom from goosewinging, that is, lifting and gybing (see Figure 3). It also prevents the upper section of the sail from twisting off and driving the masthead to windward.

On boats under 50', a rubber vang strap can be used in heavy air. It will not only cushion the shock of an unintentional gybe, but will also stretch if the boom is dragged in the water. Leading the vang to a cockpit winch allows it to be eased quickly if the boom dips; the boom may break otherwise. On a larger boat, a nylon preventer led from the end of the boom to the bow and then aft to a winch will help support the boom if it dips or the boat gybes. If it is left aft and secured, one can safely ease it off without crawling out on the bow and trying to uncleat a loaded line.

One last word about the mainsail. Do not reef the main if you are attempting to fly a spinnaker. Not only does it allow more wind to get to the chute (see Figure 4) but it will fail to provide a good blanketing effect when it becomes necessary to douse the spinnaker. In other words, reefing the main will increase your troubles.

By two-blocking the spinnaker halyard, significantly overtrimming the sheet, and slightly overeasing the pole and lowering its height, the spinnaker can be both stretched and partially hidden behind the main. Figure 5 illustrates the changes in sail shape that will inhibit oscillation. But any deep high-shouldered spinnaker will still give some problems and this speaks well for having a starcut or storm chute on board.

If you have your mainsail slightly overtrimmed and vanged, the spinnaker stretched out, the best helms-

111

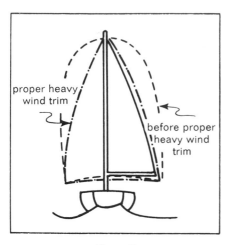

proper heavy wind trim

before proper heavy wind trim

Figure 5

man on the wheel with someone helping to call waves, and the boat surfing madly with the crew as far aft as possible, screaming with delight, what happens? The dreaded unexpected freak wave catches the boat just wrong; then comes a roll to leeward, a roll to windward, stern up, bow down, round up, lie over, and stop. What now?

How does one recover from a knockdown? Run the sheet? The halyard? The guy? Or all three? The answer is that any one will let the boat up, but I propose two basic alternatives that should be most effective.

First, assuming that all hatches not on the centerline are shut, that all gear is intact, that the crew is all aboard (hopefully attached with harnesses), it is best to *ease* the *spinnaker sheet first* (enough to spill the wind) and also to ease the mainsail vang. As soon as the boat rights herself, quickly get the vang and sheet back in to prevent renewed oscillation.

If however you decide that it's time to be conservative and drop the chute, it is better to hold the sheet and run the spinnaker guy. If the pole is eased to the headstay and the guy is run (carefully, with all the crew clear of the whipping tail as it fires forward), then the spinnaker can be

pulled in under the boom.

A second spinnaker sheet, led to a block on the rail midships, can be used to trim the flying sail into the boat. The halyard should not be eased too far until the clew of the spinnaker gets close aboard. And remember, always use the blanketing effect of the full-sized, unreefed mainsail.

The heavy air merits of the double sheet/double guy rig are obvious. The "lazy guy," that is, the leeward unused guy, can be led to a block amidships both to steady the spinnaker while running and to assist in trimming the clew aboard while dousing. In heavy weather *never* tie knots in the ends of the windward spinnaker gear (guy and lazy sheet), but *always* keep knots in the leeward (sheet and lazy guy) gear. All the gear should be neatly coiled in case of emergencies.

The windward gear must be free to run in case of severe knockdown or man overboard. The leeward gear needs knots to prevent accidental loss of both guy and sheet. The knots should be several feet from the end of the line so that if the sheet is run and the knot jams in a block, a line tied to the tail can be led to a winch.

Gybing in surfing conditions is really risky. Rather than take big risks and make abortive gybe attempts, it often pays to douse the spinnaker and reset it (or another chute) after gybing the mainsail.

A few final points. A spinnaker set in heavy weather, particularly on a large boat, always should be stopped, either with rubber bands or rotten cotton. Not only can it easily be hoisted to the masthead before filling, but it lessens the danger to the halyard crew of getting ropeburn, an override, or being lifted off the deck.

And finally, a spinnaker net is recommended in heavy air to prevent the remote, but disastrous, possibility of wrapping the spinnaker around the headstay during a collapse.

Hooking and Twisting

Leech control in various winds   Steve Falk

Beginning **sailors have** difficulty learning that their sheets do more than just control the angle of the sail with respect to the boat's centerline axis. Sheets also exert critical downward pressures that can *alter* the shape of the sail. Two somewhat related changes of shape can be induced by changing the sheeting pressure and the sheeting angle.

It's obvious, if you think about it, that the upper portion of a sail sags off to leeward some, and causes what's called *twist* in the sail. Twist occurs when the angle between upper portions of the sail and the boat's centerline is greater than an angle with similar legs formed at the lower part of the sail (Fig. 1). Twist is one aspect of sail shape that can be altered by sheeting.

A second element of sail shape that sheeting affects is the curvature of the leech (the trailing edge) of the sail — a factor beginning sailors often overlook. As downward pressure on the sail's clew is increased, the leech is tightened causing it to curve, or cup, to windward. Conversely, as the downward pull on the clew is eased, the leech opens, sagging off to leeward.

Let's look first at the principles behind what you want to do with the sail, then let's see what the mechanics are for making it happen. The principles are similar for both a jib and a mainsail.

Generally speaking, for going upwind, you want to set the sails as close to the centerline axis of the boat as they can go without losing drive. For the main on most modern boats, that means aligning the boom parallel to the centerline of the boat. For the jib, it means making the angle

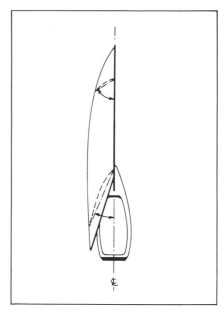

Figure 1

of the jib, measured from the tack to the jibsheet fairlead, somewhere between eight and fourteen degrees depending upon the individual boat.

As conditions get more demanding, with choppy water and gusty wind, you probably will want to sail just a little bit *fuller*, not quite so close to the wind. This brings the apparent wind a few degrees farther aft and the sails can be eased an inch or two to compensate.

When going upwind in smooth conditions, you can use all the power you can get out of the sails. This usually means you will want to minimize sail twist. In a small boat as wind strength increases, the heeling forces on the boat become more than you can control by hiking or putting weight on the rail. Here you will want to increase twist to reduce the forces

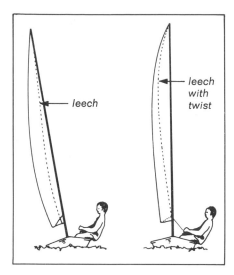

Figure 2: Twist at top of sail eases force at top of sail, reducing heeling

on the upper portion of the sails (Fig. 2).

When reaching and going downwind, rarely will you have more wind than you can handle, so here twist should be minimized. When you are running, the upper portion of the mainsail, if it's twisted, produces a lateral effort that tends to roll the boat to windward. This is a good part of the source of the downwind oscillating rolls you want to eliminate.

Now that we have established our sail shape principles, let's see how we can best achieve them. Almost all sailboats have these basic controls to work with. For the mainsail, you have a mainsheet, and a boom vang. The majority of modern designs also have a traveler that can be adjusted athwartships to allow you to vary the downward angle of the mainsheet from the boom to the traveler.

For a jib you should have jibsheet fairleads that allow you to vary the downward angle from the jib clew to the fairlead. In many modern designs you may also have a barber haul rig that allows you to vary the inboard-outboard position of the fairleads, and thereby alter the angle between the sheets and the centerline axis of the boat.

To control the leech of a mainsail and the amount of twist it has, you should apply *downward* or *upward* pressure on the boom. Increasing downward pull closes the leech and reduces twist, and vice versa.

But you want to avoid a *hooking* leech in light to middling airs. To do so try setting the traveler a bit to windward of the centerline. Then, you can sheet the boom to the centerline, or nearly so, without exerting too much downward pressure. You know the leech is right when the battens are, on average, lined up with the centerline of the boat. On average here means (if you have a sail with three battens) the lower batten is just a touch to windward of center, the next batten about on the centerline, and the upper batten just a touch to leeward of center.

If you have too much downward pressure, the leech will be cupped to windward, with two or three battens hooked noticeably to windward (Fig. 3). To correct either let off some on the mainsheet, or move the traveler farther to windward and ease the sheet (Fig. 4). If you have too little downward pressure on the sheet, the leech will sag off to leeward and there will be big knuckles at the forward end of the battens. To correct,

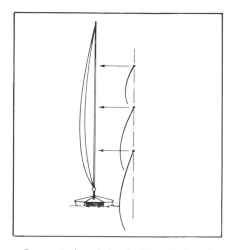

Figure 3: Leech hooked to windward. Too much downward pressure from mainsheet

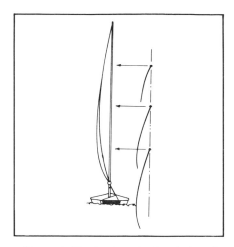

Figure 4: Moving traveler to windward and easing sheet keeps boom position the same but eases leech

ease the traveler back down to lee-ward a bit, and haul in some on the mainsheet.

As the wind blows harder, up to a point where you are heeling too much, let the leech open even more; it may do some of this by itself as the wind pressure increases. Then re-adjust the traveler so that the lower battens line up with the boom. You're apt to end up with the traveler right about midships.

Boom vangs can't help you much to get a proper leech shape when going to windward. But when you alter course to a reach or a run the boom goes outboard and there is no significant downward effort provided by the mainsheet. It is here that the boom vang takes over the function, and you can control both leech and twist with it. Set it up good and tight for all but the heaviest winds when it's desirable to let the leech open up some. Also ease it in very light winds, when too much vang can cause the leech to hook to windward.

When reaching and running, ease the traveler all the way to leeward so the mainsheet angle can help a bit to reduce twist.

To adjust the jib sheets, use the barber hauler, if you have one, to keep the sheeting angle as close to the centerline as you can in light air and smooth water. Start moving the haulers out a bit as conditions be-come rougher and you need to trade off some extra power in place of close pointing (Fig. 5).

There is an important exception. In very light air (near drifting) when you can't point very high and still keep the boat moving set the barber

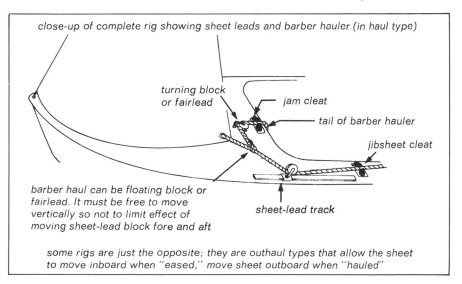

close-up of complete rig showing sheet leads and barber hauler (in haul type)

turning block or fairlead

jam cleat

tail of barber hauler

jibsheet cleat

barber haul can be floating block or fairlead. It must be free to move vertically so not to limit effect of moving sheet-lead block fore and aft

sheet-lead track

some rigs are just the opposite; they are outhaul types that allow the sheet to move inboard when "eased," move sheet outboard when "hauled"

Figure 5

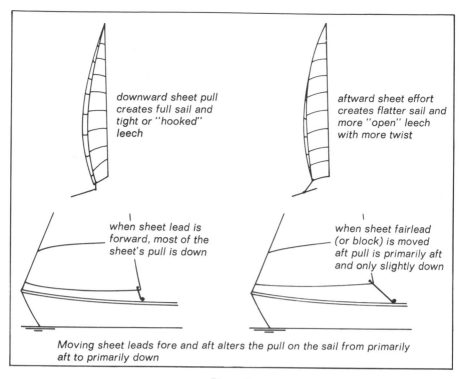

downward sheet pull creates full sail and tight or "hooked" leech

aftward sheet effort creates flatter sail and more "open" leech with more twist

when sheet lead is forward, most of the sheet's pull is down

when sheet fairlead (or block) is moved aft pull is primarily aft and only slightly down

Moving sheet leads fore and aft alters the pull on the sail from primarily aft to primarily down

Figure 6

haulers about halfway outboard. Then, set the jibsheet fairleads in the best compromise position to meet these objectives. Putting them farther forward gives you better downward pull to control the leech, but it is at the expense of giving you a fuller (rounder curve) shape to the jib. Putting them farther aft flattens the jib, but it also opens the leech (Fig. 6).

Forget the old rule about adjusting your fairleads to the position that causes the luff to "break" (begin luffing) evenly over most of its length; that puts the fairleads too far back, and you'll get an open leech in light to middling airs, just when you don't want it. Proper leech control on a jib is more important than the luff because a leech that sags off will cause the loss of much of the mainsail's drive. So go for good control of the leech *first*, then seek a smooth, fair curve to the jib. Finally, do what you can to get an even draft in the jib: a smooth arc with the deepest part of the curve at, or near, the center of the sail.

When sailing downwind, or reaching, let the barber haulers go all the way outboard to open up the slot between the jib and main and to control the leech. The principle here is very similar to the proper use of the traveler on the mainsheet.

If you seem to have trouble keeping all this straight, just remember the fundamental rule: *the harder it blows, the tighter she goes.* That rule applies to nearly all sail adjustments, mainsheet, jibsheet, boom vang, outhaul, cunningham, and halyards.

You can add one more item if you have it: a backstay, or mastbending rig. Because you want a flatter sail when the wind gets stronger, it becomes desirable to bend the mast as the pressures increase, to make the mast convex in a forward direction. This pulls the extra material built into the mainsail luff forward and flattens the sail.

If you do this with a backstay, you

simultaneously tighten the jibstay, which performs a similar mission for the jib. Some boats are even equipped with mechanical apparatus for bending the mast at the partners, shoving it forward against the mast step and the shrouds. This is the most exact method for inducing mast bend, and, in a small boat, is far preferable to a backstay adjustment. If you have this equipment, you'll need an additional adjustment to tighten the jib. You can do it either by taking up more on the halyard, or by using a cunningham or tack downhaul.

But always follow the handy rule, the harder it blows, the tighter it goes.

Concentrate on developing a feel for the boat as you experiment with sail-setting adjustments. You'll feel the pressures in the sheets and they should increase as your settings improve. You should also feel an increased liveliness on the helm.

Proper sail adjustment always is critical and demanding. The wind is varying a little bit all the time, so the best sailors are continuously adjusting — easing off on the sheets a bit when the wind lulls, hauling in a bit when it hardens. And, though it's to a somewhat lesser degree, they also are varying all the other adjustments to the running rigging, particularly the halyard, cunningham, and traveler positions. I have a slogan I keep saying to myself when I'm racing: *To win means doing everything you know how to do all the time.*

If anyone really wants to sail well, that rule applies most particularly to the time spent setting and trimming the sails.

5

Wherewithal

Basic Equipment for Mainsail Trim

The gear that shapes the sail   Peter Sutcliffe

I read regularly in sailing magazines articles that explain the latest in go-fast gear or super-rigging techniques used by the hot-shot sailors in the top one-design racing fleets. I suspect, however, that many readers are skippers and crew-members who race regularly in "not quite" one-design, or daysailer-type boats. These "not-so-hot-shots" still want to be competitive but often don't want the plethora of strings that most go-fasts seem to require.

Over the past several years I have raced regularly and gone the route of equipping my boats with the maximum number of go-fasts the rules allow. While I believe the results have justified the effort involved, particularly because I enjoyed fitting out the boats, I have been wondering just how much I could have left off and still have done nearly as well.

These mental exercises have led me to the conclusion that there is some basic equipment that will pay off extremely well in performance. Beyond this, however, the benefits must be carefully weighed against the cost, complexity, and tendency to detract from creature comfort that some go-fasts entail.

With that in mind, let's start this month with some basic equipment you should have to get maximum performance out of your mainsail. Not only can you have the necessary control adjustments to get the best out of your boat when racing, you can sail more easily, safely and precisely all the time.

Sails

You should have an appropriate suit of sails and they should be in good condition, which means they should be relatively new (four years old at a maximum).

Easy Handling

One important aspect of any sailboat, but particularly one that is being raced, is the ease with which the skipper and crew can adjust the running rigging; specifically the main, jib, and spinnaker sheets.

Almost all the force that finally moves the boom or jib clew is accounted for in friction in the blocks. In my opinion, the biggest single improvement in boat-handling equipment over the past few years has been the introduction of the ball-bearing block with non-metallic moving parts. These come in a wide variety of sizes and configurations, and are not much more expensive than the old type of plastic sheave on a plain metal pin. The mainsheet blocks all should be of the ball-bearing type; in fact I use them on all my running rigging.

Once a sheet has been pulled in tight, it is essential to be able to cleat it to relieve the skipper or crew from the load. However one must also be able to release the sheets immediately in an emergency, or make minute adjustments from time to time. The good old cam cleat takes some beating, *provided it does not slip.* (How often have you sailed in someone else's boat, got the main trimmed in to just the right spot, concentrated on getting to windward as fast as possible, only to find the mainsheet slowly slipping backwards through the cleat?)

Plastic cams are known to slip and if your boat is equipped with them, inspect them regularly, and file the teeth sharp whenever the friction of the sheet dulls the edges. Better still, use cam cleats with metal cams; they last longer than plastic. If they eventually blunt and slip, they still can be filed sharp again.

Sail Fullness Adjustment

Two basic controls affect the shape of the mainsail and are essential even to the casual racer. These are an *easily adjustable* outhaul and downhaul. The outhaul controls the tension in the foot of the sail, and through this, the camber in the sail. The downhaul controls the tension in the luff, and through this, the position of the maximum camber.

As wind speed increases, the main should be flattened and the camber brought forward; thus the outhaul and downhaul must be easy to adjust and powerful enough to make such changes when under way. On a reach or run, however, the sail

should be as full as possible and these controls should be able to be released easily once the windward mark has been rounded. They should be retightened at the leeward mark for the next beat.

There are an infinite number of ways of rigging an outhaul and it depends on the type of boat, boom, etc. I have found a 4:1 or 6:1 mechanical advantage, using wire for as much of the system as possible, to be very effective. The tail should be located in easy reach of the crew and should be cleated in either a cam cleat or a Clamcleat (Fig. 1).

The old type of downhaul pulled the gooseneck up and down a track on the mast. This, unfortunately, has the basic disadvantage that when the boom vang is tightened, it also acts as downhaul by pulling the gooseneck downward. Since a vang is tightened on a reach or a run, (which is just when the downhaul should be released) this is not a

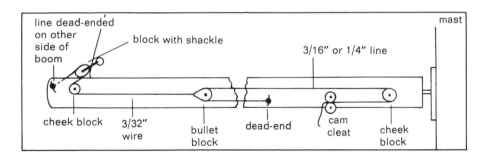

Figure 1
4:1 Outhaul System

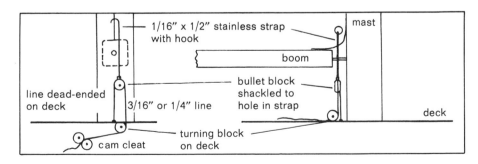

Figure 2
2:1 Cunningham System

good arrangement. The better method is a cunningham rig with a fixed boom position. This arrangement pulls the sail luff down by means of a line, wire, or strap through a grommet some 9″ to 12″ above the boom just aft of the luff rope. Again there are many ways to rig a cunningham and you should check other boats for ideas. I use a 2:1 mechanical advantage with the tail cleated at a point convenient for the crew to adjust when under way (Fig. 2).

Control of Boom Position

The in-and-out position of the boom is dependent on the mainsheet tension; however, under normal conditions as the sheet is released, the boom moves upward as well as outward. On a reach or a run it is very desirable to hold the boom down farther than the mainsheet is able to do alone. A boom vang is required for this. The vang also can be used on a beat to prevent the boom from rising when the mainsheet is released to accommodate a puff of wind.

A strong vang is essential and it should be easy to tighten. The vang should make about a 45° angle to the boom and be attached to the mast. It shouldn't be attached to the deck or keelson. In some designs the deck, or cuddy, limits the lowest point on the mast. On other boats, the vang can be mounted from the mast at the step, but then the crew may be in jeopardy from an inadvertent gybe (Fig. 3). So a compromise must be reached between power and crew convenience and safety. I like a self-contained cleat system where the lower block includes an easily adjusted and released cleat. Many vang systems offering these features are available today; look around and don't be afraid to copy one that is good.

Another desirable piece of equipment for controlling boom position, if class rules allow it, is an easily ad-

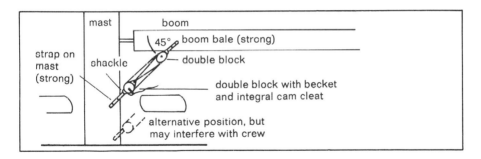

Figure 3
4:1 Vang System

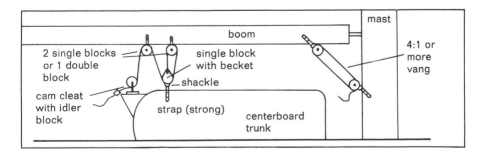

Figure 4
4:1 Mid boom sheeting without traveler

123

justable traveler. The varieties of arrangement are legion, and my advice is first to see what your class uses, then choose the one that is easiest to adjust and is least complicated.

Some classes allow a mid-boom, or "center-horse" traveler, and this is almost standard in the high-performance classes. However, it is expensive, complex, and seriously limits movement in the boat. A nice compromise is possible; this is to use mid-boom sheeting, fix the blocks to the centerboard trunk, and have no traveler at all. The tendency of the boom to rise when the sheet is released when beating can be minimized by providing an extra powerful vang that is pulled down

hard when going to windward. It also allows the same ease of gybing as the mid-boom traveler (Fig. 4).

These are just a few ways you might alter your existing arrangement to make your mainsail more effective. See what is working well with the boats in your class, use the best ideas they may have, but also see if you can improve on them. And *never* be persuaded that just because they have a lot of gear on the boat, it necessarily means they are using it to best advantage. If you think hard about the problem you will be surprised at what alternatives (and less expensive ones at that) you might come up with.

Rudiments of Luff Tension

Some considerations of draft control   Steve Colgate

The basic idea behind luff tension is to keep the position of a sail's maximum draft in the same location. Draft, or camber, as it is also called, is the shape of a sail's cross-section and it is located at a percentage of the sail's chord length. Chord length is measured as the straight line distance from luff to leech. If the chord is 120″ and the draft is 16″ deep, the sail's camber to chord ratio is 13.3%.

But as the breeze freshens, sail material stretches and the draft tends to move aft towards the leech. This movement will cause the battens

For example, the mainsheet will exert the greatest force on a mainsail, and most of it will fall on the leech. Consequently, the panels of cloth are sewn together so that the crosswise threads, or filling threads, lie along the leech of the sail. (See figure 2.)

This means that all the panels must be mast cut along the bias, where stretch is greatest. (See figure 3.) If we were to blow up a small section of the sail along the mast we would see that the threads look like a whole bunch of little diamonds at the

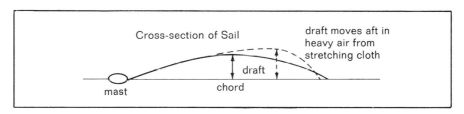

Figure 1

to cock to windward and produce a less efficient airfoil. (See figure 1.) However, increased tension on the luff can keep this movement to a minimum.

But first, just a bit about how a sail is constructed. The threads that run across a strip of sail-cloth are called the filling threads, otherwise known as the "woof" or the "weft." The threads that run lengthwise are called the "warp." Warp stretches more than woof, but the greatest stretch comes in a diagonal direction, called the "bias." Most sails are designed with this stretch in mind.

bias. As we pull down on the luff and increase the tension, each diamond elongates (the dotted lines) and pulls material in from the center of the sail. (See figure 4.)

If we pull down hard on the luff when there is not enough wind to warrant it, vertical troughs or creases will appear that run parallel to the mast.

You can simulate this effect by taking a handkerchief and pulling it at two diagonally opposite corners. The same troughs will appear just as they will when there is too much luff tension.

There are two ways to tension a

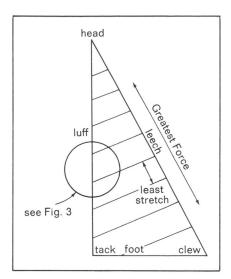

Figure 2

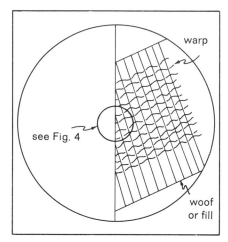

Figure 3

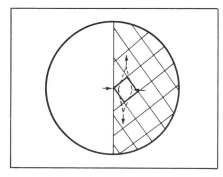

Figure 4

mainsail's luff: with a downhaul and a Cunningham. In the days of cotton sails you would buy a sail that was actually too small in light air. This would allow you to stretch it to the legal size limits when the wind velocity increased. Of course this meant you would automatically penalize yourself in light air by having a reduced sail area.

To solve this little dilemma, Briggs Cunningham, skipper of *Columbia,* winner of the 1958 America's Cup, chose the simple expedient of placing a grommet above the tack fitting and, when the tack reached down to the black band on the mast (and had been stretched as far as it could be legally), a block and tackle arrangement was attached to a line running through the grommet. When it was tightened it would add more tension to the luff, and legally so.

Some wrinkles do appear along the tack below the grommet when the Cunningham is in use, but they don't seem to make an appreciable difference in the efficiency of the sail. So just forget them.

This grommeted hole in the mainsail has become known as a "Cunningham hole" and it is now commonplace in most classes of sailboats. With a Cunningham a sail can be made full size for light air performance, and still be tensioned along the luff to keep the draft from moving aft when it breezes.

A variation of the Cunningham is also used on jibs. Many small boats have a cloth tension device attached to the jib near the tack. A wire that leads to the cockpit can be adjusted to increase or decrease the tension on the luff. Larger boats use something that looks more like the mainsail Cunningham.

A line is dead ended to the deck near the tack, and is run up through a grommet hole in the luff of the jib about a foot or so off the deck. Then it is run back down through a block and taken to a winch. The theory is the same for both a jib and a main. But the jib is much more sensitive to luff tension than is the main.

When sailing to windward the point of maximum draft on a jib should be about 30-35% of the chord behind the luff; it should be about 50% of the chord in a mainsail. If the wind increases, it's far easier for the draft of a jib to work aft of its normal location, and this means that you must constantly change the jib luff tension for highest efficiency whenever the wind changes.

Luff tension must also be changed depending upon what point of sail the boat is on. When reaching or running you want a very full sail with the draft well aft. You should ease off the downhaul and Cunningham in this situation.

Actually, you don't really have to be concerned with this high level of efficiency unless you are racing. But you should always remember that inadequate jib luff tension, with its accompanying "scallops," (an obvious slack luff between each jib hank) immediately brands the skipper as a *novice*. Not that there is anything wrong with being a novice.

But I hope this continuing series will help keep the novice-in-fact from appearing as a novice-in-effect — when he's out on the water.

The Boom Vang

Preventing mainsail twist   Don McKibbin

Whether you refer to it as a *boom vang, kicking strap, boom jack,* or *go fast,* it is the same piece of equipment. And as soon as sheets are eased it becomes a piece of essential gear on everything from dinghies to ocean racers.

It may vary in complexity from a simple single part line running from boom to mast step, to a much more complex multiple purchase arrangement that ideally leads aft to the cockpit.

Why is the boom vang so vital to good sailing performance? As the mainsail sheet is eased and the traveller reaches its limit of athwartships travel, any further easing of the mainsheet causes the boom to rise.

And this causes the sail to twist (twist is defined as the change in direction of chords of horizontal sail sections at different heights), producing a decreasing angle of incidence to the wind as the height of the sail increases.

If wind conditions are such that the boat can be kept on her feet while reaching, sail twist must be avoided for a number of reasons.

First, a sail in this twisted condition does have a varying angle of incidence from foot to head. This means it must be over trimmed in the lower sections in order to prevent luffing in the upper part of the sail.

This over trimmed lower section will be a sure cause of excess weather helm. The net effect is going to be a drastic difference in boat speed between a boat with its entire mainsail set at the optimum angle of incidence and one that has a sail with only a small upper portion in the optimum condition.

Furthermore, in a sloppy sea the boom of a boat without its sail properly vanged will rise and fall, further reducing the sail's effectiveness.

Increased use of mid-boom sheeting, which has spread in recent years from dinghies to bigger boats, has somewhat reduced the necessity of setting a vang *until* the traveller slide is eased to the point where the boom is no longer over the traveller. Of course with this arrangement the mainsheet exerts the downward force that is needed to keep the boom from lifting when sailing to windward or close reaching.

Thus far we have been looking at conditions where wind strength permits the full power of the mainsail to be utilized, and the boat kept at a good heel angle.

However, if wind strength increases to the point where this is no longer possible, then some twist aloft does become desirable to reduce the heeling forces and the weather helm that usually accompanies them. This can be accomplished by easing vang tension which allows some twist to occur aloft.

Now let's look at two boats running downwind. (See figure 1.) We see that, all other factors being equal, A is going to be faster than B because she has a larger projected sail area in her mainsail. Additionally she will have a less disturbed sail condition for her boom is steady and not rising and falling with changes either in wind velocity or lumpy sea conditions.

Another downwind condition is shown in Figure 2. This compares the chord of a sail that is twisting excessively (A) and a properly vanged sail (B). The twist aloft in A allows a force to develop that forces the top of the mast to weather.

This results, particularly as wind

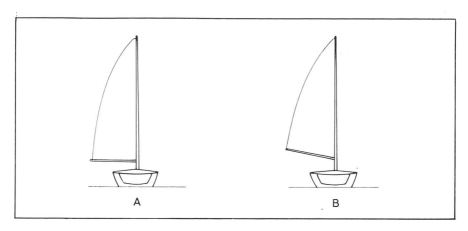

Figure 1

strength increases, either in a roll and capsize to weather in a dinghy or in the rhythmic rolling that can develop in a keel boat. It is usually amplified by the spinnaker if the trim on this sail is not correct as well.

The answer is to always *vang that boom down* to eliminate this weather force at the masthead. Doing so establishes a stable sail-carrying platform that requires a minimum amount of rudder correction to move the boat along the desired course downwind.

In most cases an offshore boat does not need a vang set when going to weather. However, in dinghies that use a bendy mast, the vang can exert force on the mast through the

boom and induce mast bending that can be controlled by blocking at the mast partner.

When going to weather in a small boat, a properly set vang can help keep the jibstay tight by, in effect, making the mainsail a backstay. Wind conditions will always dictate how much vang tension to set up. If it's set up too tight in light air the result may be an overly flattened mainsail.

When you are reaching, as I mentioned earlier, the ability to carry sail and keep the boat upright will determine how much vang tension to use. But when sailing downwind, vang tension must increase as the wind increases, to hold the boom down.

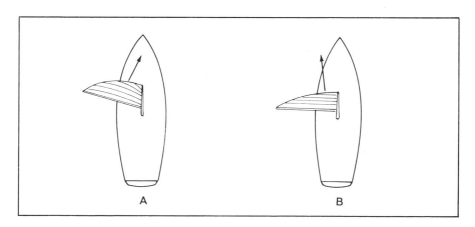

Figure 2

When a vang is set up tight, either through multiple purchase gear or by a winch, considerable loads are put on the points of attachment. Even in a small boat.

Booms, goosenecks and attachments at the mast base or along the leeward rail, therefore, must be capable of handling the loads that may be developed — up to several hundred pounds in just a small dinghy.

On larger boats the genoa sheet track may be a handy, but not necessarily ideal, place for attaching the vang. This track is capable of handling great sheer forces exerted by headsail sheets but it may not necessarily stand the vertical load imposed by the vang. The chainplates, for example, offer a stronger attachment point.

The present trend toward tall, high aspect ratio mainsails creates a sail that does develop twist very readily. And with such sails a strong vang arrangement is an absolute must.

Most fiberglass cruisers do not come with any stock vang arrangement, yet it is a very vital piece of equipment if the boat is to be sailed effectively off the wind.

One easy to rig and effective vang for such boats utilizes a rubber boom vang strap passed around the boom underneath the foot of the sail. A line runs from this strap to blocks attached to the port and starboard chainplates.

Lines are led, through these blocks, aft to the cockpit where they can be set with cam cleats or they may be led to a winch, depending upon the size of the boat. With this system the vang can be reset after each jibe without going forward and releasing a block from the lee rail, and resetting it again on the other side after the jibe.

But no matter what size or type of boat you sail, an effective boom vang is a necessity if you are interested in easier, faster, and safer sailing off the wind.

The Traveller and Backstay

Mainsail flatness and optimum speed   Steve Colgate

Most small modern sailboats are designed with both racing and pleasure sailing in mind. Very few are built strictly for pleasure sailing because it's axiomatic that if enough boats of one type congregate in an area of water, racing (even if it's informal) is the inevitable result.

So if you buy a boat, don't be too surprised if it can be equipped with a traveller, boom vang, luff tensioners on the main and jib, outhaul and backstay adjustments, fore and aft jiblead slide and possibly Barber Haulers or other athwartship jib lead adjustments.

These items aren't necessary for leisure sailing, but they do improve the performance of any sailboat and so it's useful to know their use.

Many people are more concerned with the actual adjustment than with the end result. For instance, I've seen many crew members trim or ease a sail without even looking at it. They concentrate on the winch that is doing the job and not on what the sail looks like. So let's look at two main-

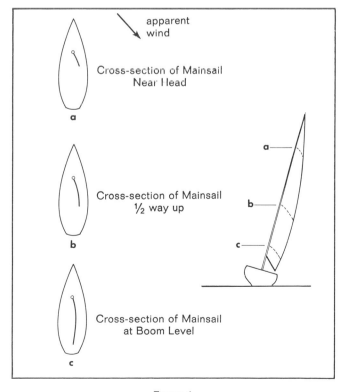

Figure 1

131

sail adjustments, the traveller and the backstay, keeping the end result in mind as we do.

The traveller is a track running across the boat under the main boom. A mainsheet block slides along it, and the better travellers have ball-bearing cars. When close hauled, the non-ball bearing types have a tendency to stick under the pressure of the mainsheet.

The traveller's function is to change the angle of the boom relative to the centerline of the boat without allowing the boom to rise. If, instead of using a traveller, we eased the mainsheet, the force of the wind on the sail would lift the boom in the air, and the top part of the leech would fall off to leeward.

Figure 1 shows the constant angle the apparent wind makes with the luff of the sail for its full length when the mainsheet is trimmed in tight. Figure 2 shows how this angle would

change in the upper part of the sail if the mainsheet were eased. The upper part can actually be luffing even though the bottom part is full of air. This effect is called twist and it is usually undesirable.

There are a couple of exceptions. The wind on the surface of the water is slowed down by friction, so the wind at the top of the mast has a greater velocity than at the deck. Thus, the top of the sail is sailing in a continual puff relative to the bottom of the sail. We know that the apparent wind comes aft in a puff. And in order for the apparent wind to have the same angle to the luff all the way up and down, a slight twist at the head of the sail is necessary.

In heavy airs this twist is always there because you usually can't get the mainsheet down tight enough to get rid of it. But in medium to light airs you can overtrim the mainsheet.

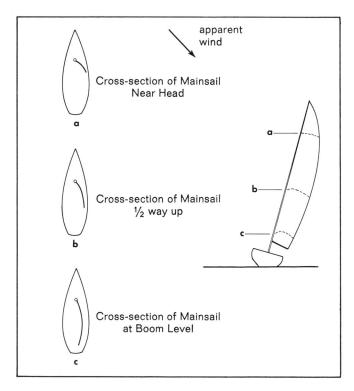

apparent wind

Cross-section of Mainsail Near Head

a

Cross-section of Mainsail ½ way up

b

Cross-section of Mainsail at Boom Level

c

a

b

c

Figure 2

Look at the battens. If the leech or outer edge of the sail is a straight line and the battens are cocked to windward, you have probably over-trimmed it.

The other exception to the harmful effects of twist is when there is very heavy air. The upper part of the sail greatly affects a boat's heeling just as weight at the top of the mast does. If you want to reduce heeling, simply reduce the effectiveness of the upper part of the sail by inducing twist. Instead of easing the traveller out, ease the mainsheet.

We all know that as a sailboat turns from closehauled to a reach one should ease the sails. (See figure 3.) If you didn't, the boat would heel way over as the wind hit the windward side of the sail at right angles to it. Forward drive would be reduced because of the lack of drive-producing airflow over the lee side of the sail. (Figure 3B.) We know that if sails are trimmed properly for a reach, the boat heels less than it does when closehauled because the drive from the sails is more in the direction of the boat's heading, and heeling force is reduced. (See Figure 3C.)

If we are heeling excessively when closehauled we can reduce the heeling by easing the traveller. Most good small boat sailors use the traveller rather than the mainsheet to adjust to changes in wind velocity. Every novice has learned that when you are hit by a puff you ease the mainsheet and head up into the wind to reduce heeling and avoid a capsize. The advanced sailor does much the same thing, but eases the traveller instead. Since the apparent wind comes aft in a puff, easing the traveller maintains the angle the apparent wind makes with the luff of the sail.

As you fall off on a true reach, easing the traveller acts like a boom vang and keeps the boom from rising and inducing twist. However, its effectiveness ends when the traveller car reaches the outboard end of the track, and the mainsail must go out

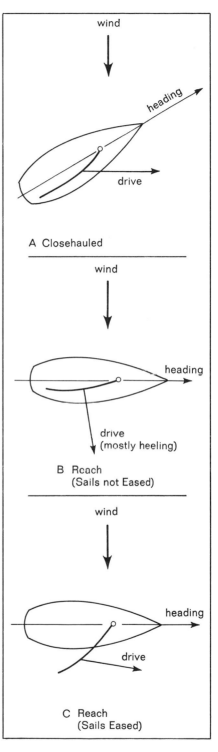

Figure 3

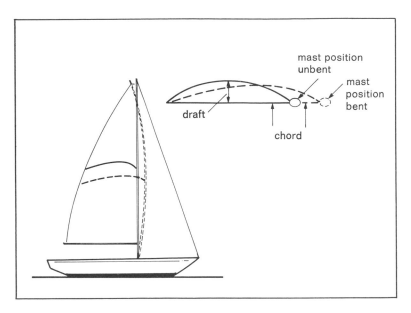

Figure 4

still further. Now the mainsheet, instead of pulling down, is angled out over the water and a boom vang has to do the work of keeping twist out of the sail.

The farther forward in the boat the traveller is located (and some boats have them in the middle of the cockpit), the farther out the boom can go before the traveller car reaches the end of the track. And the closer the traveller is to the boom, the more positive is its control.

If the traveller is mounted way down on the cockpit floor a number of feet beneath the boom, a puff may cause the mainsheet to stretch. The boom will lift, and negate some of the traveller's usefulness.

There is one other use for the traveller. You can trim the main boom up to the centerline of the boat without pulling down hard on the mainsheet. The closer the boom comes to the center of the boat the higher you can theoretically point. On a light day, however, oversheeting the main would cause the overtrimming I mentioned earlier. Battens would cock to windward and the sail would look awful.

The solution is to leave the mainsheet lightly trimmed and pull the traveller car up to windward, bringing the boom toward the middle of the boat without pulling it down at the same time. Now let's look at the backstay.

The adjustable backstay is a mast bending device. On small boats a block and tackle arrangement attached to the lower end of the backstay can produce the leverage for bending the mast with a minimum of effort. Other factors are involved in mast bend such as leech tension, angle and length of the spreaders, placement of the partners where the mast goes through the deck (if any), tension on the jumpers (if any), location of the mainsheet blocks along the boom, etc. But for now let's just analyze the backstay.

Tightening the backstay bends the mast and flattens the mainsail. But what is meant by a "flatter mainsail"? The fullness of any sail is the relationship between its chord length at a given height and its maximum draft. The chord is the straight line distance from luff to leech.

When the backstay is tensioned,

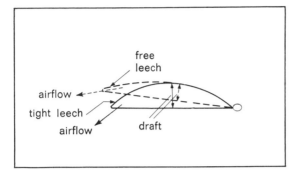

free
leech

airflow

tight leech

airflow

draft

Figure 5

the middle of the mast bows forward, lengthening the chord as the dotted lines in Figure 4 indicate. The draft will decrease. But also note the action at the top of the mast. It is pulled back and down which effectively shortens the distance between the top of the mast and the end of the boom. This, of course, frees the leech of the sail.

Figure 5 shows a sail with a tight leech. The dotted lines indicate a free leech. The free leech creates a flatter sail for the draft is less, but the chord length remains the same. The figure also shows that the drive will be in a more forward direction, which reduces heeling.

Weather helm is also reduced as the leech is freed. With a tight leech, airflow on the windward side of the sail is bent around until it exits off the leech in a windward direction.

The tight leech acts like a rudder, forcing the stern to leeward and creating weather helm. But when the leech is freed, the air can flow straight aft or slightly to leeward which minimizes turning effect of the leech.

If the wind is strong but the seas are smooth, the mainsail should be reasonably flat. As the wind goes light or seas get heavier, the boat needs more drive. Bruce Goldsmith of Murphy & Nye, sailmakers, puts it very aptly. "Full sails are like a car in low gear and flat sails are its high gear. In a lumpy sea, or right after a tack you need full sails to accelerate. But as you gain speed, you must flatten the sails, and this is where the backstay comes in." Release the backstay and the Cunningham to make the sail fuller. Then ease your traveller to increase drive.

The Jib Cunningham

Correct installation and varieties of use   John Welch

With the advent of stretchy luff genoas, the cunningham hole has become almost more valuable for headsails than it is for mainsails. The theory, of course, is the same: tensioning the luff within the luff length allows maximum sail area in all wind conditions.

The cunningham increases the wind range of the headsail. If maximum hoist is achieved in light airs, proper luff tension can be maintained, even as the wind increases. Proper tension can be held to the limits of the cloth, or the stability of the boat.

It often occurs that races around the buoys start in light airs that can become a good breeze by the time the boat is within 20 minutes of the windward mark. The ability to control the draft of the headsail in these conditions negates the necessity of a sail change. This is very desirable

particularly when the next leg is a reach. At that time the cunningham can be eased to return the fullness that is needed for reaching.

At other times, sea conditions will occur in which you will want to have a different sail shape on one tack than on another. For example, in open waters if the wind shifts 30°, then a boat hard on the wind will experience a leftover head sea on one tack and a beam sea on the other. To drive through the head chop, the cunningham should be eased to create more fullness in the sail; hence more power. On the tack with the beam sea, the cunningham can be taken down and the boat pointed higher.

In fluctuating wind velocities (under a lee shore for example) the genoa cunningham again can provide ease of sail shape control. Assume a boat is close hauled and

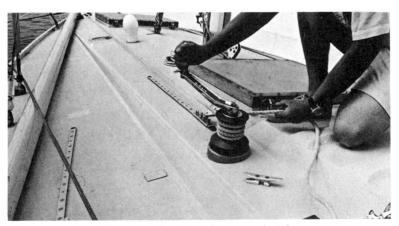

Winch controlling luff tension should be aft near cockpit for ease of handling and proper distribution of crew weight.

wind is "puffy," varying between 8 and 13 knots apparent. The #1 genoa can be sheeted home, left alone and the cunningham used to adjust sail shape.

As the wind increases, the draft moves aft and the sail is pushed away from the leeward spreader (the spreader is a good reference point for identifying draft location in a headsail). To bring the draft forward in the sail, the cunningham is brought down and the sail will regain its desired shape. The sheet does not need to be adjusted.

One big advantage of using the cunningham hole is that the genoa sheeting angle does not have to be changed as luff tension is increased. If the draft were moved forward by increasing halyard tension, the clew would be lifted which would require the genoa sheet to be moved aft to maintain the correct sheeting angle.

One thing to remember when applying luff tension to a sail under full load is that great friction is created between the hanks and the headstay. Therefore, if luff tension is applied at either the head (halyard) or foot (cunningham), it takes time for this to equalize over the entire luff length of the genoa.

Consequently, it is best to apply tension just prior to a tack so that then tension can equalize during the tack. The angle of attack that the leading edge of the sail makes to the wind will then be the same from foot to head. Another way to reduce the load in the sail is to feather the boat slightly, or ease the sheet a few inches.

Figure 1 illustrates a genoa cun-

Figure 1. Conventional cunningham rig. Snatch block is forward of tack and strain is properly distributed.

ningham rig on a typical 35 footer. A bowline is tied closely through the tack grommet, led up through the cunningham hole, back through the snatch block at the stemhead fitting, and aft to an auxiliary deck winch. The winch used can either be a cabin

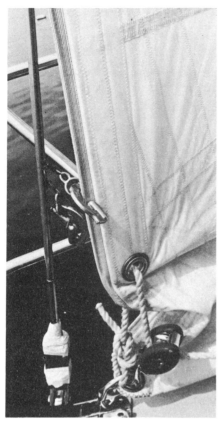

Figure 2. Snatch block is improperly lead aft of sail tack possibly putting strain on first hank and distorting sail shape at leading edge.

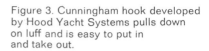

Figure 3. Cunningham hook developed by Hood Yacht Systems pulls down on luff and is easy to put in and take out.

trunk mounted spinnaker halyard winch, staysail sheet winch or a cockpit spinnaker sheet winch.

The most convenient winch location for constant trimming is in the cockpit, for a crew member will be more willing to make the continuing adjustments required to produce proper headsail shape in varying wind conditions when the winch is readily at hand and easy to operate.

Controlling genoa luff tension from the cockpit is of particular advantage in boats in this 30 foot range where fore and aft crew weight distribution and movement are critical to boat performance.

Tensioning the genoa by taking up on the halyard at the mast is a difficult two man job when a boat is heeled over with the winch located on the leeward side of the mast. The advantage of achieving the same result through one man cockpit control is obvious.

In rigging the cunningham, it is important that the line passing through the cunningham hole be *parallel* to the luff of the sail. For example, if the snatch block is located aft of the tack, then a twisting effect will be placed on the cunningham ring and

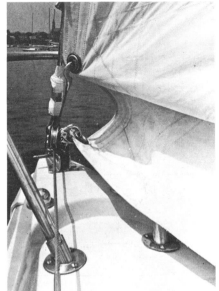

could twist the grommet out of the sail. A nonparallel pull can also put *severe* strain on the first hank, causing it to be either bent or pulled loose from the sail. (See figure 2.)

A cunningham hook is a development of the cunningham rig. It is a permanently attached wire with a specially designed hook that pulls down evenly on the cunningham ring (no twist) and allows the resultant loose cloth in a tack area to lay neatly to one side. It also reduces the time required to set up the rig. (See figure 3.)

In summary, a cunningham hole in a stretchy luff genoa can provide the following advantages:

1. Maximum sail area in all wind conditions.
2. More convenient luff tension control.
3. Increased wind range of a sail.

If your current stretchy luff genoa doesn't have a cunningham hole it would be worthwhile to have your sailmaker install one for you. It won't add to your luff length but it will give you easier and more convenient luff tension control. And you will get a lot more out of your headsail.

Upgrading the Power System

Simple, low-cost ways to more efficiency   Charles Booz

The trouble with modern sails is that they are so maintenance free, they tend to get overlooked in the spring rush — a period when maintenance turns into an obsession.

The fact is that many sail improvements can be made, many of them rather simple and inexpensive, that add just as much to boat performance as a smooth bottom and a well maintained engine.

But most meaningful changes go beyond the fix-up category and involve taking a fresh view of the entire sail system, its rigging, hardware, and the way sail inventories are utilized.

One of the best ways to start the process is to go into deep reverie about ways to simplify the rig. Remove lines and hardware if they were not used two or more times last season. Eliminate extra flag halyards. A single halyard, led to the masthead, fills most needs. During races it can be secured close to the forward edge of the mast where it will cause the least turbulence.

Spreader lights can be improved by replacing with smaller, more streamlined fixtures. Better still, take them off and replace them with a single fixture mounted on the mast and canted downward to illuminate the foredeck.

Extend the pruning process to the masthead windpennant. Exchange it for a lighter vane and check its balance at the pivot so that it will continue to read accurately while heeling.

In remounting, add an extension so that the vane is at least six inches above the masthead. This lofty perch puts it in undisturbed air and lets the masthead light do a better job of illuminating the indicator or wind sock during night passages. For downwind legs in night races this is invaluable.

In larger cruising boats, overlapping headsails can be "read" much more efficiently when a small streamer is fastened through the sail fabric about six to eight inches back of the luff. When pulled half way through and knotted it forms a double streamer that can improve your sail trim and help you properly sail close to the wind.

If the streamer is a dark color, it can be seen more easily through the translucent sailcloth. Proper air flow is indicated by a mirror image of the inner and outer streamers. When the outer streamer begins to flutter while the inner one remains pressed to the surface by airflow, the sail is approaching a stall.

Without this visual aid, a skipper

Reduced drag can result from careful taping at junction of spreader and internal tangs. Conversion to single deck light located on leading edge of mast and protected by U-shaped tubing fastened with poprivets also helps streamline spreaders.

must have unusual sensitivity to avoid blundering between sailing too high or too far off the wind. If two sets of streamers are installed, one at eye level and the second about half way between tack and head, they can be used in checking the fore and aft setting of the jib fairlead. If both streamers stall at the same time when coming into the wind, the fairlead is set properly.

If the economic squeeze has forced you to pass up additions to your basic sail inventory this year, consider ways you can make your present inventory work harder. One place to start is to dust off that seldom-used working jib, an item that comes with most stock boats but soon loses out to a 150% genoa.

This working jib, for example, can be used as a staysail on a spinnaker reach. All it needs is a tack fitting located on the foredeck about midway between mast step and the original tack fitting.

While you are at it, make this jib more effective for normal use by adding a fairlead inboard from the genoa track. A fairlead on the rail for a jib of this type creates a sheeting angle well over the optimum of about 11° from centerline.

Then there are a host of improvements that can be made just by re-deployment of lines. A set of lightweight sheets for the spinnaker pays dividends in drifting weather.

Try the new lines made of textured filament polyester, a feature that gives the feel of a spun line. Their fuzzy surface makes it much easier to hold a small diameter line without it slipping.

Control lines, particularly those that guide the spinnaker pole, can be improved by running them aft to the cockpit. This minimizes the need for people to bunch on the foredeck during sail changes and jibing maneuvers.

Speaking of jibing, every boat can profit by adopting a boom vang assembly that can remain under tension no matter what the boom position. A simple tie-down that uses a handy billy between the boom and a rail fitting does not allow this, for it has to be adjusted every time the mainsheet is retrimmed.

But the rig that does work this way runs between mast step and a bale band slotted underneath the boom about one third of the way aft from the gooseneck. It can't be used when the roller reefing is in use, but just short of the point where reefing is necessary, such a vang or kicking strap can be very valuable when beating into heavy air. It also helps

Therefore, every boat has a maximum wind velocity in which it can carry full sail, or the full sail plan. Below this wind velocity one can pile on extra-large genoas, drifters, spinnakers, mizzen staysails or what have you. But above this velocity, one begins, or rather should begin, to shorten.

Here's the way I have approached the problem. Take a sheet of graph paper and horizontally plot wind velocity expressed in knots across the bottom. Plot the sail area in square feet of your boat on the vertical scale. Now either ask the designer or draw upon your own experience to determine what is the maximum wind velocity your boat will sail efficiently at *on the wind* under your heaviest genoa, double head rig, or jib. Plot a point at the intersection of these two values. This point will be the start of a curve.

In the case shown in Figure 1, I have selected for my 56′ yawl 1,600 square feet and 20 knots respectively. From this point, I draw a curve

through other points selected as follows: at double the wind speed, its strength will be four times and the sail area, therefore, should be one fourth; at triple the wind speed, the sail area should be one ninth and so on. It does not take many points to trace a fair line; in fact, five points are all that are needed to trace a completely accurate line. This line indicates the *allowable* sail area for each wind velocity when sailing on the wind.

Now make a list of all the sails you have, their cloth weight, and their sail areas. The fun begins, and the learning as well, when you try to fit in sequence the various sails so that they straddle the allowable sail curve (Fig. 1). The surprising thing is that you quickly realize how frequently you should change sail over a relatively small range of wind velocities.

You can also learn from the graph to plan sail changes ahead so that they will take a minimum expense of energy or people on the foredeck.

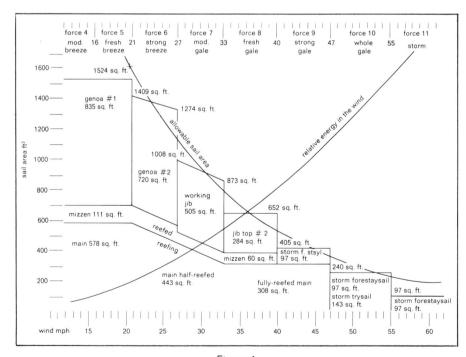

Figure 1

up to 21 knots (force 5 — fresh breeze)	main	mizzen	genoa #1
21 to 27 knots (force 6 — strong breeze)	main (down to half reefed)	mizzen	genoa #2
27 to 33 knots (force 7 — moderate gale)	main (up to fully reefed)	mizzen (reefed)	working jib
33 to 40 knots (force 8 — fresh gale)	main (fully reefed)	mizzen (reefed)	jib top #2
40 to 47 knots (force 9 — strong gale)	main (fully reefed)	—	storm forestaysail
47 to 55 knots (force 10 — whole gale)	storm trysail	—	storm forestaysail
55 to 63 knots (force 11 — storm)	—	—	storm forestaysail

Figure 2

Notice in my graph that things are arranged so that only one sail at a time is changed. The task, of course, is made easier by having reefing gear which allows considerable latitude for adjustment.

If you make a graph of your own boat, you may discover that you have some "useless" sails in your inventory; they may be too light for their sail area or they may over-lap one another. You will also discover that there may well be some serious sail deficiencies in the 30- to 40-knot wind range.

Of course you can have multiple sails for winds up to say 25 knots because that is the range in which most of the sailing is generally done. But from there on up it is important to have a few sails in good shape rather than many sails of questionable integrity.

Having a proper sail inventory, however, is not the whole solution to the problems of smooth sail changing. Having sails on board is fine only if they are easily accessible under the heavy sea conditions which usually accompany high wind speeds.

This brings me to the sail stowage problem. In many boats with cockpit lockers, the more frequently-used light sails are kept there and the heavy-weather sails are kept forward, intermingled with other gear. Often storm sails are at the bottom of a pile of gear in the forecastle. This very arrangement contributes heavily to a reluctance to change sails. If one is tired, it is easier to hope the increase in wind is temporary than it is to unscramble heavy sails stowed way forward.

To prevent such a situation I feel it is best to stow the storm sails and heavy jibs in the cockpit, and put the light-weather sails and spinnakers forward. When the weather is good, it is easy to haul the lighter sails out of the forward hatch for the boat is fairly horizontal and the open hatch does not run the risk of taking in water.

You can type a version of the sail-changing graph along the lines shown in Figure 2, though, of course, a wind velocity indicator should be aboard to give you accurate readings. With the wind indicator and the graph, sail selection becomes relatively simple and there should be little discussion or argument about what to do next.

Certain precautions must still be taken ahead of time; calculating the proper relative wind velocity the boat will encounter after turning a buoy, for example. Misjudging these wind-speeds has caused innumerable un-necessary sail changes.

Consider a boat doing 10 knots before the wind in a 25-knot breeze. The *relative* wind velocity will be only 15 knots but once she is hard on the wind and doing seven the apparent wind velocity will have risen to something close to 29 knots. Now looking at the chart, it is apparent that you are faced with a Force 7 breeze and the working jib seems the most desirable. But in the pleas-ant downwind 15-knot apparent breeze, how easy it might be to call for a #2 genoa.

There are a few people who have instincts sharpened beyond those of the ordinary seaman. I know one who always was on a winning boat. When-ever he sailed with me, I would follow his sail-selecting advice scrupulously — with excellent results. When he was on a competitor's boat, I knew my chances to get the top silver were slim.

Perhaps what impressed me most was an occurrence in the 1960 Ber-muda Race when I lost a stem casting because I failed to prevail upon an eager-beaver and otherwise experi-enced crew, to shorten enough sail. That race was won by Carleton Mitchell and when I asked him what he had done during the blow, he said: "I just kept on reducing sail, from one jib down to the next smaller one, going practically through the entire inventory."

Wind Strength and Sail Area

How to determine optimum combinations   Arthur Edmunds

One of the first decisions the owner of a new boat must make is to determine what size jib (or jibs) he should order from his sailmaker. But in order to do this accurately, he must relate the different sail areas and wind strengths that will produce optimum boat speed. But perhaps I can intercede with some thoughts so that the owner of a new boat can arrive at a "best" combination of sail area without having to sail his boat for a long period of time and determine by observation what combinations are best.

Throughout this discussion I will be using *actual* measured sail area, and Figure 1 shows three sails spread out for measurement. The figure also shows the two measurements that are necessary to determine total sail area. The first is the shortest distance from the clew to luff (perpendicular to the luff) and it is called the Length Perpendicular (LP).

The second factor is the distance from the foot to head, measured along the luff, and it is called the Luff Length. The area of any sail is calculated by multiplying the LP x ½ Luff Length; the answer is the Sail Area in square feet.

In order to have a more practical application of this problem of sail selection, let's use the dimensions of a typical sailboat of about 35' in overall length, with the following particulars:

LOA 35.0'
LWL 27.0'
Beam 10.5'
Draft 5.5'
Mainsail area   266 sq ft
Fore triangle area   308 sq ft

Displacement   15,000 lbs
Heeling Arm   19.0 ft

In any discussion of sail area and heeling, we are actually talking about the stability of a boat. Stability depends on many factors such as amount and depth of ballast, waterline beam, displacement, hull shape, height of sail plan and total sail area. I won't go into all of these factors in depth; just enough to show you how to select the correct sail size.

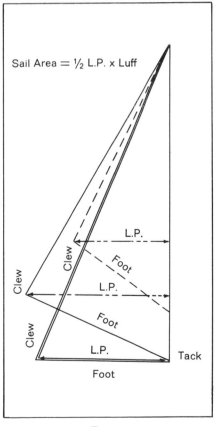

Sail Area = ½ L.P. x Luff

Figure 1

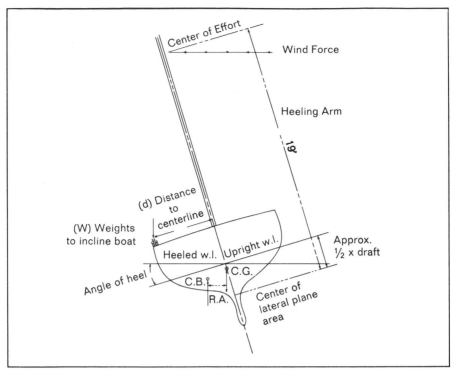

Figure 2

At any particular angle of heel, a sailboat is considered to be in a state of equilibrium for an instant, though it may not seem that way at the time! At this point the forces heeling the boat are equal to the forces that are tending to put the hull upright: this is expressed as Heeling Moment = Righting Moment (ft x lbs). The Heeling Moment is a force measured by the wind pressing on the sails (lbs/sq ft) at a particular Wind Velocity *multiplied* by the total sail area (sq ft) *multiplied* by the Heeling Arm (ft).

The Heeling Arm is shown in Figure 2 and it is the distance from the center of effort of the sails measured vertically to the center of the lateral plane area. The center of the lateral plane area is approximately ½ x draft below the waterline. Measuring on the scale drawing of a sail plan of our typical 35′ sailboat we can find that the Heeling Arm is 19.0′.

The formula for Heeling Moment (ft x lbs) is Wind Pressure x Sail Area x Heeling Arm.

You can determine Wind Pressure from the formula Wind Pressure (lbs/sq ft) = .004 x velocity squared (knots^2). Though wind pressure does vary with height above the water, the formula is a good average for the center of effort of sail area. You can simplify this formula further into the following table:

Wind Velocity (knots)	Wind Pressure (lbs/sq ft)
8	0.25
12	0.6
16	1.0
20	1.6
25	2.5
30	3.6
35	4.9

Now let's turn to the other side of our equilibrium equation, the Righting Moment. Referring again to Figure 2, you see that the position of the center of gravity of the entire boat (CG) and the position of the heeled center of buoyancy (CB) are shown. The center of buoyancy is the geometric center of the immersed portion of the hull.

This CB moves out from the boat's centerline as the boat heels over, in an amount that depends on beam and hull shape. Both the heeled CB and the CG are calculated by the designer, and the horizontal distance between the heeled CB and the CG is called the Righting Arm (RA). When the RA is multiplied by the weight of the boat's displacement, the result is the Righting Moment, expressed in ft-lbs. Looking at our typical 35' hull, the Righting Arm (RA) is calculated at 1.067' and multiplied by the displacement of 15,000 lbs, the Righting Moment is 16,000 ft lbs.

This Righting Moment can be obtained from the boat's designer, or you can get the optimum Righting Moment (at an angle of heel considered to be most advantageous) from a racing measurement certificate. A good boat dealer also should have the figure available for your boat.

The racing certificate lists the Righting Moment at one degree of heel, and you should multiply this by a factor of about 20 to get an accurate Righting Moment.

If the designer's figure isn't available and you have no measurement certificate, you can perform an inclining experiment on your boat by the following method.

The boat should be on a mooring with calm wind and water. If it is at a dock it should be tied only by the bow so that it can float freely. All gear should be in normal position with the booms secured on centerline to prevent them from swinging. Now go below and thumbtack or tape a light line, such as a nylon fishing line, to the overhead on the centerline. Make sure it can swing freely. Tie a pad of bronze wool on the bottom of the line, about three inches above the cabin sole. This high inertia-damping device works better than a conventional "plumb bob," when it is immersed in water. Now put the bronze wool into a pail of water (Fig. 3). During the inclining

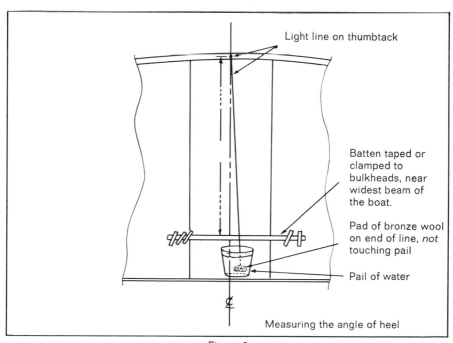

Light line on thumbtack

Batten taped or clamped to bulkheads, near widest beam of the boat.

Pad of bronze wool on end of line, *not* touching pail

Pail of water

Measuring the angle of heel

Figure 3

test, move the pail of water athwart-ships as necessary to keep the bronze wool from touching the sides of the pail.

Attach a batten (yardstick, etc.) to the bulkheads or joinerwork so that it will not move during the inclining operation. Measure the length of the line from the pivot point on the thumbtack to the top (or bottom) of the batten edge. We will assume this is 4.67′ (56″) on our 35′ boat.

Put the weights that will be used on centerline on deck and have one person (who is not being used as a weight) go below and carefully mark the batten where it intersects the line. This is the centerline, below decks, used for inclining measure-ment. Now carefully weigh the weights (or people) with an accurate scale, and have them move to the toe rail, at the *maximum beam* of the boat.

Now measure the distance from the centerline of the boat on deck to the center of the weight. If you are using people, they should stand in a fore-and-aft line just inside the toe-rail and should not move during the measurement period. In our sample boat, the weight distance off center-line is 4.44′ and the weight used is 360 lbs. About 200 lbs of weight should be used on boats up to 28′ long; 300 lbs up to 35′ long; 400 lbs up to 40′ long; 500 lbs up to 44′ long; and 600 lbs up to 47′.

When the boat has steadied down, have one man that is not being used as a weight go below and mark the batten at the spot it intersects the line. Now place the weights about half the distance outboard of center-line and again mark the batten care-fully.

Now repeat the procedure for the other side of the boat, and you will have four marks on the batten. On our sample boat, the weight dis-tances off centerline are 2.03′ and 4.44′, which makes our inclining mo-ments 730.8 ft-lbs and 1598 ft-lbs, respectively. The four marks on the batten are .074′ and .158′ (port) and .072′ and .156′ (starboard) off center-line. Before you finish, move the weights onto the centerline again and recheck the centerline mark on the batten. The whole procedure shouldn't take more than an hour once the equipment and weights are assembled.

The marks on the batten should be equally spaced from centerline mark, but if there is a great variance be-tween the marks, the procedure must be done again with greater care.

Now plot the four numbers, which represent the movement of the line at the batten, on graph paper at the corresponding points of Heeling Moment. To do this, multiply the weight used by the distance the weight is off centerline (Fig. 4) (ft x lbs). On our sample boat, this is 360 lbs x 2.03′ and 360 lbs x 4.44′. If the inclining has been carefully done, the four marks should be located on a straight line, but you can average any small variations.

You want the Moment (Righting Moment = Heeling Moment) at one degree of heel and you can find this by dividing the length of the line (l) by a constant 57.3, which is the num-ber of degrees in one radian. The ex-ample in Figure 4, which is our 35′ boat, has one degree equalling .0816 which makes the resulting Righting Moment 800 ft-lbs at one degree of heel.

As I mentioned before, you now must multiply this one degree Right-ing Moment by a factor of about 20 to obtain an optimum Righting Mo-ment for the boat. This factor of 20 is admittedly an assumption but it has been derived by studying and com-paring the Righting Moments of many boats of various lengths and types.

Once you have the optimum Right-ing Moment, you can return to the original equation and equate it to the Heeling Moment, as follows:

Righting Moment (ft-lbs) = Wind Pressure (lbs/sq ft) x Sail Area (sq ft) x Heeling Arm (ft).

The optimum Righting Moment for

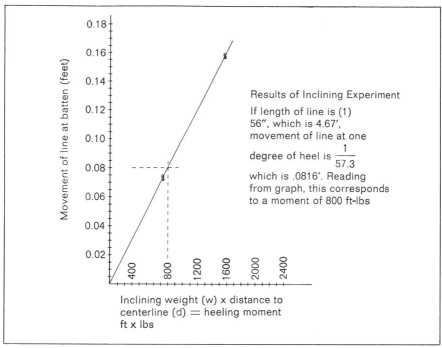

Results of Inclining Experiment

If length of line is (1)
56", which is 4.67',
movement of line at one

degree of heel is $\dfrac{1}{57.3}$

which is .0816'. Reading
from graph, this corresponds
to a moment of 800 ft-lbs

Inclining weight (w) x distance to
centerline (d) = heeling moment
ft x lbs

Figure 4

our typical 35' hull is 800 ft-lbs x 20 = 16,000 ft-lbs.

Now what you want to determine is the total sail area required for a particular wind strength to have the optimum angle of heel. You therefore rewrite the equation as follows:

Total Sail Area (sq ft) =

$$\frac{\text{Righting Moment (ft-lbs)}}{\substack{\text{Heeling Arm x Windpressure} \\ \text{(ft)} \qquad \text{(lbs/sq ft)}}}$$

Righting Moment comes either from your designer or the inclining experiment; the Heeling Arm is taken from the sail plan; and Wind Pressure comes directly from the chart. Looking at our 35' boat in a wind strength of 12 knots, we apply the above equation as follows:

Required total Sail Area =

$$\frac{16,000}{19.0 \times 0.6} = 1400 \text{ sq ft}$$

Because our mainsail area is only 266 sq ft, we need a 1,134 sq ft genoa in order to achieve an optimum heeling moment. Because this is obviously too large a sail to fit on the boat, we must use the largest sail that can properly fit. But we would *not heel over* to the optimum angle. Now using the same 35' hull in 16 knots of wind, the required sail area equals $\dfrac{16,000}{19.0 \times 1.0}$, which is 842 sq ft. Subtracting the 266 sq ft mainsail, the proper genoa size becomes 576 sq ft which is about the correct size for a large genoa for a 35' hull for use in winds up to 16 knots.

You can see that your answers will be the correct total sail area for a particular wind strength. By subtracting the mainsail area from total area, you arrive at the proper size jib that is needed. Mainsail area, of course, is obtained from the designer's sail plan.

As wind strength increases, the mainsail can be reefed and the jib changed to a smaller size in order to keep the optimum total sail area requirements you have calculated from the equation. When the mainsail is reefed and a smaller jib is used, the Heeling Arm will be much shorter and the smaller sails should be drawn on the sail plan so that the correct Heeling Arm can be measured, using the combined Center of Effort of the two sails.

A chart now can be prepared showing total sail areas, as Mr. Giannini did in his article. With this chart posted, the entire crew can see, at a glance, what sail combination is best for the boat under certain wind conditions.

Always keep in mind, though, that when you are making a chart of the correct sail combinations, the Heeling Force (lbs) really should be constant over the entire range of wind strengths, for the optimum angle of heel. While this constant will vary for each boat, you can find it by multiplying the Wind Pressure (lbs/sq ft) by the required Sail Area (sq ft) at any particular wind velocity. This constant Heeling Force is 842 lbs for our typical 35' boat. For winds over 20 knots it may be easier for you to use this constant Heeling Force to calculate the required Sail Area rather than re-measuring the Heeling Arm on a new sail plan that shows a reefed mainsail.

Once you see how this procedure works, you will have come a long way toward comprehending your boat's sail-carrying ability. And you will be able to order the proper headsails, not by guessing, but by an objective and accurate assessment of what the boat can handle.

The Virtue of "Jiffy" Reefing

A fast system for shortening the main   Peter M. Sutter

In the late '50s very few San Francisco Bay boats would bother to reef during a normal afternoon sail. Most were designed to meet the bay's rough water conditions and few really needed to reduce sail.

But the new light displacement, masthead rig, fiberglass production boats were a different story. Their owners soon found that they either reefed down or their guests would be hanging on for dear life; and they stood to lose all their mainsail battens.

Production boats soon became equipped with roller reefing. But on many boats 30' or less this merely amounted to standing on the lee side of the boat near the stern, pulling the boom out of its gooseneck attachment and rolling the sail up around it while a crew member eased the halyard.

Once the reef was rolled in and the sail stretched out, all would go well until it suddenly all rolled out again!

The final alternative was to drop the main and sail home on the jib. This usually worked, though the balance was not very good. Believe it or not, some production boats are still advertising this type of roller reefing; and buyers are still falling for it.

Larger boats did have geared roller reefing goosenecks but the reefed mainsail usually set poorly unless strips of foam rubber, etc., were also rolled in.

The leech invariably creeps forward, tightening the batten area and presenting an even fuller shape. And with geared roller reefing it's tough to vang the boom unless special arrangements are made. Many of the

sketches by Marshall Roath

How to set up the boat for Jiffy Reefing. Roller reefing (top) tightens leech, creates excessive bag in sail. Jiffy Reefing (bottom) keeps leech stretched out, sail retains proper shape.

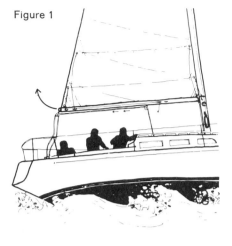

Figure 1

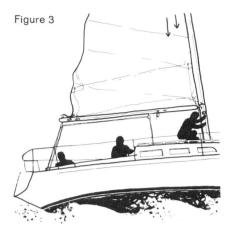

Figure 3

Figure 2

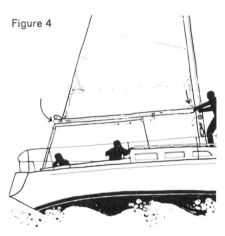

Figure 4

reefing gear pins have failed in heavy sea conditions. And what does one do when the gear handle is lost?

The answer for Bay sailors was to improve upon the old fashioned slab reefing method that could take up to 30 minutes to achieve.

Fellows like Warwick "Commodore" Tompkins, Southern California sailmaker Saint Cicero, and others worked out the bugs; and *Jiffy Reefing* was born. The word Jiffy means that if the crew takes longer than 30 seconds to throw in a reef, leave them home for the next race!

When is the right time to reef? Nine times out of ten the proper time is the moment the thought occurs. An angle of heel of 20° or more is

one good indication. A good inclinometer is very helpful for this.

Excessive backwinding from the headsail also indicates a need for a flatter mainsail, rather than an eased mainsheet. A reef will also relieve an excessive weather helm.

Jiffy reefing has three main steps. First cast off the mainsheet and let it run free but keep the boat moving with jib or genoa. (See figure 1.) Next haul the boom up to the leech reef cringle with the reef clew outhaul and make it fast to the boom cleat. (See figure 2.)

Then slack the halyard and haul down the reef tack downhaul, making it fast to the mast cleat. (See figures 3 and 4).

If the halyard is premarked it need only be slacked to the mark. Otherwise it may have to be tightened up again after the reef tack downhaul has been made fast. The mainsail can now be sheeted in again and the reefed part of the sail either tied or laced up.

One afternoon spent practicing reefing and unreefing should work out all the bugs and get the crew adept at what's required. When everything is working well it should take only 15 to 25 seconds to jiffy reef a boat up to 40 feet in length!

Here are some thoughts on setting up the gear. Just as you need to stretch the foot of a sail on the boom as the wind strengthens, the foot of the reef also will need stretching. The following procedure will achieve the proper stretch, and prevent any over stretch.

Set up the mast and boom reefing gear at dockside with little or no wind.

1. Position the boom at the bottom of the gooseneck track or at the black band.
2. Fasten an eyestrap on the port side of the mast at the band or level with the top of the boom angled toward reef.
3. Fasten a cleat on the starboard side of mast at the band or level with the top of the boom.
4. Tie a line to the eyestrap (2 × the reef depth + 2 feet). Pass it through the luff reef cringle and pull tight to position the luff reef cringle above the tack cringle.
5. With boom level, pass a line through the leech reef cringle and pull hard aft against the luff until a tension pleat is formed along the length of the reef. Mark the boom opposite the hole.
6. Fasten a strong cheek block tilted aft at a 45° angle to this mark on the starboard side.
7. Fasten an eyestrap 2-4" aft of the cheek block on the port side.

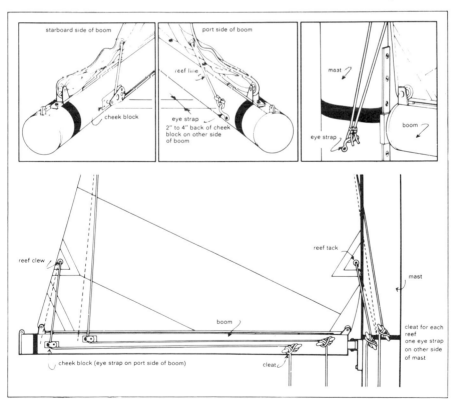

Make sure these two items are strong and well fastened as the entire load of the mainsail will be passed through them to the mainsheet.

8. Fasten a cleat to the boom's starboard side just aft of the gooseneck.

9. Provide a line 2 times the reef depth plus the boom length (0-25' boat 5/16", 25-35' boat 3/8", 35-45' boat 7/16") and tie it securely to the eyestrap. Reeve it through the leech reef cringle, the cheek block, and belay it to the cleat.

10. If you've got two or three reef points in the sail use the same gear and method of location for each, although it may be necessary to place the deepest set on the port side.

11. Don't get caught on the port tack while reefing.

A final word about the gear. The cheek blocks, eye straps and their attendant fastenings really must be healthy. On my own boat, they are thru-bolted and are not the light stamped-out stainless steel variety with light pins and nylon sheaves.

They are Merriman bronze blocks and diamond eye pads. I consider them best for this type of job.

One possible modification though is to knock the sheave pin out and replace it with a stainless steel through bolt. Most of today's booms are aluminum and few have flat sections. Therefore, use a wood or plastic cheek piece to get a flat surface for the block and pad eye to rest on.

Keep away from the "V" jam or cam cleat types for the reefing lines. Too often a cam will fail to jam or the line will jam too tightly in the "V" so you can't get it out quickly.

As with internal halyards, the reef lines may be run internally on your boom. After all it is aluminum, so why not use it as a fairlead?

Probably some will object to hauling in the reef clew outhaul first rather than the tack downhaul. We have found that the reef clew cringle positions itself better and with less strain if it's done this way. But the block and eye strap must be properly positioned or a severe load will be produced on the lower luff slides.

Which Headsail When?

Systematized sail changing   Richard duMoulin

Today, a typical ocean-racing yacht, no matter whether it is 30′ or 73′ long, may have five or even ten headsails, excluding spinnakers, reachers and staysails.

As rigs become more complex (bendy spars, hydraulic backstay turnbuckles, etc.), designs will become even more sensitive to sail trim; and headsail inventories will grow and grow.

Therefore, it becomes more important than ever to gather precise criteria for proper headsail selection.

If you are going to optimize boat speed, you must know not only the proper wind range for each headsail, and this includes learning at what point of sail each jib achieves its maximum potential, you must also know when it can be flown without permanent damage to its shape. And you should know the correct sheet lead and halyard tension for every headsail.

You must determine all this data *before* the big race, and to do so accurately, you must use every opportunity to sail against similar boats. Set each sail in its optimum wind condition, and if possible, get your sailmaker on board to look the sails over.

Keep a notepad handy to log all sail trim information for later use (Fig. 1). Log the information using *apparent* wind. This is more useful than using true wind because apparent wind is what the sail, the crew, and the anemometer (if you have one) are exposed to.

In order to quantify sheet leads and proper halyard tensions, you should have benchmarks. For proper sheet leads, numbers can be either stamped onto the track, or painted on the deck next to the track. To achieve effectively proper halyard tension, a whipping or painted mark on the halyard can be matched

LOGBOOK ENTRIES

Date	Apparent Wind	Sail	Best Lead	Best Halyard Tension	Comments
5/20	10-12 kts.	#1-4 oz.	#35	Mark 8	Sailed against sistership with leech 6″ off upper spreader, outfooted & pointed with other boat, very fast! Backstay at 6,000 lbs.
5/20	10-12 kts.	#1-7 oz.	#33	Mark 11	Pointed well but very slow, sail too heavy & flat; too little wind?

Figure 1

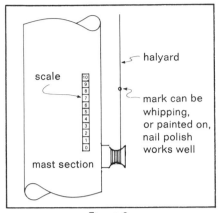

scale

halyard

mark can be whipping, or painted on, nail polish works well

mast section

Figure 2

against a scale on the mast. Sailmakers often provide plastic adhesive-backed scales for their customers, but they also are available at most stores carrying yachting equipment (Fig. 2).

Remember that sails do change shape, and halyards do stretch as the season progresses. This means you must reexamine the initial settings to make sure they are still valid.

Also remember that these settings should be based on exact wind and sea conditions. This means, however, that if you have done your sail test-

ing and log entries carefully, adjustments must be made continuously by the crew when racing.

Careful and thorough pre-season practice and experimentation with new and old sails should give a skipper and his crew enough data to construct a chart similar to the one shown in Figure 3.

If one copy is posted in the navigator's area and another on deck, the chart becomes not only a source of information on adjustments, it is a reminder to the crew on watch that a sail change might be in order. Of course, during sail changes, it also is a handy reference for crew members responsible for halyard and sheet lead adjustments.

Logbook changes must be made continuously as new sails are added, old ones left ashore, halyards stretched, and improved leads and adjustments discovered. Additional notes can be included on the chart, such as: "Maximum allowable heel 28°; begin reefing at 25 kts apparent; never use drifter in apparent winds over 8 kts; with drifter, ease backstay to half maximum load." Similar chart notations can be developed for other points of sail.

The "Sail Selection Chart," developed by the US Naval Academy

CHARISMA SAIL SELECTION Headsails — 1972

Figure 3

Sail Description	Deck Lead	Halyard Hoist (on scale)	Wind Range (apparent) 0	5	10	15	20	25	30	35
#1 1.5 oz drifter*	padeye B	2	///6					Begin Reefing		
#1 3.5 oz genoa	padeye B w/downhaul	5		///12						
#1 6 oz genoa	"	7			////22					
#2 8 oz genoa	"	5					///28			
#3 9 oz genoa	inside track #25	6						///35		
#4 topsail (& forestaysl)	rail #35	10								35-50
#5 storm jib (& forestaysl)	rail #40	8								over 50

*Never use drifter in apparent winds over 8 kts.
With drifter, ease backstay to half maximum load.

Begin roller reefing at 25 kts apparent.

MAXIMUM ALLOWABLE HEEL 28°

Apparent Wind Velocity	Close Hauled	Close Reach	Beam Reach	Broad Reach	Run
0-8 kts	#1 2 oz genoa	2 oz reacher 2 oz spin. staysail	3/4 oz chute (1.5 oz tallboy or ½ oz spin. st)	3/4 oz chute (½ oz staysail)	3/4 oz chute
8-18 kts	#1 5 oz genoa	8 oz reacher 5 oz forestaysail	1.5/2.2 oz chute (tallboy or 4 oz tall staysail)	1.5/2.2 oz chute (tall staysail, 5 oz tallboy, or 2 oz spin. staysl)	1.5/2.2 oz chute (½ oz staysail flown to leeward of spin. sheet)
18-25 kts	#1 8 or 9 oz genoa	#1 9 oz genoa 5 oz forestaysail (possibly a few rolls of reef)	2.5 oz spanker 5 oz tallboy or 4 oz tall staysl) (maybe reef)	1.5/2.2 oz chute (tall staysail, 5 oz tallboy, or 2 oz spin. staysl)	2.2 oz chute
25-33 kts	#2 8 oz genoa	#2 8 oz genoa 9 oz forestaysail reefed main	#2 8 oz genoa or #1 9 oz genoa (5 oz forestaysail) reefed main	spanker or storm chute	spanker or storm chute
33-40 kts	#3 8 oz genoa	#3 8 oz genoa 9 oz forestaysail reefed main	#3 8 oz genoa 9 oz forestaysail reefed main	#1 9 oz genoa or #2 8 oz genoa reefed main	#1 9 oz genoa or #2 8 oz genoa on spin. pole reefed main
40-60 kts	#3 jib topsail storm trysail	#3 jib topsail storm trysail (maybe forestysl)	#3 jib topsail storm trysail (maybe forestaysl)	#3 8 oz genoa or #3 jib topsail reefed or no main	#3 genoa or #3 jib topsail on pole/bare poles

Figure 4

officers and midshipmen for *Rage*'s 1970 SORC campaign, is another way to organize all information onto one chart (Fig. 4). Aboard the 52' *Rage*, all sheet leads were written on the pedestals of the coffee grinders, and all halyard tension data was marked on the mast.

Much of the value in developing one or both of these charts for your own boat lies in the fact that it forces you to examine your sail inventory as an integrated system, with many specialized sails in that total system.

Much of the indecision and tactical mistakes made on the race course can be eliminated by thinking ahead about the uses, settings and limitations of each sail. Crew communication is made easier because everyone understands the broad guidelines for sail selection; now they can concentrate fully on maximizing boat speed.

On-the-Wind Headsail Changes

The techniques of fast handling　　　　　　　　Richard duMoulin

Upwind sail changing covers two broad areas — sail selection and sail changing. *Sail selection* covers *when* to change and *what* to change to; *Sail changing* deals with the problem of *how* to change sails with the minimum loss of time. This article discusses sail changing.

An aggressively raced boat is pushed continually to her maximum speed. As soon as wind and sea conditions indicate that a sail change is needed, the crew must be ready to act immediately. Members of the afterguard and foredeck should have decided on the next jib, and it should have been lashed down on the foredeck ready for the expected change.

No time should be wasted getting the sail on deck and either hanked on or set up after the decision to change has been made. Good communication between the navigator (or whoever is monitoring and predicting weather and wind changes), the watch captain, and the foredeck chief, ensures that all pertinent information has been shared so that the best decision and earlier preparation can be made.

As a general rule, a jib that is slightly heavier should be on deck ready to go up. This is reasonable because it is easier to get a lighter jib on deck when the wind decreases than it is to get a heavier jib on deck if the wind picks up. In addition, being ready for a heavier condition may save you the heartache (and wallet-ache) of watching your light sail blow out before a heavy one is ready to hoist. The bigger the boat, the more important this foresight is.

Changing a jib should be as organized and well-executed as a play in a professional football game. Consequently, a planned "play" should be drawn up by the skipper, with suggestions from the crew. This play should be standardized for all sail changes and be understood by the entire crew.

Because any sail changing plan depends on the size of the boat and crew, the deck layout and rig, and personal preferences, I will describe a technique using four men (including the helmsman). This would be most applicable to a 30' to 40' boat, but the principles and concept of the "play" apply to any size boat.

Before I describe the technique, I want to emphasize the value of checking and *re*checking all sails, sheets, leads, halyards, etc. for readiness *before* the change begins. This will prevent loss of time and possibly equipment during the change. Every crewman should be trained — harassed if necessary — into being foresighted. Thinking ahead is not the sole responsibility of the afterguard.

The accompanying Play Card (Fig. 1) describes the change, and the diagram (Fig. 2) indicates proper crew movements. Play Cards for sail changes, gybes and spinnaker sets and takedowns are very helpful for polishing up your regular crew's coordination, and for breaking in new crew. On the card "old jib" refers to the one that has been up, and "new jib" refers to the one to be hoisted in its place.

All jib changes, except those to or from a hankless drifter, should be made either with a genoa staysail or a tallboy acting as an interim jib. Not only does an interim jib assist

	CREWMAN			
	#1	#2	#3	#4
STEP ONE: Preparation	check jib— feed luff of tallboy— unlash jib	rig tallboy— hoist tallboy	remove weather sheet, rig short sheet, attach regular sheet to new jib— trim tallboy	steer
STEP TWO: Lower Old Jib	yell "*Drop*"— unhank	lower halyard	gather jib	release short sheet— ease main— steer for speed
STEP THREE: Hoist New Jib	switch halyard— yell "*Hoist*"— run aft to trim jib	hoist jib— yell "*Trim*"	lash down old jib	steer for speed
STEP FOUR: Drop Staysail	play jib and main	drop tallboy	gather tallboy	steer for speed
STEP FIVE: Cleanup	play jib and main	clear halyards	bag and stow tallboy— attach weather jib sheet; check that it's clear	steer for speed
		Neatly flake the old jib, and have it or the next heaviest jib on the foredeck (watch captain's decision)		

Figure 1
Play Card: jib change

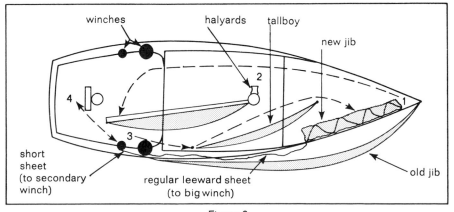

Figure 2

Spinnaker Changing on Big Boats

Procedures used on Windward Passage   Don Vaughn

It **seems every** ocean racer over 50′ has always had problems changing spinnakers in a fresh breeze with a sea running. Conventional systems are usually too slow for it's usually an all hands situation. It takes time to get the off watch up on deck, and a half-asleep crew coming up to help can sometimes be a safety hazard as well.

I first saw this type of spinnaker change on *Bolero*, when she was racing in the Southern Ocean Racing Conference (SORC) and then in England. But we have changed the original system radically since then.

The technique used is as simple as it can possibly be, especially if every one watches the foredeck, does his own job, and *stays out* of the crew man's job next to him.

Let's assume that you are on the starboard tack, main boom to port and spinnaker pole to starboard. Because of a change in wind velocity the decision is made to change the chute. The pole is secured to the mast in a standard manner: the foreguy, after guy and topping lift are secured to the pole by stainless steel screw pin shackles. These three lines control the pole's fore

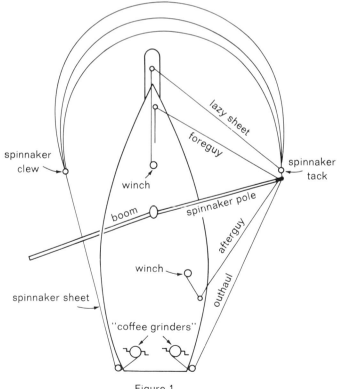

Figure 1

and aft movement as well as its up and down movement.

The spinnaker is secured to the boat by the halyard, the spinnaker sheet and what we call an outhaul that rides free through the jaws of the spinnaker pole end fitting. This means of course that any fore and aft movement of the pole must be made simultaneously by the outhaul, as well as the foreguy and after guy.

There is a lazy spinnaker sheet connected to the tack of the chute that runs forward to the pulpit through a block, then aft to a winch at the base of the mast. (See Figure 1.)

The new spinnaker that is to be hoisted is laid out on the deck (lightweight chutes are set flying; others are in stops). The tack is taken forward to the bow and the clew brought aft to about the shrouds. The balance of the chute is left in the spinnaker bag.

Dropping the old chute is controlled from three positions.
(1) The outhaul is eased forward.
(2) Taking in on the lazy sheet brings the tack down to the pulpit where the outhaul can be cast free, followed by the lazy sheet.
(3) The halyard is then eased, allowing the chute to be gathered in under the main boom in the usual manner.

As the chute is being lowered the tack of the new sail is led around the headstay and attached to the lazy sheet and outhaul. As soon as the sheet is disconnected from the old clew it is hooked to the clew of the replacement chute. When the head of the old chute is on deck the halyard is transferred to the new chute.

Note that the pole *does not change position* during the sail change. As the new sail is raised, the outhaul is sheeted home, bringing the tack of the new chute back out to the end of the pole. The pole has not moved so the trim should remain the same and only small final adjustments are necessary.

Why did we find this method better than conventional procedures?
(1) It eliminates two or three men who have to swing the pole down to the pulpit so a standard release can be made.
(2) It eliminates the struggle of trying to retop the pole while the after guy is being brought back to proper trim position.

With timing and practice we found we could make spinnaker changes during this last Honolulu Race quickly and efficiently without having the full crew topside. This not only left the off watch undisturbed but saved the time it would normally take to get them up on deck and in position.

The crew on *Passage* was as well balanced as you could find in any ocean race. Great personnel at the helm and excellent seamen on the foredeck. Combine them with a great cook, a fantastic boat and the desire to undo the unforgettable 1969 Transpac. It was this perfect combination that drove us to a new Transpac record, a win in Class A and first overall!

Spinnaker Takedowns in High Winds

Rigging and handling for smooth dousing

Warwick M. Tompkins, Jr.

Downwind **sailing induces** a euphoric condition aboard most boats, which vanishes astonishingly fast when the boat does her first deep roll or the helmsman fails to prevent a jibe or broach.

Spinnakers earned a seamanlike disfavor when they were first being used at sea. Since then spinnakers have grown larger, stronger, and more powerful, and they are carried downwind longer.

Spinnakers are difficult to handle, and are at the root of much damage to both gear and psyche. This applies to the oceangoing veteran as well as to the newcomer.

Handling a spinnaker in heavy weather is a mark of the very experienced. It requires experience, skill and judgment to extract the power available and still get it down before it causes loss of control or broken gear.

Most ocean racing craft with the pole on the headstay are capable of carrying their spinnakers in breezes up to about 25 knots. At this velocity, the boat will have a tendency to round into the wind, and to counter this tendency one must use extreme measures such as sheeting from the main boom-end, luffing the mainsail completely, or cranking in a great deal of "trim-tab," or all of these.

The same boats may carry full-size spinnakers in winds approaching 35 knots with the wind well aft. Handling a spinnaker is most difficult in these higher wind ranges for there are awesome forces involved which have numbing effects on the crew.

Most people who have worked with spinnakers have experienced a loss of control at some time. The sail receives almost universal and well deserved respect as a result.

It is, of course, the skipper's job to see that he does not carry sail beyond the ability of his craft or crew . . . and when those limits are approached, it is time for a skilled, collective effort to reduce sail.

There are a few mammoth boats today that have really special spinnaker gear and handling problems. A 160-foot schooner *Goodwill* used a five-ton coilspring on her spinnaker sheet blocks, and an eight-foot (inside-diameter) "snuffing ring" through which the sail was pulled to get it on deck!

There was also a blasting device which liberated the spinnaker tack from the pole before lowering. Mercifully, such details are beyond the experience or need of most of us!

In larger boats up to 70', the spinnaker is rigged using two sets of sheets and guys. The after guy is attached to the tack, led through the end of the spinnaker pole, and down to the rail; best rail position is somewhere just aft of the middle of the boat.

This provides the best angle of support for the pole when reaching, allows a shorter guy, and usually produces a better lead to the winches.

The pole end fitting should be designed to allow the after guy to slip freely through even if the pin has not been opened from the deck.

The windward sheet, or "lazy guy," should be attached to the tack and led over the outer end of the pole. It is called lazy guy because it doesn't take a strain until after the jibe (when it becomes the sheet). It is usually led through a block on the quarter.

Two lines are also led from the clew of the spinnaker. The sheet taking a strain should be taken to the rail at a point anywhere from the quarter to about amidships depending on course and wind velocity.

The other line can act as an auxiliary sheet or safety; it actually becomes the after guy after jibing. But as an extra sheet, or lee after guy, it has a real use when retrieving the sail.

This double set of gear evolved from the 12-meter *Vim* who used it in her almost successful bid to defend the America's Cup in 1958. It allows a neat jibe, and seems to be in general favor today except on a few boats which because of their size, rig, or other considerations use the double pole method.

Such double gear is especially helpful in dousing a spinnaker; for the lee after guy with no strain on it can be run from the clew, through a snatch block located aft of the main shrouds near the base of the mast, and then to a powerful winch.

This is required preparation before starting a heavy weather take-down. This lead can pull the sail into the quiet air to leeward of the mainsail.

The halyard, topping lift, and both after guys must of course be flaked and free to run. Flaking is infinitely superior to coiling, and the most painstaking flaking is a small price to pay for a smooth operation when the wind is very fresh.

Increasing competition in ocean racing does not allow for a course alteration to ease the work unless the conditions are severe or the evolution has gone awry . . . at that time, sailing downwind or by the lee is the only means of handling the sail.

With winds in the 30 to 40 knot range, a large spinnaker can be handled most efficiently as follows:

Use the mainsail to blanket the spinnaker. Bear off bringing the wind well aft, and adjust the main accordingly, vang and all. A mainsail not squared to the wind allows rapid wind flow across its lee side.

Do not square the pole, but commence sheeting in on the line leading from the clew through the block at the base of the mast. This should be done quickly and at the same time as the after guy and "lazy guy" are released.

Never slack the spinnaker halyard until the sail is very nearly stretched to the mast, and its foot is in the hands of the men positioned to gather it in.

The sail should be gathered until it forms a slender column of fabric, suspended by the halyard, and stretched toward the deck.

This condition keeps the sail from blowing out to leeward of the mainsail leech or filling from air blowing aft from the weather side.

Note the word "released" when I refer to the after guy and lazy guy. The two guys ought to run out freely when the sail is being hauled to the mast.

The two guys should be quickly given sufficient slack so that the sail will slip into the mainsail lee and collapse.

They should not be allowed to drag in the water on the lee side for it makes gathering the foot more difficult, slowing the retrieving of the spinnaker.

Once the tack is on board, I favor removing the after guys as soon as possible, which avoids the need for tending them further and allows more men to work at gathering in the sail. Detach them, snap them to the rail, cleat the bitter ends, and forget them for the moment.

With the guys off the sail the pole may bang for a moment against the headstay. Don't worry — the important thing is to get the spinnaker on deck. If the banging and crashing is excessive, the pole can be dropped later, steadied with the foreguy or tensioned with the afterguy. Despite the crashing noise the pole is in little or no danger.

Those gathering the sail should be stationed so that they can pull as if there is no tomorrow. The faster they get the sail to the deck, the less chance of trouble. As soon as the sail is on deck, it should be dumped below through the nearest hatch, and the attendant gear detached and cleared.

A smooth hatch located near the base of the mast will facilitate this operation, and in many boats a man stands below to receive the spinnaker. Men gathering a spinnaker should be positioned so that they bring the sail down beside themselves or onto their laps.

They should avoid straddling the gathered sail or standing in it, for if they become entangled in its folds and it fills with either wind or water there is an excellent chance they may be hurt or thrown overboard.

Taking down a spinnaker in high winds requires keen judgment, particularly by the helmsman and the man on the halyard. The helmsman must be able to keep the boat under control, steering either slightly by the lee or with the wind over the quarter, whichever is demanded by the work in progress.

With the wind by the lee, air flows around the leech of the main toward the mast, and with the wind on the quarter, it flows from mast to leech. These air flows will tug at the spinnaker and they must not be allowed to become too strong.

With the wind dead astern, the air behind the main is turbulent, and its flow largely determined by the roll of the boat. A helmsman must know all these things and be able to apply the right helm.

If he spots an impending foulup, he must be unflappable, for he is the only one who can really see the whole operation, correcting a bad situation with his voice and his steering.

In short, the helmsman must provide as stable a platform as possible, adjust course so that the wind flow is proper and do these things until the sail is safely stowed. The better he can do his job, the faster the sail will come down.

The halyard man must not slack the halyard too quickly or the sail will billow into the breeze. He must not hold up the pulling of the sail onto the deck by keeping an excessive strain on the halyard.

If he errs, to the consternation of the sail-gatherers, he must have confidence in his ability to observe and make corrections.

No two takedowns are ever the same, and a few feet of halyard held or given at a critical moment can make the difference between a clean operation and a monstrous foulup!

I mentioned keeping the sail out of the wind flow. When it is in stalled air, both corners may be easily gathered, but if the sail gets away to leeward and fills with all three corners held on board, the sail is very dangerous.

The quickest way to retrieve such a recalcitrant sail is to free all but one corner. This dictum applies whether the sail fills with wind or water.

The drag of a spinnaker in the water, attached by one end, is considerable, but possible to overcome. A sail attached by two or three corners becomes a sea anchor, cannot be retrieved, and may destroy itself and other gear.

With one attachment the sail streams freely and may be hauled aboard as a great, sodden rope, normally with all hands looking as if they were playing tug-of-war with Neptune!

For this reason sheets and guys ought to be flaked down without knots in their ends so that they may run free if it is required. When a spinnaker does go over the side, do not hesitate to release all but one attachment.

Removing the snapshackles from the sail is best for it removes the additional drag of the line, but any means of getting the sail to stream freely is warranted including cutting if necessary.

Ideally, the clew or tack will be the one corner held on board if the halyard can be released by opening the snapshackle. Failing this, one occasionally finds that the spinnaker is dragging gaily along held only by its halyard.

This retrieval problem is best

solved by sending a man to the masthead with a line. Tie one end around the spinnaker halyard and send the other to the deck, where it can be used to haul the halyard aboard, and thereby the spinnaker.

One should have several spare spinnaker sheets, guys, and even a halyard on board. All are cheaper than a split spinnaker, and sacrificing such minor piece of gear can well prevent a chain reaction that might cripple the boat or her crew (literally).

In a really heavy air takedown, I see little need for setting a headsail on the headstay. It is an additional piece of gear to rig and unrig, and will not draw properly anyway as the takedown evolution is in progress. The sail might prevent some wind flow across the leeward side of the mainsail, but if it does, it's probably too large for the conditions anyway.

A headsail alternately backing and filling in the lee of the main in such winds can throw a man many feet if it hits him. This risk, coupled with the effort and organization involved, makes the presence of a staysail in the foretriangle undesirable until the spinnaker is completely down and cleared. Then rig whatever headsail seems right.

There is some dismay at the way in which ocean racers carry on with spinnakers in heavy air. This, in my opinion, is justified, for there is real danger inherent in so powerful a sail.

Attempts have been made to limit the number or weight of spinnakers a vessel may carry. But little satisfaction has resulted, and all that has really happened is that the better seaman-racers continue to reap the benefits of their skill.

I wish to emphasize that simply learning a list of do's and don'ts is not the answer when driving hard up wind or down. Ocean racing success requires great skill and seamanship. A skipper's judgment of his boat and crew remains the ultimate arbiter on how long and how much sail can be carried.

So, learn how to carry the spinnaker in plenty of wind, but master its lowering so that you can stop when your judgment — and conditions — demand it.

Watch Out for Heavy Weather

Mainsail and spinnaker trim in a breeze　　　　　　Steve Colgate

Heavy weather is the time when previously unimportant things become important. A helmsman who doesn't *quite* have the timing becomes a disaster in heavy weather. The mainsail you're keeping for "one more season" becomes a bag. The spinnaker guy with the little chafe marks lets go. The small leaks in the hull become big ones. And the crew member with a tendency toward seasickness — he will become seasick.

The one way to feel really at home in heavy air, and to have an edge on the competition, is to practice in it. The person who sails in San Francisco Bay is going to feel more at ease in heavy going than the sailor from Long Island Sound. He knows what he, his boat, and his crew can take.

If a lot of heavy air practice is impossible, here are a few things to remember about sailing in it when it occurs. Upwind, keep the boat upright to reduce weather helm. This is usually done by easing the traveler out, bending the mast to free the leech and tightening the cunningham on the mainsail to keep the draft from working aft in the sail. If the sea is lumpy and the wind quite strong, at some point you may want to ease the mainsheet thereby allowing the boom to lift. The top of the mainsail near the head will be luffing relative to the bottom of the sail, but the result will be less heeling.

Off the wind in heavy air, the mainsail becomes a large factor in control, particularly on small boats. A strong boom vang is a must. If the boom is allowed to lift in such conditions, the top of the leech will fall off so far that it may actually

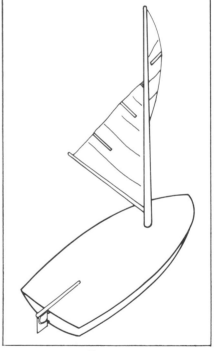

Figure 1

point forward of abeam or at least be folding over the spreader and shrouds. Figure 1 shows what happens when you have a main with inadequate boom-vang tension.

174

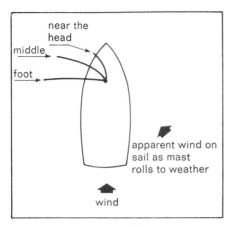

near the
head

middle

foot

apparent wind on
sail as mast
rolls to weather

wind

Figure 2

Figure 2 describes a cross-section of the sail near the foot, in the middle, and near the head. Note that while the foot of the sail is in a stalled condition, which is symptomatic of downwind sailing, the head actually is getting airflow over the lee side. This creates lift which will tend to pull the top of the mast to windward. And this, of course will start the boat rolling.

When it rolls far enough to windward, the boat's stability will start to roll the boat back again. Once this sequence starts, each subsequent roll is a little more severe. Apparent wind will move forward on the sail each time the mast rolls to weather. The faster the boat rolls, the farther forward the apparent wind will go. And the farther forward the apparent wind, the greater the portion of mainsail area that will develop airflow and lift on the lee side. The greater the lift, the faster the mast swings to windward, and so on, until the boat is rolling madly.

The solution is to vang down strongly at first and if the vang can't handle the forces, trim the mainsheet in a little so the top part of the sail also is in a stalled condition.

When a spinnaker is hoisted, a rolling situation can become greatly aggravated. The spinnaker may roll around to the weather side of the boat, again pulling the mast over to windward. The boat now develops a lee helm because the center of effort of the sails now is to windward of the hull. The helmsman will try to steer the boat up again, but this actually heels the boat even more. Try to imagine a boat that is blown almost flat to windward. The rudder really is pushing down on the water and *lifting* the stern rather than turning the boat.

The spinnaker may then roll around to the leeward side of the boat, and this will cause the boat to broach. It's almost impossible to dampen this rolling completely if the winds are strong, but it can be reduced. Probably the biggest cause for spinnaker oscillation is an eased halyard. If the halyard isn't two-blocked, or if it has stretched (which is often the case), the spinnaker is free to spin in an arc. Pulling the halyard up again very tightly will reduce the possibility of rolling.

In such heavy weather conditions you want to *reduce* the effectiveness of the spinnaker. By easing the pole ahead of a 90° angle with the apparent wind and over-trimming the sheet (Fig. 3) you can roll part of the spinnaker in behind the mainsail which will blanket it to a degree.

This will also keep the spinnaker from picking up airflow on its lee side. This flow will, just like the mainsail, pull the spinnaker over to the weather side of the boat, and roll the mast to windward.

Some say that lowering the pole also helps keep the spinnaker under control. But lowering it does make the spinnaker luff fuller and makes it more likely to collapse. In heavy winds, the jolt of a spinnaker's refilling after such a collapse easily can break something.

Finally, always make sure the spinnaker pole foreguy is tightly secured so that the spinnaker pole can't swing around if the boat does heel to windward in one of those rolling motions.

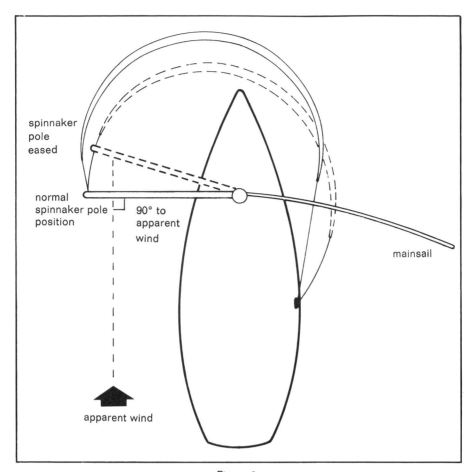

spinnaker
pole
eased

normal
spinnaker pole
position

90° to
apparent
wind

mainsail

apparent wind

Figure 3

Sail Locker

Optimize Your Sail Plan

Pointers on applying the IOR rule Bob Barton

Virtually all offshore racing involves boats of different sizes and designs; generally each has a different speed potential. In order to make legitimate competition possible, the bigger (theoretically faster) boats give time handicaps to the smaller ones. The amount of handicap depends on the amount of difference in rating and on the "length" (in the United States, distance is used to determine length) of the race.

The key to this handicapping process is the *rating* of boats according to their performance potential. The two most widely used rating rules in this country are the International Offshore Rule and Midget Ocean Racing Rule.

Because of the time handicapping process, an important tactic in ocean racing is to have your boat rate as favorably as possible. This means improving the relationship between *rating* and *speed potential*. Such improvement can come either through reducing the rating, without comparably reducing speed potential, or increasing speed potential without comparably increasing the rating. The art of achieving rating improvement through either of these techniques is called "rating optimization."

Although a rating is affected by many factors, most of the rating analysis and optimization is done using variables that are related to the sailplan. Concentrating on the sailplan to achieve an optimum rating results from a number of factors:

First, a "stock" sailplan may not be ideal for every different sailing condition around the country. Certain areas have heavier than average winds; other areas may have very light air. Sea conditions also can vary a great deal. These diverse conditions can make a great difference in how the sailplan is designed.

Second, in practically all rating rules there are certain obvious sailplan penalties that must be avoided and you are badly handicapped if you don't make sure your boat is free from these pitfalls.

Third, generally speaking, it is far less expensive to change the rating through modifying the sailplan than through modifying the hull shape (the other major determinant of a boat's rating).

Under the IOR, a boat's rating depends on seven factors: Length (L), Beam (B), Draft (D and DC), Freeboard (FC), Sail Area (S), Stability (CGF), and a factor for propeller drag (EPF). Though there are quite a number of mathematical steps required to compute a rating, the last two are:

$$\text{Measured Rating (MR)} = \frac{0.13L\sqrt{S}}{\sqrt{B \times D}}$$

$$+ \, 0.25L + .20\sqrt{S} + DC + FC$$

Final Rating (R) = MR $\times$ EPF $\times$ CGF

Don't worry too much about all the mathematics, but do notice that Sail Area (S) appears twice in the Measured Rating (MR) formula; and it has a *positive* influence on MR in both instances. This of course means that, when sail area is increased, the rating also increases.

Sail area can be increased, or decreased, in a number of ways. The IOR rule recognizes this, and in fact the *sail area* (or S in the formula) is "short hand" for the sum of:

179

1. The foretriangle sail area — measured by the height of the foretriangle (I), the rated foretriangle base length (JC) (from the forward edge of the mast to the headstay, or the spinnaker pole length — whichever is longer) and the amount of overlap of the biggest genoa (LPG) (Fig. 1).

2. The mainsail area measured by the length of the luff (P) and the length of the foot (E) of the mainsail (Fig. 2).

3. A penalty for mainsails that are undersized relative to the foretriangle sail area. This factor is called SATC.

In mathematical terms, the rated sail area (S) equals all three of these factors added together, i.e., S = Foretriangle Area + Mainsail Area + SATC.

The only time you will not use this equation to determine S is when the area of the spinnaker (SPIN) is larger than the sum of the three factors described above. In this one case, the spinnaker area will be used instead of S.

While I know these remarks are not entirely complete, they do give you a general idea of the relationship that exists between the various elements of the sail area formula. Knowing this will make it easier for you to understand and apply the following rules of thumb to your own sailplan. None are hard and fast, but chances are good that if you don't follow them, you run the risk of having a higher rating than you need to have.

1. The spinnaker pole length (SPL) should never be *less* than the measured foretriangle base (J) (Fig. 1). It can be greater, but you will carry a higher rating if it is.

2. The maximum width of the spinnaker should never be more than 1.8 times the rated foretriangle base (JC).

3. The upper limit of the spinnaker pole (track) (called SPH) should never be above deck by more than 25% of the foretriangle height (I) (Fig. 2).

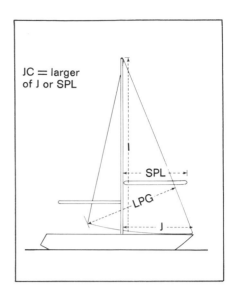

Figure 1

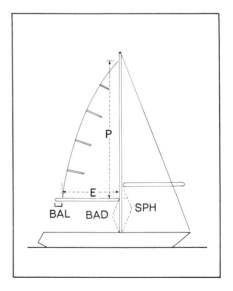

Figure 2

4. Spinnaker luff lengths (SL) should never exceed their limit (LL on the certificate).

5. The overlap of the largest genoa (LPG) should never be less than one and a half times (150%) the length of the rated foretriangle base (JC).

6. Staysail overlap (LPIS) should never exceed LPG.

7. The area of the spinnaker (SPIN) should never exceed the rated area of the working sails (called RSAT on the certificate).

Mainsail

8. A bale or padeye on the end of the boom for sheeting of headsails never should be more than 6″ outside the black band. (BAL on the certificate must always be less than .5).

9. Batten lengths must never exceed the maximum allowed. Battens #1 and 2 must be not greater than 10% of the foot length (E) plus one inch. Battens 3 and 4 must be no greater than 12% of the foot length (E) plus one inch.

10. The lower black band on the mast should never be above the deck more than 5% of the mainsail luff length (P) plus four feet. This distance is called the BAD on rating

certificates (Fig. 2).

11. A mainsail headboard (HB) never should exceed the maximum unpenalized width which is 4.5″ or .04x E, whichever is greater.

12. The top batten (BLP) never should be closer to the head of the mainsail than 20% of the mainsail luff length (P).

13. The mainsail area (RSAM) should never be less than the minimum limit (RSAMC on the certificate).

Ratings are computed to four decimal places, then rounded to the nearest tenth. For example, a boat with a rating of 24.5499 would have a rating of 24.5. But another boat with a rating of 24.4500 would also receive a rating of 24.5. If all other things are equal, the first boat should have a slight performance advantage, for it measures .0999 feet higher. But because of the rounding that takes

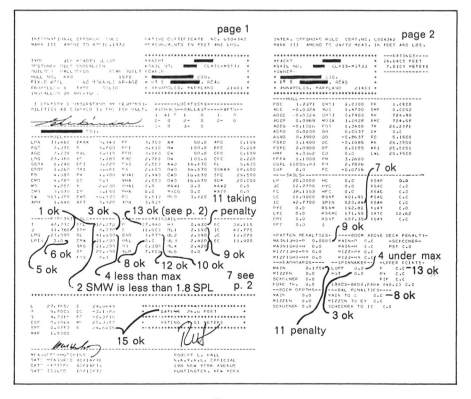

Figure 3

place, the first boat will rate just the same as the second boat even though it has more "power" (15).

This means, of course, that to optimize your rating you should take advantage of the rounding element in the certificate and have your decimal rating come out to .x499, or something slightly less; anything down to .x400 is acceptable. If you think this is pushing a point, in a sense you are right. But remember that even if you don't want to worry over such fine points, someone you are racing against will.

I have drawn up a sample certificate and each rule of thumb is keyed by number to the rating certificate. If you study your own certificate you may be surprised to discover that your boat isn't set up according to the "rules" just presented (Fig. 3).

If you find discrepancies, you can unquestionably improve the relationship between your rating and speed potential simply by having the offending variable adjusted (by your sailmaker, boat yard, or on your own). Once the adjustment is made, call your local IOR measurer and ask him first to remeasure the variables you have changed, and then to get you a new certificate (about $25).

This certainly isn't all there is to rating optimization — I purposely haven't gone into the complex subject of tuning a sailplan to local wind and sea conditions. This is a subject left to an expert sailmaker or designer. What I have tried to do here is give universal rules of thumb which anyone can apply to an IOR boat.

If you have understood this discussion, you can make an initial start at scrutinizing your own rating certificate. And you certainly will be in a better position to know if you need expert help.

Sail Plans and Performance

Aspect ratios and efficiency John R. Stanton

Every yachtsman would like to have the most effective sail plan possible, but at present there is no simple accurate technique which permits a designer to quickly design an optimum sail configuration.

During the initial phases of the design effort, the required sail area is estimated. Several methods are available, but the one most commonly used defines the anticipated sail area as a function of the hull's wetted surface.

Any preliminary estimate merely establishes a base line from which further refinements can be made as the design evolves. However, final sail area usually falls within 5% of the original estimate.

A designer should consider four factors when he defines a sail plan configuration. They are:

1. Drive required
2. Heeling moment
3. Sail distribution
4. Rating rule

The "wetted area" estimating technique shown in Figure 1 considers the first two categories. Sail distribution and rating are computed separately.

Years ago the lion's share of a boat's sail area went into the mainsail. They were huge, often gaff-rigged with or without topsails. Jibs were used primarily to balance the craft.

Only a few venturesome souls dared to suggest that jibs could develop drive in their own right, and clean up air flow over the luff of the mainsail.

Even the use of Marconi mainsails did not affect sail area distribution practices for quite some time. It wasn't until 20 years ago that a marked trend to large foretriangles began.

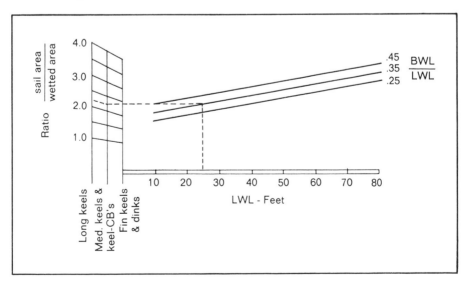

Figure 1 "WETTED AREA" METHOD OF DETERMINING SAIL AREA

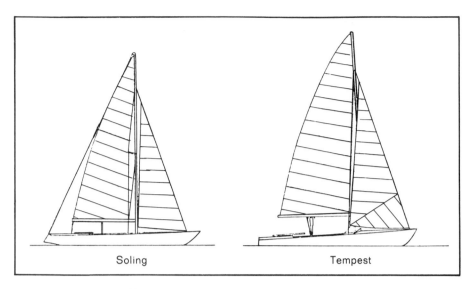

Figure 2 EXAMPLES OF MODERN
FRACTIONAL FORE-TRIANGLES

Today the foretriangle usually accounts for 40% or more of total area (excluding overlap), and it may go as high as 60% in racing/cruising boats with masthead rigs.

Smaller foretriangles are still very much with us, especially in class boats. Even relatively new one-design craft such as the Soling and Tempest have not strayed very far from the fold.

In my opinion a masthead rig with 50-60% of the design sail area in the foretriangle has many positive features, and few disadvantages.

Assuming an "inboard" rig, a 55/45 foretriangle-to-mainsail distribution will put the mast position at about 45% of the overall length. At this station the beam is sufficiently wide to provide good structural support for the shrouds, without imposing high column stresses on the mast, a condition common to narrow shroud bases.

The 55/45 configuration also places the sheet turning block of a genoa with a 150% LP at about 65% of overall length. Maximum beam on deck normally falls slightly aft of midships so one has considerable flexibility with the block's athwartship adjustment.

My design studies show that the optimum genoa sheeting angle is 8° to 12° from centerline, depending on

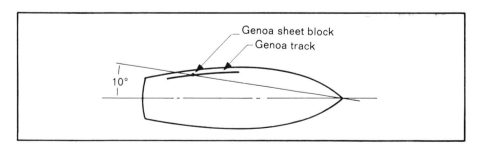

Figure 3 METHOD FOR ESTIMATING LOCATION
OF GENOA SHEET BLOCK

the boat. Analyzing a few consistently high performance boats supports this conclusion.

In my last article I discussed sail interaction and the favorable influence a masthead genoa has on the flow over the mainsail's leeward surface. Obviously, these benefits are not as great with a rig that has a ¾ or ⅞ foretriangle.

With a ¾ or ⅞ rig, the mast contour above the headstay tang is usually tapered. This is possible because stresses in the top section are lower than those in a masthead sail plan of equal height.

Although the mast wake losses are proportionately less, the shortened foretriangle configuration is less efficient in reducing separation than the masthead rig. See Figure 4.

One possible disadvantage of the 55/45 sail plan is the tremendous power inherent in large headsails. It usually requires a somewhat larger and more skilled deck crew to set, trim and douse these sails with speed and precision.

So far we have not considered the influence of aspect ratio on sail distribution although it weighs heavily in any sail plan design decisions.

The performance of any airfoil in unrestricted three dimensional flow is, in large part, a function of the aspect ratio. Test data confirms that an airfoil's effectiveness increases with an increasing aspect ratio, but at a decreasing rate.

Imagine a genoa joined with its mirror image along the foot (see Figure 5). The span of the sail is doubled as is the l/J ratio, the area and the aspect ratio.

Type	Degrees to centerline
a) Fast, narrow-beamed keel boats and planing centerboarders	∢ = 8
b) Fast, medium beam, keel boats and nonplaning centerboarders.	∢ = 10
c) Fullbodied, heavy displacement cruising craft.	∢ = 12

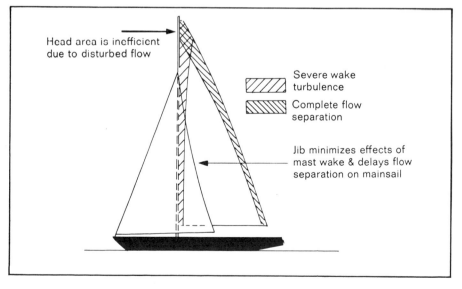

Head area is inefficient due to disturbed flow

Severe wake turbulence

Complete flow separation

Jib minimizes effects of mast wake & delays flow separation on mainsail

Figure 4   EFFECT OF SHORT FORE-TRIANGLE ON MAINSAIL FLOW

185

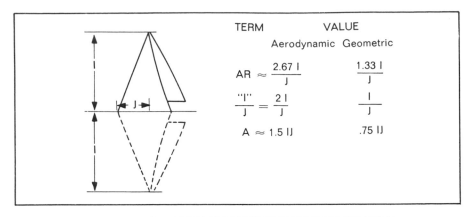

TERM	VALUE	
	Aerodynamic	Geometric
$AR \approx$	$\dfrac{2.67\ I}{J}$	$\dfrac{1.33\ I}{J}$
$\dfrac{\text{"I"}}{J} =$	$\dfrac{2\ I}{J}$	$\dfrac{I}{J}$
$A \approx$	$1.5\ IJ$	$.75\ IJ$

Figure 5 "MIRROR IMAGE" TECHNIQUE FOR DETERMINING
AERODYNAMIC VALUES OF 150% LP GENOAS

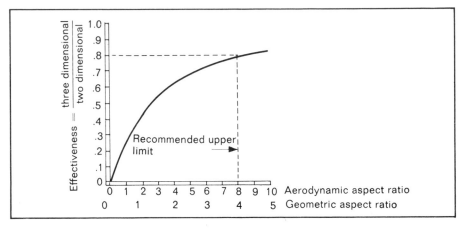

Figure 6 EFFICIENCY OF A 150% LP THEORETICAL
GENOA AS A FUNCTION OF ASPECT RATIO

Theoretically the aspect ratio of an ideal genoa with its foot adjacent to the deck is equivalent to a genoa combined with its mirror image. We should, therefore, evaluate a sail on the basis of its *aerodynamic* aspect ratio rather than its *geometric* aspect ratio.

Figure 6 displays effectiveness versus aspect ratio for a theoretical 150% genoa. The geometric aspect ratios have been adjusted to reflect their equivalent aerodynamic values.

Two significant characteristics are clearly displayed. These are:

1. Efficiency is very low at small aspect ratios.

2. Efficiency increases very slowly beyond the aspect ratio of 4.

The aspect ratio for a "deck sweeper" 150% LP genoa can be determined by the equation:

$$AR = \dfrac{I}{.75J}$$

Using this equation we can produce the following table.

I/J	AR
2 /1	2.67
2½/1	3.34
3 /1	4.00
3½/1	4.66
4 /1	5.33

186

If we consider an aspect ratio of 4 to be the practical upper limit for 150% LP genoas, we see that the I/J ratio should not exceed 3:1.

In actual practice the optimum aspect ratio is somewhat less than the theoretical value, usually falling between 3.0 and 4.0. Because of wind gradient along the luff, negative twist from foot to head, and "leakage" at the foot, the aerodynamic loading tends to be most intense in an area bounded by the chords at 10% to 60% of luff height.

With less loading at the head and foot, it is not necessary to provide as large an aspect ratio to minimize three dimensional losses at the ends.

The actual optimum I/J ratio should be computed for each boat instead of relying on a "rule of thumb". A precise value is not too important for these discussions, but I do want to make the point that extreme values of aspect ratio, whether very high or very low, should be avoided.

We can also apply the mirror image technique to the mainsail. The treatment is similar to a high aspect ratio airfoil with a gap in the center of the span. If we neglect mast turbulence, the losses at the head are largely a function of aspect ratio similar to the low cut genoa.

The apparent aerodynamic aspect of a typical mainsail and its mirror image is about 10. The equivalent corrected geometric aspect ratio is, therefore, 5.

There would appear to be a difference between this value and my earlier statement which suggested a practical AR limit of about 4.0. Actually there is no discrepancy.

Sail twist and low efficiency induced by the mast wake greatly reduce the aerodynamic load intensity near the head, making the potential for leakage considerably less than if it were a clean airfoil with no twist.

Therefore, the mainsail's usefulness closehauled is rather negligible above 80% of the luff. If we compute mainsail aspect ratio using .8P ($P =$ mainsail luff length) or even .9P the values of AR will usually be found to

be 4 or less.

No aspect ratio discussion is complete without talking about the influence of the rating rules. Most contemporary boats are designed to a formula, whether it is a class rule, such as the 12-meter, or a handicap rating system, typified by the new IOR rule.

The IOR formula de-emphasizes aspect ratio somewhat. Under the CCA rule P/B (B = mainsail boom length) ratios in excess of 2:1 were heavily taxed at 30% of the excess. The IOR reduces the penalty to 20%. In spite of these reduced AR penalties, inequities still exist.

Some designers have interpreted the new rule as encouraging very high P/B ratios and there has been an increasing number of new designs with very tall sail plans.

This characteristic is particularly noticeable on some boats with short overhangs where mainsail P/B ratios of 3:1 and more have been specified.

This is an unfortunate trend since it is not the intent of the rule to promote a specific configuration.

Actually, the lower assessment is a partial recognition of the fact that higher aspect ratios are not as beneficial as some people had thought.

At the risk of being accused of preaching, I feel the penchant for all-inboard rigs has been overdone in some cases. Short ended boats would be better off equipped with optimum lower sail plans supported by stub bowsprits and boomkins, if necessary.

The IOR assesses 150% LP genoa and mainsail areas at about 80% and 70% respectively. The foretriangle I/J and mainsail P/B ratios are taxed at 20% of the excess over 2:1 and then added to the basic sail area rating.

One of my recent studies compared the AR effectivity versus the assessed rating over a broad range of aspect ratios. A summary of the results is plotted in simplified graphic form in Figure 7.

Part 7 (a) shows that high and low aspect ratio mainsails are at a de-

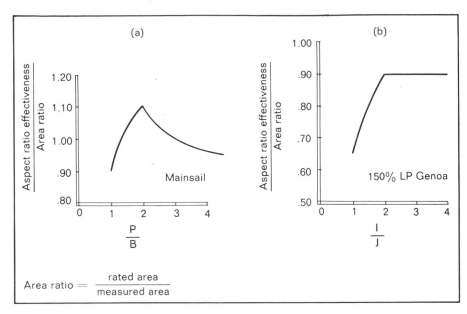

Figure 7 COMPARISON OF ASPECT RATIO EFFECTIVENESS
VERSUS IOR RATING PENALTY FOR GENOAS
AND MAINSAILS

cided disadvantage when compared to a moderate (2:1) plan form.

Any equitable rule should have a constant aspect ratio effectivity/ area ratio value. I feel the mainsail assessment under the IOR should be reduced from 20% to about 10%. Furthermore, an aspect ratio credit should be given to sail plan configurations which are less than 2.0.

In 7 (b) we see that the IOR genoa handicapping formula appears to be correctly proportioned at I/J values of 2 or more. It is quite apparent, however, that short foretriangle con-figurations should receive AR credits to account for their lower efficiencies.

There are two morals to every sail-plan story:

1. Designer and/or owner should carefully evaluate the impact of an extreme sail plan upon performance and rating before committing himself to a design which is not in harmony with the rating rule.

2. Any rating rule can and should be changed whenever and wherever it runs contrary to good design practices.

Heavy Weather Genoas

Design considerations of #2 and #3   Charles Ulmer

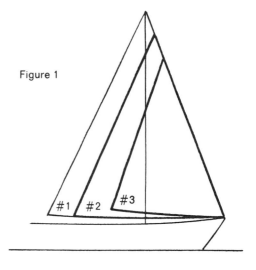

Figure 1

Probably the least understood, yet in their own right the most important, sails on an ocean racing yacht are heavy weather genoas, specifically its #2 and #3. Since these sails are not her last resort in "survival" conditions, many skippers don't realize the importance of their proper design, cut, and construction.

The common conception of a proper #2 and #3 is a sail of slightly heavier cloth than the #1, with substantial overlap and a shortened luff. (Figure 1). This, so the theory goes, lowers the center of effort to reduce heel and maintains overlap (and thus slot effect) to give the boat maximum drive.

Nothing could be farther from the truth! To understand this fully, let's consider the above paragraph item by item.

First of all today's boats, particularly those with light displacement, have high ballast-displacement ratios and, through wider beams and hull configurations, they develop a tremendous amount of stability from their hulls. Both these factors lead to greater loading on sails. Thus substantially heavier cloth weights are indicated in order to maintain proper shape.

Second, let's consider overlap. A quick glance at Figure 2 shows that overlap in a heavy air genoa restricts traveler movement unless one is willing to accept severe backwind in the mainsail and a closed up slot. A restricted traveler results in excessive heeling due to the force exerted by the mainsail. Obviously neither situation is desirable.

The really important factor comes to light when we consider the actual shape of a wide, low genoa in heavy

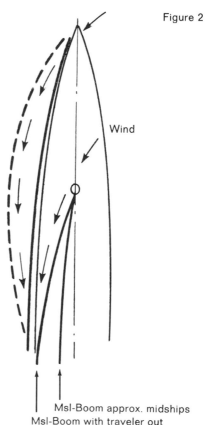

Figure 2

Wind

Msl-Boom approx. midships
Msl-Boom with traveler out

air. This is shown by the dotted line in Figure 2 and is exaggerated for clarity. As you can see, the point of maximum camber moves aft, resulting in less forward drive, more drag, increased backwind in the mainsail, and finally a far greater heeling moment. It is obvious that the wider a sail is made, the more cloth there is to stretch on the bias, and the more aggravated this condition becomes.

Finally, add to this the fact that sail interaction, or slot effect, decreases drastically in importance as a boat is overpowered.

What is the answer to all this? Simple! Figure 3 shows the effect of less overlap. By moving the clew forward there are no traveler or backwind problems. There is less stretch, because the sail is narrow,

Figure 5

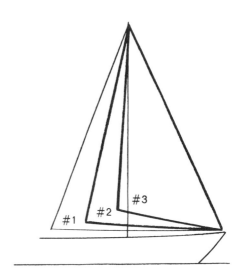

#1 #2 #3

Figure 3

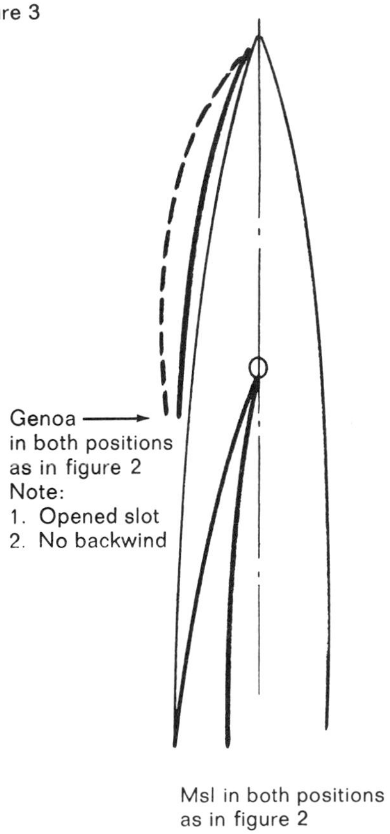

Genoa ⟶
in both positions
as in figure 2
Note:
1. Opened slot
2. No backwind

Msl in both positions
as in figure 2

Figure 4

F_T = Total Force
F_F = Forward Force
F_S = Sideways Force

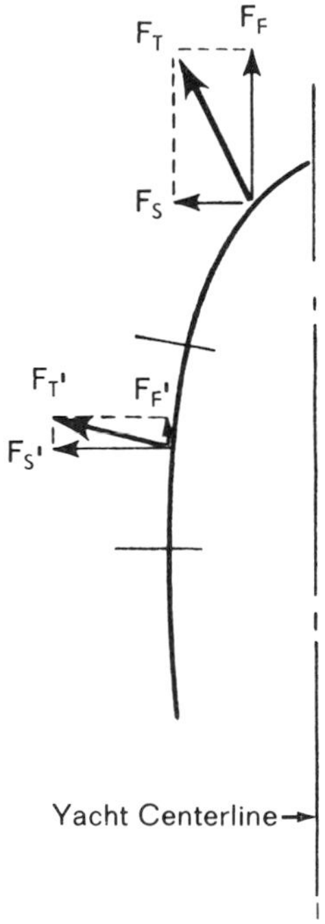

F_T F_F
F_S

$F_{T'}$ $F_{F'}$
$F_{S'}$

Yacht Centerline ⟶

and the sail has a better windward shape with less heeling moment and a desirable amount of sail interaction.

Last, we have luff length. Figure 4 shows a section of a well-shaped genoa. By vector analysis or simple eyeball, it is obvious that the forward thrust of any sail comes from the forward third, or luff area. It stands to reason, then, that by shortening the luff we reduce the amount of horsepower pushing us ahead.

Furthermore, that portion which so many people are prone to cut off is, because of its height, in the area of maximum wind velocity and probably the most effective part of the entire sail. In most cases, when these sails are used, sea conditions are proportionately bad and we need more power, not less, to maintain our speed.

In addition, the lower part of the sail is in the lee of the seas when in a trough and its effectiveness is further decreased. The old argument that a higher sail has a higher center of effort and therefore more heeling effect is somewhat true. However, the case against the lower, fatter sail is far more condemning.

What, then, should a proper #2 and #3 look like? This depends on a number of variables starting with the type of boat, ending with the area you intend to sail in, and encompassing a great deal in between. Figure 5 clearly demonstrates the principle of reducing area by reducing overlap, and this is the key to better heavy air genoas.

The Star-Cut

A spinnaker for the racing wardrobe   Hubert Dramard

Although **it has come** into widespread use on offshore racing boats only in the last year or two, the star-cut started its life ten years ago. It was the product of the combined thinking of a civil engineer and a journalist. The civil engineer was, of course, Bruce Banks who at that time was just starting his sailmaking business. The journalist was Ken Rose, a former Banks customer who then was making a study of spinnaker geometry as a hobby.

Progress was slow in the early days of spinnaker design. No matter how carefully a shape was evolved mathematically, the sail that was made rarely performed as predicted because the need to use the lightest possible cloths inevitably led to considerable distortion of the designed shape. The answer was to design an entirely new system of cutting a spinnaker, to make distortion virtually impossible.

Theoretically this should be easier for a spinnaker than for any other sail. Being supported only by its three corners, the forces on a spinnaker are easy to define, unlike other sails where the forces are sometimes partially distributed along spars or luff wires. With these point loadings at each corner it is reasonable to assume that the forces in the sail radiate like a fan from each of the corners. If, therefore, the weave of the cloth can be made to do the same thing, the result should be the ideal way of stabilizing shape and eliminating distortion.

The idea was first tried on dinghies ten years ago and the first results were encouraging. Shape was indeed well controlled — perhaps too well controlled. Little star-cuts became quite popular in the interna-

tional 505 class at the time, but the first real stimulus for development came in 1963 when the British were preparing to challenge for the America's Cup.

Before making any spinnakers for this project, Bruce Banks spent hours at the top of the mast of a 12-meter with his camera, photographing the extraordinary patterns of uncontrolled distortion taking place in the heads of all the spinnakers. An analysis of these with Ken Rose resulted in the decision to work entirely with the star-cut principle. On spinnakers of this size they worked out that an ordinary crosscut sail would stretch 6-10″, possibly even more, from the clews to the center of the sail on the diagonal of the weave.

The first 12-meter star-cut was a sensation. Made for *Flicka II* in 1962, it was still being used on the French 12-meters at Hyeres seven years later, even though the basic design had been vastly developed and improved. Seven star-cuts were made during the development program for the 1964 British challenge and the best sails were retained in England when *Sovereign* and *Kurrewa* were sold to France.

After 1964 further development of the star-cut became secondary to the improvement of shapes from simpler cuts, for the star-cut was extremely laborious to design, took a long time to cut and resulted in a lot of wasted material.

The next milestone was reached in 1968 when a genuine attempt was made to evaluate the true potential of the cut on offshore boats. Ken Rose was racing that year in David Macaulay's new *Longbow II,* and he persuaded the owner to let him use

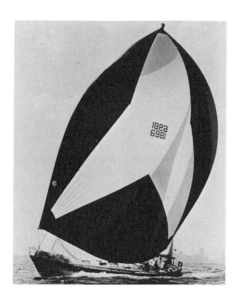

star-cuts. The results, once again, were quite shattering. *Longbow II* won the RORC Championship that year and even though she was not designed as an all-out racer, it was decided to enter her for the British Admiral's Cup team in 1969. New star-cuts were made to take advantage of all that had been learned in the previous season.

The lessons learned were, in fact, predictable. The conditions that caused the greatest distortion in conventional spinnakers were those in which the star-cut proved to have an undoubted superiority. By far the most critical was on a close reach.

As the boat's course comes closer to the wind, the apparent wind speed increases and the forces distorting the spinnaker magnify. This is aggravated by the fact that the flow of air becomes more and more transverse from luff to leech, causing the build-up of a high pressure pocket close to the luff.

The effect on the sail can most easily be seen by looking at the angle between the luff and foot at the tack when close reaching in a stiff breeze. The sail may be cut so that this angle is perhaps 100°; but on a close reach, the loading at the tack corner might well halve that angle, indicating the huge distortion that has taken place in the sail. Such distortion causes the sail to become fuller and more baggy at the very moment when you want it flatter.

It was therefore decided that the star-cut should be developed on offshore boats primarily for close reaching and *Longbow*'s new spinnakers for 1969 were developed with this in mind. Their performance was more than up to expectations. When conditions were just right, she sailed past 20 to 30 boats at a time, either because they could not carry spinnakers at all or were forced to sail a more leeward course as soon as they hoisted them.

Longbow did not make the 1969 Admiral's Cup team, but as soon as the team was selected, team captain Geoff Pattison insisted that all the British boats carry star-cuts in their wardrobe. Since then they have become accepted as a vital part of the sail wardrobe in any serious racing boat in Britain and a steady output is finding its way as far afield as Australia, South Africa and the United States.

The sail is basically a close reaching and heavy weather spinnaker. But with the experience gained in the last two seasons, there are now definite rules about how and when a star-cut should be set. The basic technique is not markedly different from that for any other spinnaker except for one major consideration. The sail is designed to work as close to the wind as possible, and the correct sheeting position needs as much thought as the location of a fairlead for a windward headsail sheet.

This location is invariably a great deal further forward than the aft sheeting position used for most running spinnakers. The easiest method of locating this is to use the spinnaker boom as a measuring stick. When the spinnaker boom is placed along the side of the boat with the front end just touching the capshrouds abreast the mast, the aft end will be located at the proper sheeting point for the star-cut. (See figure 1.) This position should always be used for close reaching unless the boat becomes over-powered. If this occurs, move it aft to raise the clew and open the upper leech.

The sail should always be hoisted with the sheet running through a snatch block at this position. To set the pole height correctly, the man on the sheet should keep the luff just on the verge of breaking while pole height is adjusted so that the outboard end of the pole is just fractionally *lower* than the clew relative to the deck. If the wind is very strong and the boat is hard to hold on a reach, the outboard end of the pole should be pulled down even further. This brings the flow of the sail further forward and causes the upper leech to open.

Only *after* this maneuver is found to be inadequate to maintain control should the sail's sheeting position be moved aft. If it is moved aft unnecessarily some of the driving power will be wasted, just as it is when sailing to windward with a genoa sheet lead too far aft.

When the sheeting position is moved aft, the clew will lift and it might be advantageous to raise the pole slightly again. This becomes a significant factor in a very strong wind on a broad reach with a headsail inside: easing helps maintain directional stability.

One general rule about headsails is that a *full size* genoa should *never* under any circumstances, be set inside a star-cut. When close reaching, the pole is so low that the gap between luff of the genoa and the luff of the star-cut is too small to allow the star-cut to work properly. If the star-cut collapses, it becomes almost impossible to fill it again.

For broader reaching in winds too strong to carry a big high-flying spinnaker, a No. 2 or No. 3 genoa inside the star-cut will greatly help in maintaining directional stability and preventing an updraft from forming in the spinnaker if the boat heels too far. But when sailing very close on

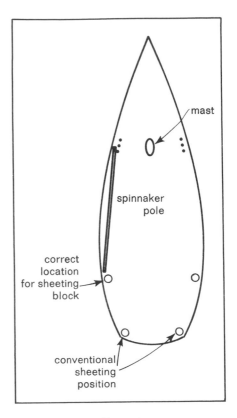

Figure 1

the wind, the only sail to set inside a starcut should be a tall staysail, tall-boy, or slotsail.

Only when the wind is far enough aft for the pole to be well away from the forestay can a #1 genoa possibly be set inside. But under these conditions the spinnaker sheet tends to foul the big sweep of the genoa, spoiling its flow.

When running in really heavy weather, the lazy spinnaker sheet should be brought into operation as a second sheet and should be led through a block on the leeward side, preferably forward of the mast. In this way the double sheet on the clew fixes the clew height rigidly so that it cannot rise and fall in such a way as to amplify the rolling of the boat.

Under such conditions a lot of downward pull should be exerted on the second sheet; the pole should also be strapped down to the same height. To further help prevent rolling, the mainsail should not be squared off but sheeted nearly half way in and strapped with a boom vang. This insures that the wind will always cross the windward side of the sail in the same direction.

Always remember the star-cut is very much a purpose sail. To fulfill its purpose properly, its designed shape is fractionally smaller than the size built into a working spinnaker. It should, therefore, only be used when the course is too close for a working spinnaker or when the wind is too strong to enable the boat to be kept under control with a working spinnaker.

The Close-Reaching Spinnaker

Construction and selection of the star-cut　　　Tony Johnson

Unlike most sails, the history of
the Starcut is easily traced. Bruce
Banks developed its design over the
past ten or eleven years, but it wasn't
until two years ago that it became
very popular. The Starcut's popularity has been helped by the fact that
a great many new IOR boats were
emerging at this time that were at
their worst when they were close
reaching.

The pinched-in after sections on
those IOR designs seemed to hinder
them on this point of sail; and the
Starcut's popularity really stemmed
from its racing success. But this success was not just a case of having
another new gimmick on the right
boat. The Starcut was successful because it *really was* a faster type of
reaching spinnaker. Curiously, it was
only after extensive research was
done that it became evident why it
was faster.

The two major differences between
the British Starcuts and their close-
reaching counterparts of conventional construction were the stretch
characteristics of the sail, and its
overall shape. This still is true today.

Generally speaking, the overall
design of the Starcut is flat and
broad shouldered. This differs greatly from the more conventional close-
reaching spinnakers which are generally flat and very narrow shouldered. Starcuts hold their girth higher
and this results in a larger, more
projected sail. They are easier to fly
because these broad shoulders allow
them to curl more on the leeches
before they collapse. Once they do
collapse, they are easier to fill again.
Figure 1 shows the basic design differences between the two types of
reaching spinnakers.

But making a Starcut is an inter-

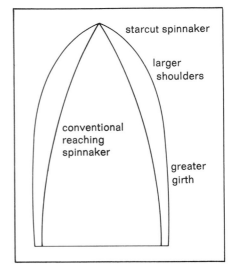

Figure 1

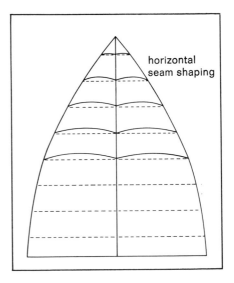

Figure 2

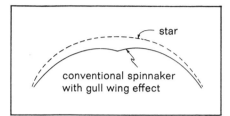

Figure 3

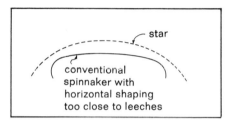

Figure 4

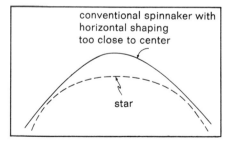

Figure 5

esting proposition for it is virtually impossible to duplicate the flat, broad-shouldered shape with a conventional mitre or crosscut construction. To support the broad shoulders, the seams must be shaped horizontally (Fig. 2).

But the more shoulder that is built in, the more shaping is required. Eventually, this can result in a gull-wing effect (Fig. 3). If too little shaping occurs, the shoulders will not stand up and large wrinkles will radiate out from the head.

If the horizontal shaping is put too close to the leeches, the sail's angle of attack is increased. Now the sail will be hard to fly because the shoulders roll in and collapse too readily (Fig. 4).

If the horizontal shaping is done too close to the center, the spinnaker will end up being pointed in the center (Fig. 5).

All these problems become more acute as the sail stretches; and stretch is going to be considerable with either the crosscut or mitre cut construction. Even if heavier materials are used, a good amount of bias stretch occurs; bias stretch, inevitably is two to three times greater than stretch along the grain line. This means that a conventionally cut reaching spinnaker must be designed with a stretch allowance. Unfortunately, this results in a sail that either has to be "stretched in" or one that eventually will stretch out.

The now famous Starcut construction eliminates virtually all of these problems. Because it contains vertical head panels, it is possible to have a *greater* number of panels each with smaller amounts of shape. This results in a much more uniform configuration at the head. Opponents of the Starcut claim that its vertical head panels and the diagonal clew panels below create a *washboard* effect. However, even if a small amount of washboarding does occur, it will be very minor compared to the stretch and design problems that are going to occur with other types of construction.

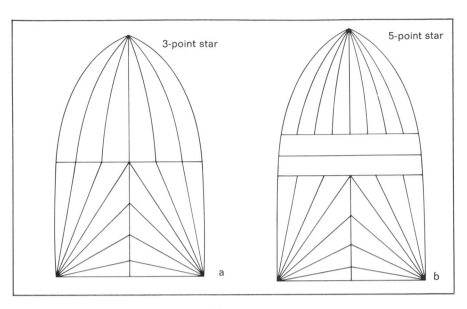

Figure 6

Perhaps the best compromise, and one that is practical for boats 40' and under, is a spinnaker with a radially-cut head and a flat, horizontally-cut bottom. In short, this is a radial-head spinnaker that is designed specifically for reaching. Its advantages are:

It has the same good overall shape as a true Starcut pattern.

It has lower panels and seams that run with the air flow across the sail. This eliminates wash-boarding and air-flow disturbance.

It has considerably fewer seams. This reduces cutting and sewing time which should reduce the cost of the sail.

It has minimum head distortion because of its strong, non-bias head panels.

The only disadvantage is that bias stretch can occur in the clew areas, but this problem can be solved in several ways. On boats in the 20' to 25' range, a heavier weight cloth (0.96 oz. Stabilkote Nylon) can be used throughout the sail, and the bias stretch held to a minimum by using large specially designed reinforcements at the clew.

With boats in the 25' to 30' range,

the head section can be cut out of 0.96 oz. Stabilkote Nylon and the lower panels constructed from something around 1.5 oz. nylon. Boats in the 30' to 40' range require 1.5 oz. nylon head sections and 2.2 oz. Dacron lower sections. Actually, the spinnaker could be constructed entirely out of 2.2 oz. Dacron, and it appears that Dacron reaching spinnakers could become a very common item.

The construction of a Starcut does alleviate bias stretch completely in all three corners, and the end result is a spinnaker with two to three times less stretch than a conventionally cut spinnaker. Heavier cloth materials can be substitutes of course but more weight aloft means more heeling, and this is seldom if ever helpful on a close reach.

There are several schools of thought on the Starcut's exact construction, and when one attempts to equate and measure different types, it becomes evident that many of them differ not only in construction but also in their overall shape. The fuller draft and broader-shouldered models, ironically, do test out the best. The flatter designs, especially those

198

Figure 7

with completely flat bottom panels, are the least efficient and the hardest to fly. It is possible to build well shaped Starcuts using both a three point and a five point method (Fig. 6A and B).

If you intend to buy a Starcut, give special attention to both the boat's sailing characteristics and the local weather conditions the boat is to experience. Tender boats usually get more overall use from a Starcut which is reduced both in its size and in its draft. Boats with shallow or small rudders, and usually centerboard boats as well, also require smaller Starcuts.

More stable boats can get a lot of use out of a full-sized Starcut because they steer well. But pay very close attention to your local weather conditions for this can be as important a factor as the boat's sailing characteristics.

Despite the progress made to date, the Starcut concept continues to look open to continued development. Very lightweight Starcuts, built with full shoulders for normal broad-reaching and running, also should prove to be a popular sail. The 0.5 oz. spinnaker in Figure 7, for example, is stronger than a 0.75 oz. Stabilkote spinnaker but is almost half its weight. While it is more expensive to build than a 0.75 oz. spinnaker, it is far less expensive than two chutes: one heavy and one light.

Initial apprehension over this sail — that the increased numbers of seams would make it unstable when flying in light air and a chop — proved to be false. Less shaping was needed in a greater number of panels, which gave it a more uniform shape and steady flying characteristics. When close reaching it seems to be better than either a conventional 0.5 oz. or 0.75 oz. because it has consistently less stretch.

There is another application for the Starcut design that also has proven very effective. It is a smaller model designed to fly outside a genoa or a double-head rig. Its primary use occurs when the wind is too great to carry a large Starcut, or when you are in close competition and cannot afford to risk a broach or having to fall below course. The sail is designed with shorter luffs and a narrower girth so that it flies farther above and away from the genoa.

This combination often is faster than a large Starcut in heavier breezes because it allows more total sail area to be carried at a lower angle of heel. In addition, this "ministar" combination eliminates a lot of time spent by the crew on the foredeck for the time required to drop the genoa and raise a staysail is eliminated. So is the time spent later on in dropping the staysail and reraising the genoa. The time saving could make a difference of several places in any close race.

It is hard to tell what the future holds in store for this unusual type of sail. But since the first Starcut arrived, sailing *and* sailmaking have become even more exciting.

Filling in the Foretriangle

The case for multiple headsails   John R. Stanton

Most boats equipped with a 150% LP genoa are underpowered in wind conditions of 7 to 10 knots. But I would suggest that you weigh the rating penalties and take a hard look at multiple headsails before committing yourself to an LP greater than 150%.

Years ago, when cutters were the rage, two, three and sometimes four jibs were carried by cruising/racing craft. With the introduction of low stretch sailcloths and camber control devices and techniques, multiple headsails fell out of favor. Huge, masthead, overlapping genoa jibs dominated the scene (see Figure 1).

There was ample logic for the development of large headsails. Theory and tests have shown them to be more efficient, area for area, than smaller multiple jibs.

The International Offshore Rule also recognizes this fact by taxing the foretriangle rather heavily in accordance with the following formula:

$$RSAF = .5I \times J \left[1 + 1.1 \frac{(LP - J)}{LP} \right] + .125J (I - 2J)$$

where:

RSAF — Foretriangle Rated Sail Area (the actual rating uses the "corrected values" IC and JC which may vary slightly from the measured terms I and J).

The individual nomenclature is defined in Figure 2.

Because of the current method of rating foretriangles, multiple headsails are enjoying renewed interest in order to circumvent high assessments made on large LP genoas.

The most common configuration is popularly known as the double head rig. It consists of a 150% jib topsail and a 150% staysail. This combination increases total headsail area by

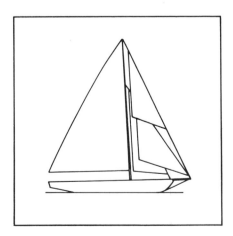

MARCONI RIGGED CUTTER

Figure 1

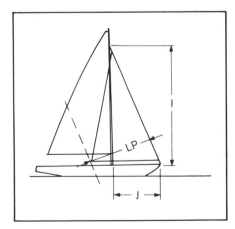

FORETRIANGLE NOMENCLATURE

Figure 2

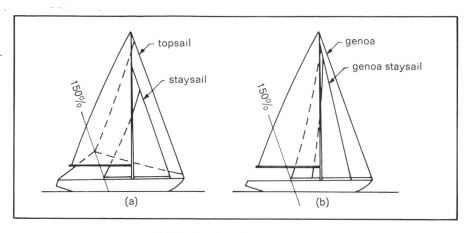

TYPICAL DOUBLE HEAD RIGS

Figure 3

about 50% without incurring any penalty (see Figure 3a).

Another effective arrangement, though less common, consists of a 150% genoa and a tall, low overlap staysail. This combination increases without penalty total headsail area by about 35% (see Figure 3b).

Potentially, this is also a very powerful combination, but its full potential is seldom achieved because the staysail is usually cut too full; and it is often improperly sheeted.

The objective of any multiple head-sail combination is to increase thrust without incurring an added penalty burden. It is interesting to look at some parametric thrust curves $C_t A$ for various headsails.

Figure 4 shows performance curves for a moderate displacement masthead sloop sailing alternately with a 150% genoa, 170% genoa and a 150% genoa and genoa staysail combination.

Note that on a heading of 45° to

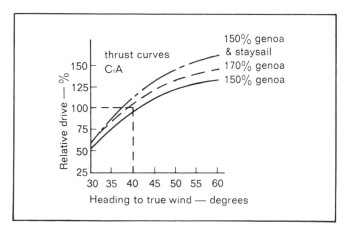

COMPARATIVE DRIVE OF THREE HEADSAIL CONFIGURATIONS

Figure 4

the true wind, the 150% genoa and staysail combination develops about 12% more drive than the 170% genoa. This is equivalent to a 2-3% increase in speed. When this is combined with the lower rating it can become a significant elapsed time or rated speed advantage.

The margin becomes even greater on a close reach. And, when one considers that 60% of most offshore racing is reaching, the potential for improving one's fleet position with this combination is obvious.

Multiplane aerodynamic theory has never been highly developed. The data that is available is of vintage reference and most applies to configurations which, unlike sails, have geometrically similar elements.

In my own studies of sail performance and sail plan optimization, I have found that the effort required to analyze a double head rig is three to four times greater than that required for just a genoa and mainsail combination.

Introducing a staysail into a sailplan greatly complicates the relatively simple interaction which does exist between a genoa and a mainsail.

The interaction between the genoa or topsail, and the staysail, limits the aerodynamic force developed by either sail. The degree of interaction is largely a function of chord lengths, angles of attack and the gap between the adjacent chords. Gap is measured as a ratio of the average length of the two adjacent sail chords. As the gap ratio increases, the sail efficiency increases and vice versa.

Theoretically, a tall staysail set inside the genoa or jib topsail and run all the way up the mast to a point just below the genoa halyard block provides the best configuration close hauled.

The optimum gap/chord ratio is established near the foot and maintained along the full height of the foretriangle. Thus, every square foot of sail in the foretriangle is functioning at the same level of efficiency.

But practical considerations often require us to deviate from the ideal situation and multiple headsail selection is no exception. The theory is predicated upon the sails being paper thin and doesn't provide for the necessity of shifting the genoa or jib topsail from one side to the other as the boat tacks.

The finite thickness of the sail, especially along the luff, does have a choking effect on air flow near the head. It also impedes the smooth transition of the head of the outer jib as the boat is brought about.

The solution is a compromise which locates the staysail halyard block at a point about 10% of I below the genoa or topsail halyard block (see Figure 6).

As noted earlier in this article, sail interaction causes sail efficiency to become progressively lower as the gap/chord ratio is reduced. This suggests that there is an optimum relationship between the total headsail area and the thrust coefficient.

The secret of optimization is to trade off area for efficiency until the drive force represented by C_tA is at its maximum for a given installation.

Starting with a genoa and mainsail, installing a ribbon staysail will provide a modest increase in area with a negligible reduction of genoa efficiency. Assuming small staysail overlap, the downwash from the leech of the staysail reduces the effect of mast turbulence, especially below the first spreader, and thereby increases mainsail effectiveness.

Staysail sail area can be increased by lengthening the foot and the amount of overlap. A point is soon reached, however, beyond which an increase in area is more than offset by the decrease in sail efficiency.

As a general rule the most favorable staysail configuration for close-hauled work places the staysail tack about 40% of J abaft the headstay with an overlap (LPIS) of 110-115%. Drive here is maximized when close-hauled or even when sheets are cracked a bit (see Figures 5, 6a).

Proper sheeting of the staysail can be a problem, especially if there is

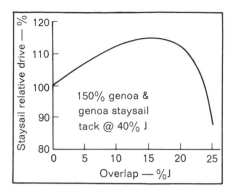

COMPARISON OF THE EFFECT
OF STAYSAIL OVERLAP ON
DRIVE — CLOSE HAULED

Figure 5

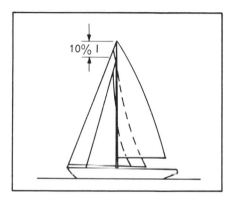

AN EXAMPLE OF A PRACTICAL
GENOA & GENOA STAYSAIL

Figure 6

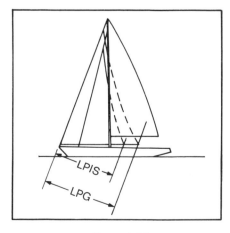

Figure 6 (a)

much overlap. The ideal athwartship location of the sheet turning block is about midway between the boat centerline and the rail; but interference with the forward lower shrouds then becomes a likely possibility.

There are at least four ways to circumvent this dilemma:

1. If it is structurally feasible, locate the lower shroud chain plates on the sides of the deck house.
2. Reduce the overlap to clear the shrouds.
3. Cut the leech very hollow to clear the shrouds.
4. Remove the forward lowers, replacing them with a single jackstay running on centerline to the foredeck.

Undoubtedly there are other ways of accomplishing the same end, but these are the exception and are peculiar to a specific boat. I leave it to you to judge which is most suitable for your installation.

As previously noted, the most popular form of double-head rig consists of a 150% jib topsail and staysail as shown in Figure 3a. There is little question about sheeting practices in this configuration. The jib topsail must be sheeted well aft and the 150% staysail sheets are usually led between the upper and lower shrouds.

It is not uncommon to see 150% staysails sheeted between upper and lower shrouds located at the rail, although this is not always good practice for all of the sails, jib topsail, staysail and main, suffer some loss in efficiency.

Figure 7 shows the relatively small gap/chord ratio that exists with the staysail sheeted to the rail. The normal low pressure area on the leeward side of the staysail is immediately adjacent to the high pressure side of the jib topsail.

The tendency for the air to flow the short distance from the high to the low pressure area in order to attain equilibrium severely limits the pressure differential over each sail which

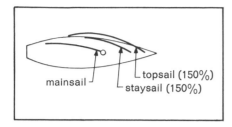

RELATIVE SAIL POSITIONS FOR A
DOUBLE HEAD RIG AS MEASURED AT
THE TOPSAIL CLEW HEIGHT. STAYSAIL
SHEETED TO THE RAIL.

Figure 7

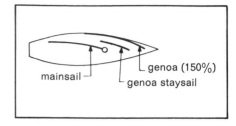

RELATIVE SAIL POSITIONS
FOR A GENOA AND STAYSAIL.
STAYSAIL SHEETED "INBOARD".

Figure 8

in turn reduces the driving force developed by the rig.

There are other aspects of this sheeting arrangement which might degrade performance. The upward and rearward shifting of the topsail clew establishes an excessive overlap which denies the mainsail of most of the benefits normally derived from the genoa downwash. Only the mainsail head can enjoy the full influence of a leading edge slat effect.

Any staysail, whether flown with a genoa or jib topsail, operates in a header. This means that the staysail should be cut with low camber and trimmed inboard.

Now, if the 150% staysail is sheeted to the rail, not only is the force developed by the headsails lessened, but the intensity of the staysail downwash onto the main is reduced also. In the latter case, the possibility of flow separation over the mainsail is increased, especially near the foot.

In short, proper staysail sheeting always requires a rather acute angle, that is, close to the centerline when sailing on the wind (Figure 8).

Although the staysail drive to heel ratio F_d/F_h is less favorable, the improved mainsail performance more than compensates for the low staysail drive so that, on balance, the overall drive force is increased. The heeling force increases also, but in light winds it is of little consequence.

As previously noted, even with proper sheeting, the 150% LP staysail may not be as effective as a genoa staysail. On the other hand, the jib topsail and its staysail is an excellent reaching combination in moderate to strong winds, surpassing the genoa and its staysail when sailing beyond a close reach.

Since the staysail does add another dimension to sail interaction, most helmsmen find that the performance of a double head rig is somewhat sensitive to changes in course and trim.

If you have any mathematical inclination you might try a series of experiments to determine best performance on various relative headings and at different wind velocities. On each heading and at a given wind velocity, vary the trim of each sail one at a time.

Record the speedometer reading for each trim setting. When you have recorded sufficient data, plot loci of maximum speed versus heading and wind velocity together with the respective sail trim settings.

In effect you will be creating a speed polar with the optimum trim angles superimposed over it. You will find that this plot is a great tactical aid and can help to sharpen your sail changing decisions.

The Double Head Rig

Jib topsail and genoa staysail   Arvel Gentry

The double head rig is experiencing a revival. One area in particular is its use on level class, or ton boats, to improve their beating and close-reaching performance in light and medium winds. To keep their rating down, these boats frequently are measured with a 150% genoa instead of a 170% to 180% headsail. The 150% is great for medium-to-strong winds but when the wind drops, many of the boats suffer from a lack of sail area. The double head rig, with a high cut jib topsail and genoa staysail, is a popular way of trying to get back some of the lost sail area.

I have applied aerodynamic analysis techniques to the double head rig, and hopefully the conclusions presented here will shed some new light. If nothing else, you will see why the staysail is such a sensitive sail to handle.

To understand the effect of adding a staysail, we must move in for a close-up and study in detail the flow streamlines *between* the genoa and the main. An accurate streamline drawing is essential to obtain a true understanding of this sail interaction problem.

Figure 1 shows an accurately calculated set of streamlines about a jib topsail and mainsail combination under beating conditions (without the staysail). This is the same basic sail combination I have used in earlier parts of this series except that the mainsail is sheeted in 2.5° closer to the centerline, and the genoa is let out 5°. I did study the flow with the genoa out only 2.5°, but the conclusions did not vary from those presented here. Other sail angles and shapes might give differing amounts of sail interaction but I rather doubt that significantly different conclusions would be reached.

If you were going to add a staysail between this jib topsail and the main-sail, just where would you put it?

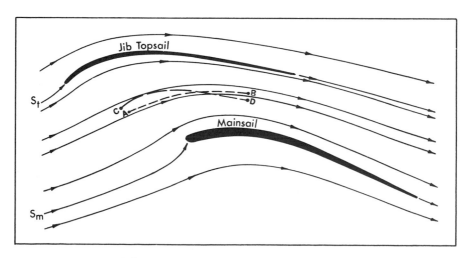

Figure 1

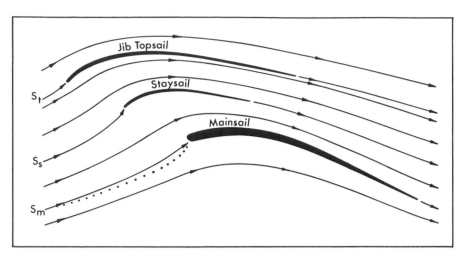

Figure 2

Let's first assume the staysail has its luff at point A in Figure 1 and that it is sheeted so that it has a shape indicated by the line A-B. You can see this shape lies exactly along an existing streamline in the flow between the topsail and the mainsail.

Therefore, even though this staysail will hold its curved shape like the other airfoils, the pressures will be the same on both sides of the airfoil and it will not contribute any lift at all to the sail combination. Similarly, it will not have any effect either on the topsail or the mainsail. You can see this situation aboard a boat when the staysail appears very "soft" in shape, and obviously does not seem to be carrying much load. In some cases the whole staysail may seem soft, but usually it is just a part of the sail that is affected.

Therefore, if the staysail is going to contribute any lift at all, it will have to be placed at an angle of attack to the local curved flow field created between the topsail and the main. In Figure 1, the line C-D fits this requirement. This sail is placed at an angle to the local curved flow and should, therefore, cause the flow field picture to change. As a result, it will have a pressure difference

between the two sides of the sail and it will hold its shape and not luff. Finally, it *may* contribute to the total driving force of the sails. Note that I have said *may*, for, as we will see, the staysail has some strong effects on both the topsail and the mainsail.

An accurate flow diagram for this three-sail combination is shown in Figure 2. If you compare Figures 1 and 2 very carefully, you will see some interesting things. First, the streamlines downstream of the leech of the topsail and the mainsail are almost exactly the same in both diagrams. Only the streamline passing right through the area of the staysail shows any change at all. Apparently, this staysail has not affected the downstream flow either of the topsail or mainsail.

Next, you will observe that the stagnation streamline for the mainsail (S_m) is a little straighter as it approaches the mainsail. In Figure 2, the dotted line is the mainsail stagnation streamline when the staysail is not present. The addition of a staysail seems to have reduced the upwash flow coming into the mainsail; however, it is important to note that the level of the mainsail stagnation streamline well out in front of the sail is about the same. In other words, the staysail apparently has not had a great effect on the total amount of air that is made to flow on the lee side of the mainsail (including the lee side of the topsail).

In other words, this means that the total lift obtained from the three airfoil combination is about the same as it is with just the topsail and mainsail! We have added sail area, but the lift does not increase.

This conclusion is also verified by a comparison of the stagnation streamline for the topsail in Figures 1 and 2. They are almost exactly the same. The staysail itself has not altered the upwash of the topsail stagnation streamline. But don't throw away your staysail quite yet.

Despite the fact that the staysail has little effect on the flow in front of, and downstream of the sails, it does have a significant influence on the streamlines *between* the sails. The general effect is that the staysail just plays with the air that is flowing between the jib tip and mainsail but does not, in general, change the actual amount of air flowing between these two sails.

The primary thing a staysail does do is to cause a slight redistribution of the slot air by taking some of the air flowing near the lee side of the mainsail and shifting its flow path so that it is closer to the windward side of the jib topsail. The streamline on the forward-lee side of the mainsail

becomes further away from the sail while the streamline on the windward side of the topsail becomes closer to the sail.

If we remember Bernoulli's principle, we realize that the forward-lee-side pressures on the mainsail will be higher and the lee-side pressures on the topsail will be lower which means that the *theoretical* lift contributed by both the topsail and mainsail will go down. This is what we mean when we talk about sail interference.

All these effects are clearly shown in the pressure distribution plots shown in Figures 3, 4, and 5. In each plot the solid line shows the pressures with the staysail set, and the dashed line shows the pressures without the staysail.

In Figure 3, note that the lee-side suction pressures (negative pressures) have not been affected by the staysail but the jib topsail windward-side pressures have been strongly affected by the staysail. The lifting force on any part of the sail is represented by the difference between the lee-side and windward-side pressures and the total lift is represented by the area between the lee and windward pressure curves. This jib topsail suffers a large loss in lift because of the presence of the staysail.

Mainsail pressures are shown in Figure 4. The staysail has caused a

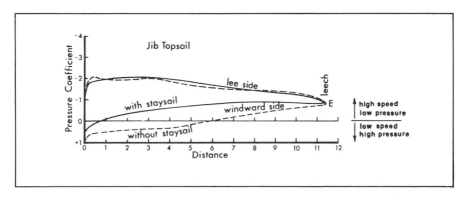

Figure 3

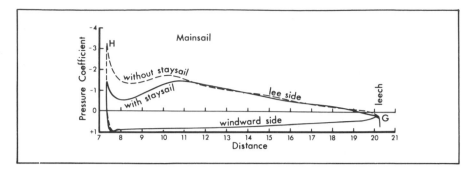

Figure 4

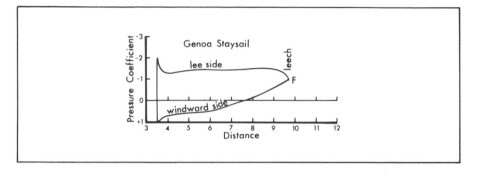

Figure 5

significant reduction in suction pressures over the forward-lee part of the sail, and has slowed down the air in this area. This produces a loss in the mainsail's theoretical lift.

Pressures for the staysail are shown in Figure 5. Again, the lift of the staysail is determined by the area inside of the lee and windward side curves. In this example, the lift of the staysail is just enough to offset the lift losses from the interference on the topsail and the main. However, there are some strong positive effects the staysail has as we will see later.

I do not mean to imply from this analysis that *no* staysail will contribute additional lift. The airfoil shapes I used for this study were rather arbitrary in shape, and were selected only to illustrate the types of effects that can occur between the three sails. Other airfoil shapes and positions would give differing

amounts of interference but the types of effects that occur would probably not change much.

You might well ask the following question at this point. If a mainsail causes an increased upwash of the flow into the jib, then why doesn't the staysail do the same thing for the jib topsail instead of actually reducing it? The answer seems to lie in the fact that the staysail leech is *ahead* of the leech of the topsail and does not significantly affect the flow conditions at the topsail leech. If the staysail were going to affect the lee-side velocities of the jib topsail, it would have to be through some change in the leech flow of the topsail. The staysail is not positioned to do this.

The leech of a jib is in a high-speed flow region created by the mainsail and this creates increased velocities, reduced pressures and more lift all along the lee side of the jib. I call this the "bootstrap" effect, and its effect is present in both a two-sail and a three-sail combination.

Look at the leech pressure in Figure 4 (point G). This pressure level (near zero pressure coefficient) represents a mainsail leech velocity that is near freestream as is required by the Kutta condition (by which air leaves the airfoil at the leech smoothly with the same speed and pressures on both sides). The leech pressure of the topsail (point E in Fig. 3) is negative, about -1, which means the velocity of air coming off the topsail leech is much higher than freestream. This is beneficial because the velocities all along the lee side of the topsail will also be higher.

Note in Figure 5 that the staysail also has a high leech velocity (point F) about the same level as for the topsail. This occurs because the leeches of both sails are in the same high speed region of flow created by the mainsail. However, if the topsail were much smaller, and positioned so that its leech was located at about the maximum camber point of the staysail, as with a cutter rig, then we would get a double bootstrap effect. The mainsail would help the staysail, and the staysail in turn would help the topsail instead of hindering it. This combination would have less sail area, but I wonder what its resulting performance would be.

Before you cut up your staysail for a duffel bag, I should tell you of some of the positive benefits of the staysail. After all, we do know the double head rig can be an effective sail combination. First, in these illustrations the mainsail was sheeted in rather tightly. In this position it gave a strong upwash flow field for the topsail and created large increases in the topsail lee-side suction pressures. But this meant the lee-side pressures at the leading edge of the mainsail had very high negative values (about -3 in Fig. 4, point H). This suction peak was followed by a rapid increase in pressure to the positive side. The boundary layer

probably would not like this rapid increase in pressure; it would separate and the mainsail would be stalled.

However, with the staysail present, the suction peak is not so high, and the pressure rise not so steep, and the boundary layer is able to withstand this change. Accordingly, it remains attached and does not stall. The staysail has suppressed the high velocities around the mast which allows the main to be trimmed tighter without stalling. The flow field created by this unstalled mainsail gives an increased upwash into the topsail and furnishes a higher velocity flow region that favorably influences the leech and lee-side velocities of the topsail. It is the staysail that permits the main to do all of this!

From practical experience we also know there are other beneficial effects that help compensate for the staysail's possible interference with the windward-side pressures of the topsail. The jib topsail is cut with a high clew which increases its overlap on the mainsail. This helps the mainsail lee-side flow in the upper part of the sail.

However, with the high clew, the foot of the topsail loses the end plate benefits earned by a low deck-sweeper genoa. This is where the genoa staysail apparently fits in again. Because it is tacked low with a low clew, it makes use of some of this air. Additionally, the foot of the staysail does not have much topsail area to interfere with, for the topsail is high cut in this area.

In this discussion I have not distinguished between the different types of staysails that could be used. It is obvious that when a short hoist genoa staysail is used, it will have its maximum interference with the topsail and its suppression of peak velocities on the mainsail will be only in the lower portion of this sail.

Up high, above the staysail, we will have to rely on the large overlap and close proximity of the topsail leech to help the mainsail lee-side flow remain attached.

When bearing off from close hauled to a reaching course, the topsail is let way out and it is no longer able to keep the tightly trimmed upper part of the main from stalling. To remedy this, you must let out the mainsail and allow the upper section to twist off more. Another approach would be to change to a tallboy type of staysail. If the tall staysail goes near the top of the main, it will help suppress the peak velocities on the mainsail and keep the upper part from separating. All these arguments, of course, assume the wind is not high enough to create either excessive heel angle or weather helm.

A close-reaching condition is where the three-sail combination really comes into its own. The staysail helps control the separation on the mast and mainsail, it also carries a high lift because of the bootstrap effect, and the topsail now is sheeted out so far that staysail interference with it is at a minimum.

This all leads me to one important conclusion. The staysail is a very tricky sail to handle. If the mainsail is not trimmed so that it can benefit from the interaction effects created by the staysail, then the staysail may not increase the total driving force of the sail combination at all, even though considerable sail area is added.

The staysail does reduce the efficiency of the topsail if they are too close together. However, the side benefits of the staysail I have already mentioned do make it a useful sail; but it must be used with great care.

Roller Furling Headsails

The answer to simplified sailing Herb Hild

Faced with the problems of vanishing crews and inflationary dollars, every skipper should grab at a good idea that makes life easier aboard ship.

Roller furling genoa gear is one solution which is enjoying an unprecedented burst of popularity. But it's no innovation. The device has been used for 30 years or more, even though the current boom only gained momentum two or three years ago.

Today, we see roller furling gennies on everything from the International Tempest two-man keelboat to 100-ton cruising ketches. And before long, it might even be fashionable as auxiliary gear on some of the current crop of out-and-out ocean racers.

If you are considering roller gear, it's first necessary to distinguish between roller furling and roller reefing. Some people don't stop to think. They hear the word roller and it all sounds the same.

Roller furling means that you furl the genoa completely to get it out of the way for ease and convenience. Roller reefing is being able to set any portion of the sail for varying wind conditions.

In other words, reducing sail area. Roller furling is wonderful, while roller reefing is great . . . if you can accomplish it successfully.

A lot of people have been misled. They think you get a sail and gear, set it up and presto — roller reefing. Certainly there are all kinds of advantages. Ease of handling, no need to be on the foredeck, no lugging of sails. You just put it up at the beginning of the year and leave it there.

But whether such a sail can be successfully roller reefed is questionable. They can be reefed, of course, but it leaves a lot to be desired.

When you build a sail, you select a piece of fabric that's suitable for the use for which the sail is intended. If you are making a spitfire jib you use the toughest cloth you can get and if you are making a 170% genoa you choose an appropriately lighter fabric.

But once you start to reef that genoa and start to sail it in 25 knots of breeze, that fabric is not designed for that type of exposure. So, even if you can successfully roller reef it down to a smaller area, you are disturbing and hurting the cloth tremendously.

Of course, you can say "let's build it out of a heavier piece of cloth." But why do you want to sail with your full jib if it is constructed out of a thick, heavy piece of dacron. You are defeating the purpose of a genoa.

It's also difficult to keep the proper shape when you roller reef. As you roll the sail, you develop extra thickness of cloth on the leech and on the foot. This builds up to cause a full shape in the sail at the very time in heavy going that you really need a very flat sail.

You end up with something that has all the billowy look of a pudding bag. When it comes on to blow, you always want to be able to handle your boat. However a misshapen sail with a lot of draft will merely knock the bow off the wind. And if the sail is really baggy, you'll be dismayed to find that you can neither point nor come about.

The current trend towards roller furling jibs is due to the use of dacron sailcloth as well as the wide

211

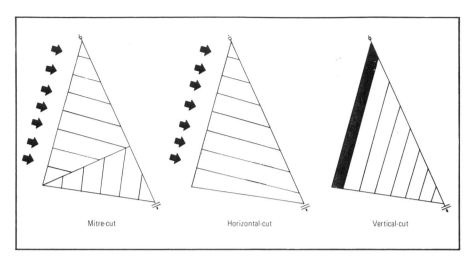

Mitre-cut   Horizontal-cut   Vertical-cut

Arrows indicate seam ends left open to ravages of sun, salt
and water on old-fashioned mitre-cut genoas and currently popular
horizontal-cut sails. Protective panel outlined in grey on
vertical-cut genoa completely covers the sail when furled,
can be easily replaced if it becomes worn or
damaged.

variety of companies now offering well designed and built roller furling gear.

Years ago, with cotton sails, roller furling played hell with the canvas. Two years use and the leeches were all shot. And when the jib was rolled up tight it would retain moisture and then begin to mildew. A little prolonged weathering and dampness and all the stitching rotted and broke. Now, with dacron sails, the material stands up extremely well.

When installing roller furling gear, the most important requirement is luff tension. Without adequate tension it will never work well.

Perhaps the reason that roller gear never really made it years ago was the rig configurations we had then. The modern day masthead rig lends itself to better luff tension because it is backed up directly with backstays that guarantee positive results.

In order to get adequate tension, you'll need a wire halyard for the roller jib and a winch on the mast. Put five or six turns of wire on the winch and then get the luff as tight as possible. If using a winch is impossible, then a two or three part tackle on the fall of the halyard is the other alternative.

The other big decision is how you'll get that new furling gennie up there. Should you use rod or wire luff? Should you eliminate the headstay or leave it standing? One thing is clear. If you want optimum performance at any price, put your genoa onto a rod and use that to replace the headstay. It is undoubtedly the most efficient way of doing it.

You get the required tension on the stay, minimize the windage and there are no winches or blocks to worry about. But, because you eliminate the headstay, you have no auxiliary stay or halyard as a backup. In the event of any failure, you could find the mast in your lap.

Rod has an advantage when it comes to twisting moment. You take a rod and twist it at the bottom and it responds identically at the top. Just what you want for roller furling.

Rod gets costly though when you add the initial expense of buying it

— about $135 for the rod alone for a 35-footer — to the cost of preparing it for a genoa.

Years ago when we started working with stainless rod and dacron, there were rusting problems with stainless. First the rod was blamed.

Then we found that any kind of stainless and dacron in contact together in a salty environment would also set up rusting in the stainless. So, we protect stainless steel by wrapping it or coating it.

First the rod is wrapped with tape, then it is hitched with light line over its whole length to prevent the sail from slipping. Finally the sail is stitched on by hand.

You can also use 1 x 19 stainless steel wire locked in with a very thick, tough vinyl covering so in a sense it is almost a rod. There is no trouble with unlaying or untwisting. It is locked in there by the vinyl.

It also eliminates the wrapping, hitching and stitching process required for rod. For any boat up to about 40′, it is only necessary to seize the sail to wire at selected intervals. The seizing grabs into the vinyl and holds the sail firmly in place.

Repair and maintenance is another point to be considered by any prospective purchaser. Should trouble arise, the best safety combination is a roller jib and a separate forestay, be it wire or rod.

The free standing headstay lets you safely lower the sail and slip it off for repairs. A wire luff roller jib can be lowered quite easily at sea or when tied up. Rod is a good bit more stiff and unyielding.

Any way you look at it, the roller furling jib has definitely come into its own as a good practical answer to simplify sailing.

Triple Roller Headsails

A cruising rig with strings attached   Charles H. Vilas

It is hard to realize that a new generation has taken up cruising knowing only the gospel of the overlapping jib, high aspect mainsail and masthead spinnaker. Racing this rig can be lively and a lot of fun, but I question whether it is any more suitable for cruising than the sandbagger rigs of the Nineties.

I even wonder if the day may not come when present fashions in sail may look just as ridiculous to the practiced eye as the excessively long bowsprit and overhanging boom of an old sandbagger.

If the double headrig is good today for the cruising man, then the triple headrig, complete with three roller furling jibs, must be better yet.

My 13½-ton Colin Archer double-ended cutter is equipped with a roller furling jib topsail, a roller furling jib, and a self-tending roller furling club-forestaysail. Combined area of all three approximate the area of my marconi mainsail. This means that I can reduce my total sail area in half merely by pulling strings from the cockpit.

The three roller furling gears have been in constant use for more than 20 years with only two minor failures. I have cruised the waters of Long Island Sound, Nova Scotia, and Newfoundland with complete confidence in the safety and reliability of the rig.

In fact, I consider the hazards of the roller furling gear, implied or real, to be far outweighed by the dangers of going forward in a seaway to furl headsails on a plunging bowsprit or pulpit. This is especially true if you cruise short-handed or single-handed as I frequently do.

The three headsails are set on Wyckham-Martin #3 roller furling gears. Twenty-five years ago when I began installing them one by one they were the only gears that were not enclosed and did not require the use of wire on the spool.

Because I was among the early ones on this side of the Atlantic to try out roller furling gears, I had no one either to lead or mislead me in their installation so I had to figure it all out myself, perhaps a lucky happenstance after seeing some present day installations.

My first consideration was the pendants holding the tack of the jibs down to the bowsprit on a cutter whose rig had been designed more than a century ago. The original pendants were manila line and hardly satisfactory for a roller furling system. Even wire rope might come unlaid when transferring the torsion of the gear to the sail.

To solve the problem, I substituted bronze rod with eyes welded to each end. The rod for the topsail was 12' long, the jib 2' and the staysail 10". I also had short pieces of rod welded to the pendant at right angles for winding up the sails by hand should the line at the furling drum break or foul (Detail Fig. 2).

The jibs were secured to the halyards and rod tack pendants with snap shackles. I also made up wires with thimbles in the ends the same length as the luff ropes in the sails, so that in case of a hurricane I could quickly unshackle the rolled-up sails and substitute the wires to reduce windage and the risk of damaging the sails.

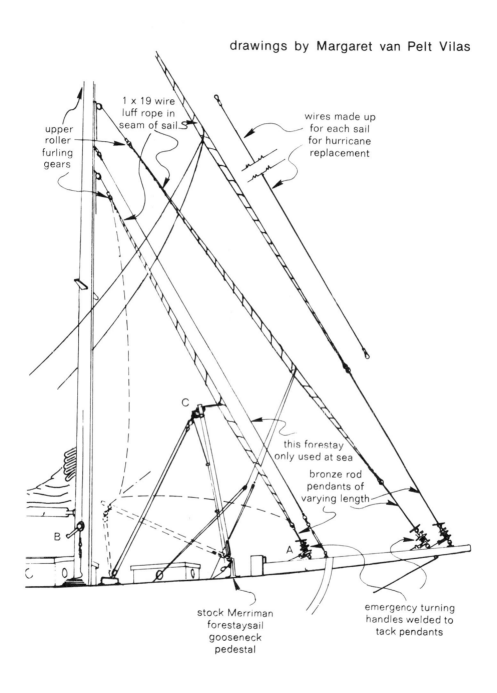

Figure 1

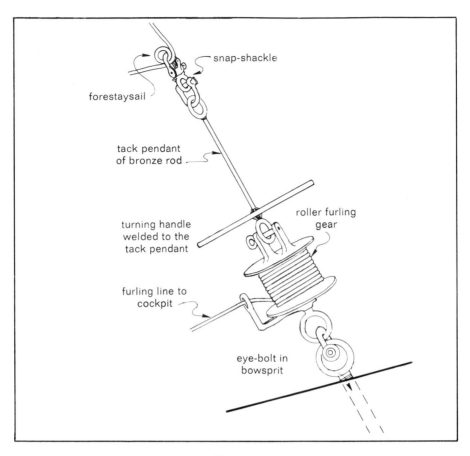

figure with labels:
snap-shackle
forestaysail
tack pendant of bronze rod
turning handle welded to the tack pendant
roller furling gear
furling line to cockpit
eye-bolt in bowsprit

Figure 2

The one-part halyards are 7x19 stainless steel wire and the thimbles on both ends are fastened with Nicopress fittings rather than splices that might fail were torsion to unlay the wire.

These halyards pass through blocks on the mast and lead down to #2 Merriman winches where seven turns are taken around the drums. Rope tails of ⅜″ nylon are tied to the lower thimbles of the halyards. With no strain because of the seven turns of wire, the light nylon is adequate for cleating to the mast and for lowering the rolled-up sails (Detail Fig. 3).

An important feature of this rig is the single-part halyard. In my opinion, the two-part halyard presents a serious hazard.

More than one skipper has had the experience of fouling the wire in an enclosed furling drum, then in a bit of panic lowering the half furled sail and having the torsion twist and jam the two-part halyard when the sail is part way down.

The wind always seems to be piping up when this happens, and the half-lowered jib unrolls and takes charge, leaving the harassed skipper in real trouble.

To eliminate this difficulty, most roller furling rigs have a fitting attached to the halyard block at the head of the jib. This fitting rides on a fixed forestay set forward of the jib and prevents the two-part halyard from twisting as it is lowered.

This helps to keep the halyard from twisting but when the sail gets

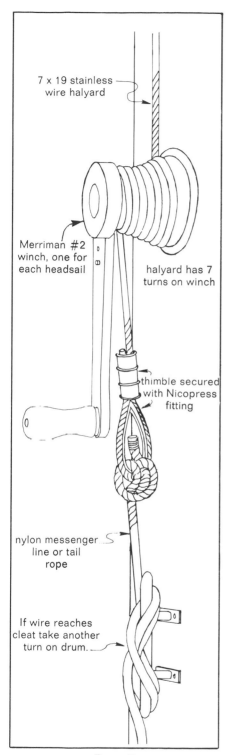

7 x 19 stainless
wire halyard

Merriman #2
winch, one for
each headsail

halyard has 7
turns on winch

thimble secured
with Nicopress
fitting

nylon messenger
line or tail
rope

If wire reaches
cleat take another
turn on drum.

Figure 3

rolled up off the wind, an inexperienced crew may roll up this stay inside the sail, especially if they are set close to each other.

I feel strongly that the only foolproof system for boats under 40' is to use a single-part halyard heavy enough to take the load and a sheave of proper diameter in the block to take the size of wire.

The line that winds up on the roller furling drum is ¼" nylon. If I cannot break the line with my hands, it is strong enough for any pull I might make in furling the sail and it is much easier on the hands than wire. Should it break, which has never happened to me, I could go forward and wind the sail up with the cross rod welded in place for just that purpose.

A wire with a rope tail tends to foul every fairlead, stanchion and deck fitting as it travels along the deck. Wire loosely wound on an enclosed drum gets hopelessly fouled where it can't be untangled. More and more I am convinced that simple nylon line wound on an open accessible drum is best.

If proper tension is not maintained on the line as the sail is unfurled, the coil gets larger on the drum until loose loops slip off and take a turn around the drum fittings. When this happens, I go forward and wind the sail up with the bronze handle until I have enough slack to clear up the tangle.

On the starboard side of the head and foot of my jibs I have sewn an eight-inch strip of the same material as the sail. It is not made an integral part of the sail but can be easily removed by snipping the threads much as a tailor does when altering a new suit.

This strip is my automatic sail cover and is the only material exposed to the weather when the sail is furled. After several seasons, my sailmaker replaces it during the winter with a new strip.

My self-tending roller furling club-forestaysail is virtually unique. Stafford Johnson once asked a well-known sailmaker if he would make him a roller furling club staysail. The sailmaker said quite firmly that it was impossible.

"Don't tell me that!" Stafford exclaimed, "I have just been cruising with one."

In certain respects, the sailmaker's reaction was justified. I confess that I could not work the device out on paper. Instead I had the roller furling forestaysail made up and installed loose footed. I then measured the vertical from the rolled-up clew to the deck. I next measured the horizontal distance from the unrolled clew to its intersection with the vertical line. This distance was to be the length of the club and was 14" less than the vertical dimension. I then ordered a 14" high Merriman pedestal gooseneck, a stock item.

The pedestal gooseneck plus the club made a perfect fit from deck to clew with sail furled. The club also just cleared the mast when the sail was unfurled. To get proper lead for the clew pendant (or staysail out-haul), the club must extend well beyond the clew.

I have spliced a short length of half-inch dacron to the clew. It leads down through the outer of two holes drilled through the end of the club, then back up through the inner hole, then around again through the loop between the two holes (Detail Fig. 4).

Like a clove hitch on a post, its own pressure holds it in place, and, like adjusting a clove hitch, I can easily alter the length of this clew line. Once it is set properly, I marl-hitch the leftover line to the club just to get it out of the way.

If the staysail is dry and the sheet is slack, it rolls up perfectly in spite of the arc described by the club in its travel from horizontal to the vertical position. If the sail is wet or is rolled up before a strong following wind, the furl may be quite messy, but nevertheless a furl.

On conventional roller furled jibs, the lead of the sheet bisects the miter of the sail and the jib rolls tightly and evenly. However, with the

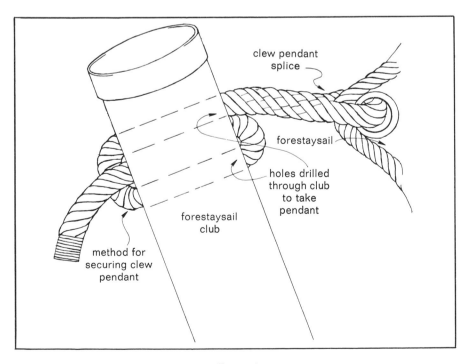

Figure 4

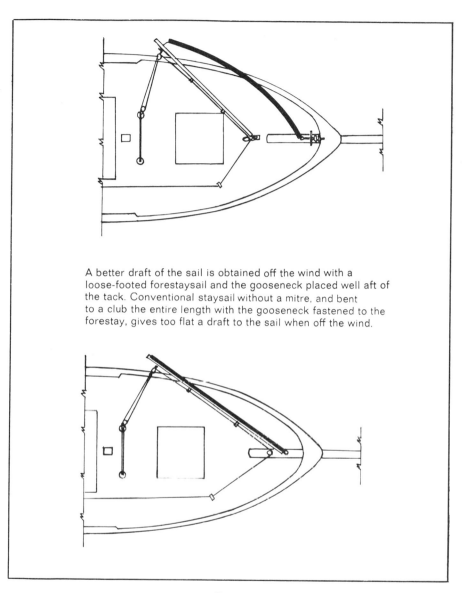

A better draft of the sail is obtained off the wind with a loose-footed forestaysail and the gooseneck placed well aft of the tack. Conventional staysail without a mitre, and bent to a club the entire length with the gooseneck fastened to the forestay, gives too flat a draft to the sail when off the wind.

Figure 5

increased tension on the foot created by the angle of the clew line when nearly furled, my staysail furl may be a bit messy with a tight foot and loose leech. If I get such a bad furl, I ignore it until I am at anchor when I can re-roll the sail into a neater harbor furl.

To control the notorious tendency of roller jibs to sag off to leeward, I can tighten up my running backstay with the help of a deck winch. Boats with tight permanent backstays don't have this problem.

When sailing off the wind, the fore-staysail behaves as if it had no club at all because of the position of the gooseneck well aft of the tack. The sail gives much better draft off the wind than a conventional staysail (Fig. 5) where the sail is bent to the club and the club secured to the forestay.

So much for the details of the rig. But how does she sail? Without an overlapping headsail, I do not get the slot effect one gets with a genoa. Performance with a number two or even a number three genoa would be much better. However, once I unfurl the jib, it is simply amazing how this heavy old boat perks up.

And when the topsail is set, wow! With all the talk about leading edges, just look at what she has.

And slots! The boat has enough to keep any aerodynamicist happy.

I have often been tempted to borrow a masthead genoa to set in place of my jib topsail just to see what would happen. Brad Ripley did this on his Rhodes double-ender *Wagtail* and promptly cleaned up in Off Soundings Club racing. But I would lose too much of my cruising advantage, so I have done no more than dream of such an idea.

You have to sail with my rig to be able to appreciate what it does for the singlehander. True, to tack I have to scramble around with jib sheets. But the staysail is on a traveler and the running backstays are both set up when close hauled and hence neither needs tending, leaving only the jib and topsail to be cast off and sheeted.

My technique is to get the jib around as the boat luffs, leaving the topsail aback until I have cleated the jib sheet. Then I release the weather topsail sheet and scurry to cleat the leeward sheet before the wind fills the sail and I have to struggle with it.

For short tacks, I roll up the two outer jibs and convert my boat into a knockabout, relaxing in the cockpit with nothing more to do but flip the tiller over. If there is promise of a longer leg, I unroll the jib or even the topsail for a while, knowing full well that as soon as I come to the next short leg it will be no effort at all to roll them up again.

For Long Island Sound sailing, I removed my original forestay as it was too close to the staysail and it was apt to roll up in the sail. That left no forward support for the mast but the three roller furling rigs. When later I took the boat to sea, I set a new forestay with about eight inch clearance and never rolled it up in the sail again.

I have standard plastic chafing tubes on this stay to save wear on the jib sheets when tacking. The topsail sheets rub against the luff of the jib which is reinforced.

There never is any need to reef a headsail. The foretriangle is already broken up into three nearly equal increments. Should it come on to blow, the first thing I do is to tie a very deep reef in the mainsail instead of rolling up any headsails. I do not have roller reefing gear on the main boom as I would have to sacrifice my gallows frame and inboard mainsheet, both of which I consider more important.

If the wind pipes up still more, I roll up the jibtopsail, next the jib. If the wind lightens, I can unroll them again with no effort and roll them up once more if it is merely a lull.

Under a deep reefed main and forestaysail, I have a well-balanced knockabout rig comfortable in winds over 30 knots and safe in blows to 40. By then, however, if there is any build-up of sea, a Colin Archer design, with her deep forefoot and full body forward, may hobby horse. If, under these conditions, I am anxious to get to weather, I turn on the engine and motorsail. In the protected waters of the Bras D'Or Lakes where most of my day sailing is now done, however, I rarely do this as the boat sails quickly and comfortably in any kind of wind.

I am currently conducting a test between canvas and terelene (dacron) to see whether water rot or sun rot gets one or the other first. The jib is made of khaki duck and the forestaysail and topsail of maroon terelene. Another few years should prove which is the more durable when left out in summer sun and rain.

Without roller furling gears, the triple headsail rig can be a handful and requires an active crew. But although it may be out of fashion, this rig is no more obsolete or outmoded for cruising than the good old-fashioned and much maligned kedge anchor.

Roller furling gears have been used in England for more than 60 years and only comparatively recently have they taken hold on this side of the Atlantic.

Just imagine yourself sitting in the cockpit and pulling strings to furl or unfurl any combination of small, easily handled headsails while your competitive friends struggle with unwieldly genoas on wet, slippery foredecks.

The gospel of the modern rig has been dictated by the competitive spirit of racing. To extend it into the field of cruising, however, is to deprive the cruising sailor of the comfort and safety he so sorely needs.

To combine the 60-year-old tested and proven jib furling gear with the centuries-old multiple headrig is merely to return to the dictates of the sea learned from generations of experience by our ancestors and only forgotten in the past 40 years.

Having lived with this rig for more than half of those 40 years, I would never consider changing.

Care and Maintenance of Synthetic Sails

A regimen for hale and hearty Dacron   Bernard A. Goldhirsh

In the U.S., we call it Dacron. In England, it's Terylene; in France, Tergal; in Japan, Tetoron; and in Russia, Lavsan. But whatever its trade name, the chemical composition is exactly the same — polyethylene terephthalate. The polymerized molecule of this petrochemical substance is strong, hard, and dimensionally stable, but for all its wonderful properties, Dacron (and other synthetics such as Nylon) is not without its share of weaknesses and needs proper handling and treatment. To appreciate this point fully, it will be helpful first to see how Dacron is made into sails.

From Polymer to Cloth

Getting from polymer to actual sailcloth is basically a four-step process involving careful judgment on the part of all concerned, especially of the sailmaker, who must specify many variables for the cloth he will eventually sew into a sail. Simply speaking, in the first step the polymer is extruded into a long filament, its properties being the inherent properties of the polymer. In the second step, these filaments are mechanically twisted together to form a Dacron thread. Its properties are now a function of the original polymer plus the number of twists per unit length of thread. The greater number of twists, the greater number of physical bindings holding the filaments together and therefore the stronger the thread. Because a twisted thread will always unwind and elongate when stressed in tension, the greater the twisting of the thread the greater its elasticity.

Elasticity, however, is a property we do *not* want if the sail is to hold its shape. Consequently, the choice in the amount of twist in the weaver's thread requires a delicate decision on the part of the sailmaker to maximize strength yet minimize stretch.

In the third step, two sets of threads are chosen, one set to be the warp, the other to be the weft. (The properties of the warp need not be identical to those of the weft.) The warp is woven under and over, and in a direction perpendicular to, the straight weft. Small squares are thus formed by the crossing threads, and the resulting weave takes on the characteristic grid observed in sailcloth. The number of threads per square inch on this grid is known as the tightness of the weave. Tightness is exceptionally important to the ultimate effectiveness of the cloth, as it determines such crucial properties as porosity, surface smoothness, and dimensional stability (see below).

In the fourth and final step of completing the sailcloth, the fabric is treated with resin fillers to take up the spaces between the threads and thus decrease the porosity of the cloth. The sailcloth is then passed between heated rollers, a process called calendering, which fuses the warp and weft together to increase the dimensional stability and impart a smooth, glazed finish. A tight weave, having more threads to the square inch, will gain more by this process than a looser weave with its fewer threads. In any event, the less filler the better, as the filler tends to be brittle and cracks slowly with age (and faster with bad treatment), impairing the smoothness and effectiveness of the sail's surface. If you examine a Dacron sail closely, you will see thousands of these cracks throughout the filler.

Though cloth may be either tightly woven or loosely woven for any given weight, the former is preferable for the following reasons:

Porosity. Porosity is the relative ability of air to pass through cloth, and is a critical factor in performance, as the driving force of a sail depends on the ability of the cloth to maintain the pressure differential that exists between the windward and leeward sides. A tightly woven sail having many thin threads per square inch presents more cross-sectional area of thread per unit than does a loosely woven sail. Therefore, there are less open spaces for the air to pass through. This tighter weave, with its lower porosity, will be able to maintain the pressure differential better and thus be a more effective sail. Furthermore, tightly woven cloth requires less filler than a loose weave to achieve the same degree of minimum porosity.

Surface smoothness. Ideally we would like our cloth to be perfectly flat and smooth, so that the airflow immediately adjacent to the sail is not disturbed. But an absolutely flat sail is an impossibility, since the warp necessarily travels up and down the straight smooth plane of the weft. However, for a given weight sail, this departure from flatness can be kept to a minimum by using thin threads in a tight weave.

Dimensional stability. The extent of pressure differential between the windward and leeward sides of a sail is determined by such factors as porosity and surface smoothness, but most importantly by the designed shape of the sail itself. The ability of a sail to hold its designed shape is a function of the dimensional stability of the sailcloth. When a sail is set, the warp and woof find themselves in a state of tension. To completely understand the different directions of potential elongation involved under this tension, we must look along the axes of the warp, the woof, and the diagonal (45° to the warp and weft). If a small, square piece of sailcloth is placed in tension applied equally along warp and weft, the warp dimension will increase more than the weft dimension. The reasons are twofold: (1) the warp, being curved, is longer than the weft, and since threads stretch so much per unit length, the longer warp stretches further; and (2) again because the warp is curved, it will tend to straighten and elongate somewhat when in tension, whereas the weft is already as straight as it is going to be.

The greatest dimensional instability, however, is along the direction of the diagonal. If tension is applied along the diagonal (or bias), the normal rectangular grid will transform into a diamond-shaped grid and the diagonal dimension will increase substantially. A simple but enlightening experiment will illustrate this phenomenon. Take a handkerchief in both hands and put it in a state of tension by pulling first along the warp and then along the weft. Now try pulling it along the diagonal. Notice the severe stretching and elongation in the diagonal direction. Also notice the folds that appear when pulled this way. This is exactly what happens to a sail stretched along the bias by improper sail handling.

To review, going from the most stable to the least stable directions, we have the weft, the warp, and the diagonal. The sailmaker, aware of these stretch directions, designs his sails for minimum elongation and maximum dimensional stability by cutting the sails in accordance with the magnitude and directions of the forces that are operative when the sail is used properly. Improper sail handling — that is, applying forces in the wrong directions — will stretch and ruin a sail in short order. On the other hand, if properly handled, a Dacron sail will maintain its designed shape and give many years of effective performance.

Sail Care

Given a basic understanding of the nature of sailcloth, we can now look at some of the dangers that synthetics are susceptible to, and which you should always be on the lookout for. These will be chafe; slatting or flapping; creases and folds; dampness, dirt, and mildew; salt; and stretch.

Chafe. Unlike cotton, Dacron is a very hard material. For this reason, the stitching of Dacron cloth, rather than being protectively sheltered within soft fibers, necessarily sits on the outside of the cloth exposed to whatever may abrade against it. Thus the stitching of a Dacron sail is especially susceptible to chafe, and should be continually inspected as a matter of normal routine by the skipper. Getting into this habit will prove invaluable, since if worn stitches are caught early enough, the area can be taped or resewn before the rapid undoing of the remainder of the thread takes place. Adhesive-backed spinnaker tape can be obtained at any sailmakers and should be kept on board at all times for such purposes. It will do an excellent job as a temporary repair on any sail under almost all conditions.

The areas of a mainsail which take the greatest beating and which therefore should be watched most frequently for chafe and stitch deterioration are:

• Where the main bears against the lee shrouds and running backstays. A boom vang will help keep the main from working against the lee shrouds. Also, if you have running backstays and will be on one tack for a long period, a running backstay which is chafing should be lashed forward out of the way of the mainsail.

• Along the leech where the sail bears against the topping lift. A shock cord rigged between the topping lift and permanent backstay will keep the topping lift out of the way of the leech.

• At batten pockets, both at the leech where the battens are forced down into the pocket, and at the forward end where the batten can chafe through the sailcloth. As a general rule, battens should fit snugly and be tapered down toward the inner end. Wooden battens should be varnished to prevent their absorbing moisture, and taped along their whole length to prevent splintering. Always remove battens before bagging or stowing a sail.

• At sail slide seizings. The waxed twine used for attaching slides should be checked regularly. Slides at the headboard are especially vulnerable to chafe and should be seized with wire rather than twine. When sail slides must be replaced, make sure they are tied on at equal distances from the luff or foot rope to insure even tension and proper sail set.

Similarly, the areas of headsails that should be watched carefully are:

• At the leech and clew, especially on overlapping sails, where each time the boat tacks punishment is meted out by spreaders, shrouds, and mast projections (cleats, winches, spinnaker fittings, etc.). An often overlooked area is along the headsail foot, which is apt to be chafed by lifelines or snagged by stanchions. Headsails should be hoisted and marked at the potential chafe points and taken to a sailmaker to have anti-chafe patches sewn on. For added measure, spreaders should be taped at their outside ends.

• At the lower jib hanks, which take a great deal of strain, particularly on larger genoas.

Nor should possible chafe to spinnakers be ignored. Places that should be kept under constant scrutiny are:

• At the foot tape and clew rings where they may abrade against the forestay.

• At the head swivel, where a shackled-on swivel inevitably will chafe the head stitching.

Slatting and Flapping. It should be noted in this context that the filling and calendering process mentioned earlier can never be repeated once a sail is sewn. Because a flapping sail will accelerate the cracking of the filler and the breakdown of the fused bonding between the warp and weft, it must be spared such treatment before it loses its designed shape and its effectiveness decays beyond saving. The forces of a flapping sail also will hasten chafe and quickly finish off the beginning of a rip or a broken stitch. Therefore, flapping should be kept down to a minimum. Never leave sails up when your boat is at a mooring or dock and a fresh breeze is blowing. The little extra effort to raise and lower sail is well worth it in terms of the life of your sails.

Creases and Folds. Creases imparted by improper folding, bagging, stowage, and storage of sails will impair the smooth finish that is so valuable to a fast, effective sail. Badly creased sails should be washed down with fresh water and hung up loosely along the luff to dry. *Never hang a sail by its leech,* as this will cause it to stretch. If the creases are stubborn and do not come out by this process, take the sail to your sailmaker for further treatment. *Do not iron a synthetic sail yourself.* This is a most delicate procedure, as Dacron is thermoplastic and will undergo deformation at temperatures over 160 degrees Farenheit (as those who have furled sails with a cigarette in hand will sadly testify).

Dampness, Dirt, and Mildew. Although finished to a seemingly smooth finish, Dacron sails still have surface irregularities which can harbor moisture, dirt, and other foreign particles. These particles act as nucleation sites for the development of the mold growth called mildew. Mildew does not grow on the Dacron itself, nor does it affect the strength of the fibers. It does, however, discolor the fabric and is hard to remove (see later). Batten pockets tend to retain moisture longer than any other parts of the sail and thus are likely places to look for the beginning of mildew formation. Likewise, and for the same reason, batten pockets are the best place to check to determine if your sails are dry enough to bag or stow. To prevent mildew, always keep sails clean and never store them until they are perfectly dry. In any event, keeping sails clean is a matter of pride. A step in this direction is to clean all surfaces the sail will contact — spars, stays, and deck in particular. Spars should be cleaned with bronze wool and warm water to remove the oil and dirt that tends to accumulate and get transferred to the sail. Stays can be cleaned by running a cloth soaked in heavy-duty detergent down their lengths. Decks should be washed down whenever possible before handling sails.

Salt. After a hard day's sailing in spray, sea water will evaporate from sails, leaving a layer of salt crystals which will tend to absorb moisture from the air and keep your sails damp. Additionally, the salt layer adds unnecessary weight aloft and makes the cloth stiffer. Both will adversely affect a sail's performance. Whenever possible, sails should be hosed down with fresh water to remove salt deposits, and then completely dried before stowing.

Bending On, Hoisting, Dowsing

Breaking in New Sails. Unlike cotton, Dacron needs no breaking in period. Bend your sails, hoist them to their marks, and you are ready to go.

Bending on the Mainsail. A properly bent-on mainsail will insure that the sail takes the shape designed by the sailmaker. The halyard should lead fair off the sheave to the headboard. If the sheave is too far forward, for example, and pulls the headboard in toward the mast, creases will appear up by the head of the sail. Unlike cotton, which would stretch and absorb these creases, Dacron is stiff and unforgiving, and will take it upon itself to faithfully reproduce (and sometimes amplify) every error introduced into the sail. As already mentioned, sail slides must be equidistant from the luff rope and, again, from the foot rope; otherwise uneven forces will be set up causing creases at the stressed slides. Also, make certain that the clew and tack are fastened so that the foot sets in a straight line.

Bending on Jibs and Genoas. Similar to the slides on the main, jib hanks should be fitted so that the luff sets equidistant from the headstay. Otherwise you will be flying an inefficient sail with creases by the hanks too far away from the luff, and areas sagging away from those too close. The jib hank pistons should be rewarded with a drop or two of oil periodically to keep them operating freely.

Hoisting Sail. While hoisting the main, never leave the boom unsupported, or you will, in effect, be asking the leech to carry the weight of the boom — a job that it will have to stretch (a long way) to accommodate. On a large boat, use the topping lift; on a smaller boat, hold up the boom by hand until the main is hoisted to its mark.

Lowering Sail. Once the halyard is set free, the sail should come down by its own weight. Never pull a sail down by its leech — it will stretch! If a sail needs help, work the halyard and luff to ease it down, and then determine the cause of the resistance. Whatever the reason — a loose slide seizing causing a jam in the track, a loose track screw, accumulation of dirt, etc. — chase it down and correct it immediately. The next time you may have to get the sail down in a hurry. Once the mainsail is down, it is good practice to loosen up on the outhaul. Since you'll be readjusting the tension the next time out according to sailing conditions, you might as well ease it immediately and preserve the spring in the foot rope.

If the main is to be left furled on the boom, it is most important that a sail cover is used to keep sunlight and dirt from damaging the exposed sail. If battens are left in (though it is better not to), they should be aligned fore and aft when the sail is set on top of the boom. If it is to be bagged, make sure that the sail is dry and the sail bag as large as feasible to minimize cramming and creasing. Likewise, there should be plenty of room in the sail locker to accommodate the bag. Also, fiberglass boats can accumulate moisture through condensation on the hull wall inside the locker and communicate this dampness to your sail bag and sails. As a mildew preventative measure, always stow sails in an area where there is good air circulation and a minimum of dampness.

Small jibs, if taken off the boat, should be hosed down, dried, and rolled along the luff from head to foot and then once again from luff to clew. Light genoas and jibs should be rolled if possible also, but if not, care must be taken in bagging and stowing as the lighter sails are more susceptible to being creased than the heavier working sails.

When sails are stored for the winter they should be washed thoroughly, dried, and rolled or folded in a clean, well ventilated, and dry area. Many sailmakers offer this service, along with performing a check-up on overall condition.

Cleaning

Small sails (under 120 square feet) can be washed in a bathtub, using soap or detergent in water no hotter than what your hand can bear. If the sail is too large to handle in a tub, it can be laid out on a clean concrete floor, washed down with a scrubbing brush, and then hosed off with **fresh** water.

Stains which will not readily **wash** off can be removed by the following methods:

Mildew Stains. As previously explained, mildew does not attack Dacron fibers directly, but grows on the moisture and dirt particles lodged in the sail, leaving an unsightly stain. Keeping sails clean and dry will discourage mildew formation. However, if through neglect mildew stains do appear, try to remove them as soon as possible. Once a nucleation site has taken hold, the mold will grow rapidly. Scrub the infected area with a stiff brush to remove as much of the mold as possible. Then place the stained portion in a 1 percent cold water solution of bleach and let it stand for about two hours. Wash thoroughly and rinse with fresh water. Repeat if necessary.

Oil and Grease. These can be removed by applying trichloroethylene to the stained area. Metallic stains that remain — generally oil and grease containing small metal particles in suspension — or rust stains, can be removed by soaking in a 2 percent warm water solution of concentrated hydrochloric acid. Wash thoroughly and rinse with fresh water.

Varnish. Varnish stains can be removed by first wiping the stained area with trichloroethylene and then with a 50 percent mixture of acetone and amyl acetate.

Theory

Is High Aspect Ratio Efficient?

A cruising man casts his doubts   Murray L. Lesser

Variations on the theme *high aspect ratio sail plan* play an increasingly prominent role in the descriptive literature concerning the newer *racer/cruiser* sailboats. One even finds the words "offering the advantages of a modern high aspect ratio sail plan" applied to boats intended solely for cruising. While nobody actually spells out what those "advantages" might be, it is generally believed (at least by most sailors) that high aspect ratio sails are "more efficient."

Having a healthy skepticism about fads in sailboat design, I decided to look into the matter. Here, then, are the answers to the questions: What is aspect ratio? What are its effects on sail efficiency? Are "high aspect ratio sail plans" good, or bad, for us cruising sailors?

The term *aspect ratio* (AR) means *length-to-width ratio*. It's a convenient concept for the aerodynamicist, because it fits neatly into his lifting-line theory for wings of finite span. He defines AR as the wing span divided by the average chord. Because he deals with wing planforms of many differing shapes, he calculates AR by squaring the span and dividing by the wing area (b^2/S).

If you want to apply the same measure to a sail, you can square the height of the sail and divide by its area. But most sailors calculate an AR simply by dividing the height by the length of the foot. The numbers in this article are based on the latter version — the "sailor's measure."

The usage does vary among authors on yacht design, and you must be very careful when you are making comparisons. For example: Marchaj, and Henry & Miller, use the aerodynamicist's version; both Kinney and Illingworth use the sailor's measure.

For a rectangular sail, both versions get you the same number for the same sail. For a triangular sail, the aerodynamicist's AR is exactly twice the sailor's AR, for the same sail. It doesn't really matter which version you use, as long as you remember how to translate between them, when necessary.

So much for how to calculate the aspect ratio. But what part, if any, does it play in the design of a sail plan? What is the effect on sail efficiency of variations in aspect ratio?

For the aircraft aerodynamicist, aspect ratio is a major (but not the only) factor in laying out a wing planform. His analytical theory, backed by experience, tells him the values of both the positive effects (less drag due to lift) and the negative effects (heavier structure and less internal space to put it in) as a function of increasing aspect ratio. Given a set of performance criteria, he has a fairly straightforward analytical approach to designing the optimum wing planform for a particular airplane.

The sailboat aerodynamicist (designer) isn't as fortunate. Sailboats are not airplanes! Operating conditions are such that theory valid for airplane design analysis is good only for predicting general trends in sailboat performance. However, by making a stab at rational analysis, by looking at data from wind-tunnel tests on sails, and by remembering what has been learned from experience, one can lean on the theory to come to a few conclusions.

First, you must stop and ask yourself what possible meaning can be attached to the words *sail efficiency*. After all, according to the engineers, "efficiency" is the percentage of the energy put into the system that comes out as useful work. In our system that which moves the boat through the water is the useful work. The energy put in comes from the wind, and it is free.

But sail area itself is a limiting factor — especially if you have to hand a sail by yourself. The bigger the sail the more energy you, personally, have to expend in keeping the boat sailing well. So the only meaningful measure of sail efficiency is the relationship between sail plan and how fast a boat will move in the direction you want to go, assuming a fixed amount of actual sailcloth area, and taking all factors into account.

As will become evident, there is much more to sail efficiency than just aspect ratio. However, all the indicators agree that high AR sails are *most efficient* only for beating to windward. Even here, increasing the AR much above 3 is not very helpful (except for very light air) since such an increase adds more heeling moment without adding much more drive.

Much lower aspect ratios, around the gaff rig's 3/4 or 1, are *best* for beam to broad reaching. In part, this is because the aerodynamic drag due to lift is now helping us, since it has a component in the "drive" direction as soon as the apparent wind is abaft the beam. This lower aspect ratio sail can develop more total aerodynamic force before stalling out, and more of it is usable when reaching since the heeling component is no longer a limiting factor.

If one wishes to compromise between performance to windward and

performance on reaches, one can't have the best of both worlds. But, for the general sailor, one *could* have second best, for both. If aspect ratio is the only design consideration, an aspect ratio of around 2 is probably about right for most cruising sailors. It's not as good as either 3, or 1, when they are at their best. But it's better than 3, or 1, when sailing on a point where the *other* would have been the best.

Thus, theory leads us to the conclusion that a high aspect ratio sail, per se, is more efficient (if not overdone) only for the 'round-the-buoys racing skipper because he's the only one for whom speed made good to weather is the most important design criterion. From an overall performance standpoint, the high aspect ratio sail is more likely to be a detriment to the rest of us.

But there's a more important aspect of high aspect ratio sail plans that we should examine. We can expand our theory by looking at some results of design techniques that have been used by serious racing sailors in their attempts to maximize their chances of winning. For example, consider the Bembridge Redwing class:

As reported by Henry & Miller (*Sailing Yacht Design*), the Bembridge Redwing class was based on one-design hulls — 27' single-masted fin-keel racing boats. All actual sail area was measured, and was limited to 200 square feet of canvas. But its distribution fore, aft, and up the mast was the skipper's choice. The choices varied wildly, each skipper trying to maximize his chances of winning according to *his* version of the conventional wisdom.

When the smoke cleared at the end of the season, it was found that the two consistent leaders had each chosen *a mainsail area twice the jib area*. The best light-air boat of the two had a mainsail AR of 3.6. But the overall fleet winner was the other, with a mainsail aspect ratio of 3.0. And the boat with the big overlapping genoa was the slowest one of all!

If you look at the sail plans of the recent clutch of *racer/cruisers,* you will find that none of them look anything like either winner of the Bembridge Redwing class. In fact, they all look like the over-all loser.

In spite of the conclusion that should be drawn from the evidence, big genoas are *not* the least efficient sail plan for ocean-racing boats. The reason is simple. There is no interest in maximizing the efficiency of the *actual* sail area; the idea is to maximize the effectiveness of the *rated* sail area. Thus, sail area that goes unmeasured, or otherwise doesn't contribute toward increasing the rating, is the most efficient kind of all — if you are ocean racing.

It is clear that the Rating Rules, not Mother Nature, have made the fore-triangle a premium area.

Each of the various Rating Rules puts a different constraint on what the designer can do to maximize the actual sail area corresponding to a given rated area. So each of the Rules produces a different characteristic sail plan. I have a great deal of difficulty in understanding the non-intelligible mathematical forms favored by Rule-framers, so I won't attempt a detailed explanation.

However, we began to hear the drums beat for high aspect ratio sail plans just about the time the IOR Rule was adopted. Mainsail aspect ratios went up from around 2¼, for stock boats built to the CCA Rule, to an average of 3; and they are still climbing. And, as anyone can see just by looking at the sail plans of the boats produced since the IOR went into effect, there must be something in the new Rule that favors even larger fore-triangles (relative to the mainsail area) than were profitable under the old Rule. The relationship between these statements is not hard to find.

If we assume that the rating "profit" under the new Rule is made merely by removing *measured* area from behind the mast and putting it into the fore-triangle, we can find the aspect-ratio catch. The Rule still requires that the measured luff of the mainsail cannot be smaller than a very large (nearly constant) percentage of the height of the fore-triangle.

For reasons that are certainly more historic than scientific, designers apparently continue to prefer drawing a fore-triangle having an aspect ratio of around 3; that average hasn't changed between "before" and "after" IOR. But the designers are now increasing the relative area of the fore-triangle. So the mast is taller (and thicker, to carry the added load). Thus, the luff of the main must be longer, while its area is smaller. The only thing that can give is the boom length. So it is shorter.

Eureka! High aspect ratio mainsails! But they're not on purpose; they are the unfortunate result of another design decision. If anything their actual efficiency, even on a beat, is lower than before due to the added blanketing effect of the thicker mast on the narrower sail.

So we can conclude that the words *high aspect ratio sail plan,* featured in the brochures, describe a sloop that carries a mizzensail-sized main — essentially a close-coupled ketch. The vestigial mainsail can barely balance the boat, while all the power is coming from the large fore-triangle full of multiple, oversize, hard-to-handle headsails. The design may insure that the new stock boats can sail *up* to their IOR ratings. But this design change is in the wrong direction if we're interested in the *cruiser* part of racer/cruiser.

If we choose one of the new ones, we have lost the lazyman's best point of sailing. Gone forever is a high speed reach under working sail in a gentle breeze — the crew resting and the big main doing all the work. In spite of its upholstered, carpeted, teak-trimmed interior, the new breed is too slow (without extra sails and a lot of hard work) to be a good cruising boat. It's good only for winning races.

Sailboat design is not a recent art.

Success is still based 98% on experience, 2% on science. Common sense ought to be enough to tell us that the *mainsail* is properly named. If it isn't the *main* sail, we don't have an efficient sailboat.

Some Basics of Sail Dynamics

Forces applied to a mainsail   John R. Stanton

General purpose sails such as mainsails and working jibs operate in two basic aerodynamic states:
(1) close hauled and close reaching and
(2) reaching and running.

In the first, the airflow closely follows sail contour, while in the second the sails are "stalled," which means that severe flow separation exists on the lee side. See Figure 1.

The mainsail, versatile as it is, cannot provide maximum efficiency on all points of sailing. Windward performance is most sensitive to sail shape and set; consequently, the mainsail is designed to maximize its close hauled characteristics.

In order to be effective on other points of sailing, sail designers and sailors resort to a variety of camber control devices and adjustment techniques. These include zippers, reefs, leech lines, downhauls, boom vangs, clew and halyard tension adjustment and mast and boom bending. With these, the sailor can adjust the amount and location of camber to suit the wind condition and broad points of sailing.

The lateral force coefficient Cl increases rapidly with increasing camber while the drag coefficient Cd increases slowly at low angles of attack. Variation of these parameters controls the amount of driving power we can extract from our sails.

When sailing to windward the thrust component is a small fraction of the total sail force. Most of the force develops heeling moment. These are the forces (thrust and heel) that are of primary interest to sailors.

In Figure 2 the lateral (Fl) and drag forces (Fd) are seen to be perpendicular and parallel, respectively, to the relative wind in accordance with accepted practice. A resultant force Fr is derived from the component forces Fl and Fd. Drop a line from the apex of Fr perpendicular to the course line. The component forces developed by this line are thrust Ft and heel Fh.

The critical factor in the illustrated parallelogram of forces is the angle between Fr and Ft. When "on the wind" the angle (call it ε) is large, typically 65 to 80 degrees. Thus, the

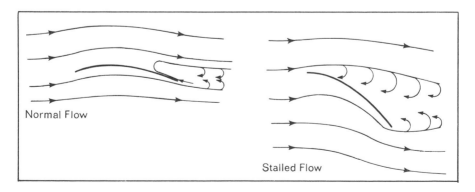

Normal Flow

Stalled Flow

Figure 1

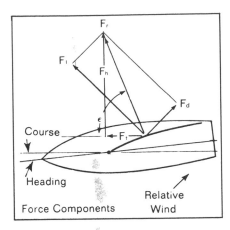

thrust component Ft is relatively small compared to Fr. Small changes to the angle ε greatly increase or decrease the thrust force Ft.

The angle ε is controlled by Fl and Fd. As you can see from Figure 2, small changes in either Fl, Fd or both can cause ε to change and ultimately make a large change to thrust Ft.

Sailors can vary the lateral force Fl over a broad range by adjusting the sail camber and trim, but control over drag is, regrettably, largely beyond his control.

The basic drag, that is the windage of the hull, spars and rigging, is established by the sailboat designer during the preliminary design. The designer is also largely responsible for the extent of the sail drag since he establishes the sail plan, the boom height and the outhaul and halyard locations, etc.

When the sailmaker appears on the scene, he usually finds that the sail plan has been largely determined by the designer without the benefit of a sailmaker's suggestion or comment. Therefore, there is little he can do but establish the basic camber by the "cut" of the sail and provide two or three camber control devices such as a zipper or foot reef and a leech line.

Let's assume your boat has a nice set of sails with a main cut to give 12 percent camber in a 10 knot breeze. In a light breeze you'll find your boat is underpowered; she isn't making much headway. You ease the clew outhaul a little; and, if you have a foot reef or a two-position zipper, you let out on the foot a bit.

This increases your maximum camber to about 15 or 16 percent. Your lateral coefficient Cl will increase from 1.6 to 1.75. A 9 percent increase may not seem much, but remember, races are won and lost by seconds and minutes and a ten (or even a two) percent difference can mean a lot in close competition. See Figure 3.

What do you do if the wind picks up, the sea gets lumpy and you heel excessively in gusts? You ease the sheets a bit to reduce the angle of attack and you tighten the clew outhaul and take in the foot until you've reduced camber to 9 or 10 percent.

Now you've reduced Cl to about 1.3. You are developing all the sail power the craft can effectively carry on this point of sailing; heel is reduced and sail drag is reduced which partially offsets the added resistance of the choppy sea.

The airflow phenomena which we have considered so far have been two dimensional only. One might

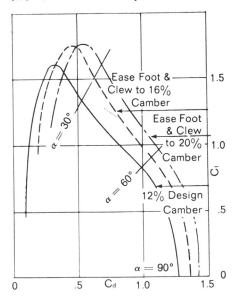

Figure 3   Effect of Camber Adjustment

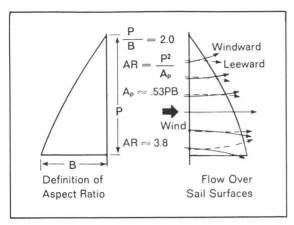

Definition of Aspect Ratio	Flow Over Sail Surfaces
Figure 4	Figure 5

draw parallels between the two dimensional state and an airfoil of infinite length; or, in more down-to-earth terms, an airfoil extending fully across the throat of a wind tunnel.

A practical airfoil quite obviously has a finite length to it which makes it three dimensional. The introduction of another dimension further complicates an already complex physical phenomenon.

Some skeptics doubt that there is a correlation between classical aerodynamics and sail aerodynamics, but there is good agreement. Three dimensional theory, when properly adjusted to account for sail assymmetry, provides an accurate analysis of sail aerodynamics.

Regettably, very little valid analytical work has been accomplished and published. It is to be found chiefly in the heads and notes of a few individuals.

In sailing circles it has been the custom to refer to the luff length to foot length ratio, P/B, as the aspect ratio. This is acceptable terminology as long as you recognize the limitations. I think it is an unfortunate definition, however, since it is at odds with the accepted aerodynamic definition which takes into account the planform of the airfoil.

Aspect ratio as applied by the aerodynamicist (Figure 4) is defined as:

$$AR = \frac{P^2}{Ap}$$

where

AR = Aspect ratio
P^2 = Luff height squared
Ap = Projected sail area

By this definition a Marconi mainsail with a luff-to-foot ratio of 2.0 has an aspect ratio of about 3.8.

Even the aerodynamicist's definition loses some of its meaning when applied to sails. Classical three dimensional flow theory has been developed for symmetrical air foils, without tip constraints, operating in uniform winds. The Marconi rig exemplifies the exception to the ideal airfoil. It is nonsymmetrical; flow at the foot is restricted; the sail twists from head to foot; and the air velocity is greater at the head than the foot.

The origin of the use of "aspect ratio" in sail aerodynamics is vague. The point to be made, however, is that too much emphasis has been placed on aspect ratio. I don't wish to belabor the point at this time. Let me just say that the optimum luff-to-foot ratios, P/B, for modern Marconi rigs lie between 2.0 and 2.5.

The air pressure on the leeward side of a sail is below atmospheric pressure whereas the pressure on the windward side is usually slightly higher than the free air. The difference in pressure $\triangle p$ measured in pounds per square foot presses against the surface of the sail and provides the aerodynamic force which drives and heels the boat.

The existence of an unconfined pressure difference is not a stable condition; therefore, the higher pressure air flows toward the low pressure area in order to achieve equilibrium.

On the windward surface the air flow develops lateral components which move toward the foot and head. On the leeward side the movement is inboard toward the aerodynamic center of the sail which is usually about 30 percent of the luff height above the boom. See Figure 5.

The tendency of the air to move in a lateral direction causes the air to "spill" over the foot and the upper leech which imparts a circulatory motion to the air. The swirling air passes downstream and becomes what is known as "trailing vortices."

The air flow around the foot is quite obvious because of the abruptness of the geometric boundary. The head is another matter, however, and requires further explanation.

Imagine, if you will, a point about two thirds the way up the sail at which the air flow begins to develop a curl as it passes off the leech. Initially, this swirling action is weak and is carried off as "added turbulence" to the basic flow.

As we approach the head, the lateral flow rapidly picks up in intensity until a pronounced vorticity is in evidence. Unlike the foot, there is no clear cut demarcation of the point at which the head vortex begins. It is somewhat arbitrarily defined, and there is no established standard to measure it against. See Figure 6.

The load distribution from foot to head is relatively complex. There is a strong similarity between the sail outline and the load profile. Nevertheless, factors such as tip effect, twist, varying camber, velocity gradi-

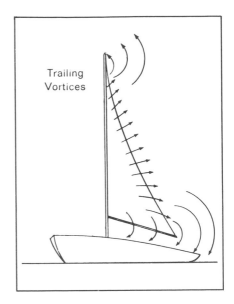

Figure 6

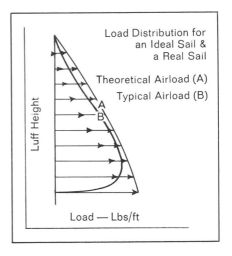

Figure 7

ent and mast interference alter the pattern, especially near the foot and the head.

Figure 7 displays the load distribution curves for an ideal and a typical Marconi mainsail. Curve A represents a theoretical sail. Curve B is typical of a real mainsail and includes the effects of changes in section, velocity gradient, end effect, twist and mast turbulence.

The disparity between Curve A

and Curve B demonstrates that sails, as we know them, are not the efficient devices we would wish them to be. It follows that our current design and fabrication techniques and materials have not developed to their full potential, or that they are inadequate to the task, or both.

In either event, it is quite apparent that more scholarly solutions to these problems are required if we are to achieve a higher level of sail performance.

Interaction of Sails on the Wind

Extreme sail plans and their performance   John R. Stanton

Sails usually attain maximum lateral force values at angles of attack which lie between 15° and 20°. Beyond this point the lateral coefficient C_l diminishes rapidly while the drag coefficient C_d increases significantly (Figure 1).

The foot of the average mainsail is trimmed at angles of attack of 20° or more. Thus, the flow over the lower chords is potentially separated. In the case of cat-rigged boats this is precisely what happens.

Let's turn our attention to Figure 2. In part (a) we show a modern sloop sailing close to the wind with only her mainsail set. Part (b) displays the relative wind and the mainsail angle of attack at various positions along the luff. Note that the lower 20% is at or slightly beyond the stall point. This means we have high lateral and drag forces in the foot area. The resultant drive force is low and, conversely, the heeling force is high.

As we move up the mast we see that the chord angles of attack gradually decrease to values which are below the stall point. Concomitantly,

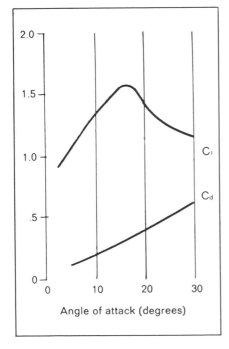

Figure 1

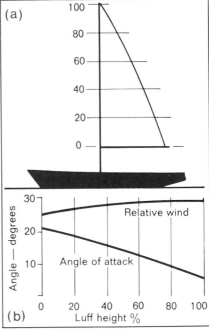

Figure 2

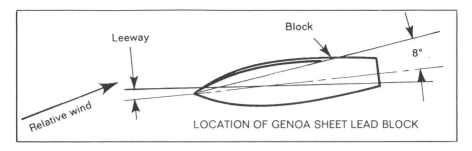

LOCATION OF GENOA SHEET LEAD BLOCK

Figure 3

the thrust-to-heel ratio becomes more favorable.

When we sum up all the factors involved: the angle of attack, the thrust ratio, mast disturbance, twist and end effect; we find that the mid-luff area provides the greatest drive force, which is about what you might expect.

The genoa is a powerful sail in its own right. As a rule of thumb, the yachtsman can expect his "jenny" to develop about twice as much driving power per square foot of sail area as the mainsail.

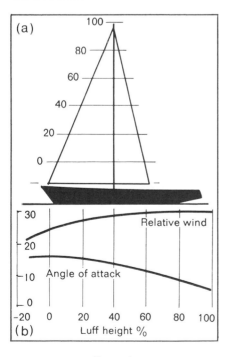

Figure 4

Genoas are usually flatter than mainsails. As a consequence, genoas will develop flow separation at angles of attack beyond about 15°.

A well set genoa has its sheeting blocks set 8° to 10° off of the boat's center line (Figure 3). This means that the angle of attack at the foot is about 15°, which corresponds to the angle at which the maximum lateral force is developed.

Note in Figure 4 (b) that the angle of attack varies from a high of 16° at the foot to $7\frac{1}{2}°$ at the head. Thus, we see that the genoa is capable of developing a very high lateral force at a favorable drive-to-heel ratio.

As the relative wind approaches the luff of a single sail, the pressure differential induces the flow to follow an arc-shaped path similar to the contour of the sail. The wind's reluctance to change direction is precisely the reaction which develops the lateral force on the sail. This characteristic is accounted for in the section lateral force coefficient C_l.

The relative wind passes on either side of the luff of the sail at the same speed. Immediately thereafter, the velocity and pressure on both sides of the sail begin to change essentially in accordance with Bernoulli's law. This is one of the basic laws of fluid mechanics. It states that pressure is a function of velocity squared. In other words, the local pressure is equal to that atmospheric pressure plus or minus the dynamic pressure according to whether the velocity is decreasing or increasing, respectively.

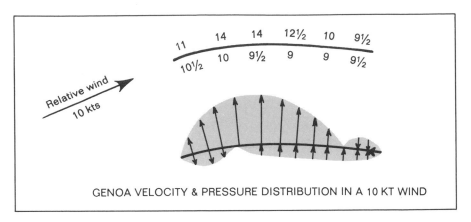

GENOA VELOCITY & PRESSURE DISTRIBUTION IN A 10 KT WIND

Figure 5

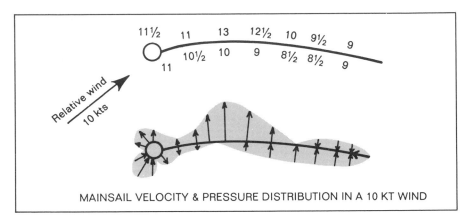

MAINSAIL VELOCITY & PRESSURE DISTRIBUTION IN A 10 KT WIND

Figure 6

Figures 5 and 6 display the velocity and pressure profiles for an isolated genoa and mainsail. They should be studied as a basis for comparison with the values obtained when interaction is considered.

The sharp dip in the profile immediately aft of the mast is due to local flow separation which occurs along the aft section of the mast. The maximum intensity of this disturbance is felt about one mast diameter downstream from the luff.

Sail interaction exists whenever two or more sails are set in close proximity to one another. This rule applies without exception.

The classic, and perhaps the most illustrative, example of sail interaction in modern boating is the combination of genoa jib and mainsail.

Figure 7 shows the potential circulation around a genoa and mainsail. The most striking feature is the counter circulation which exists in the slot between the sails. This seems to be contrary to the popular notion that the genoa and mainsail form a giant nozzle which greatly accelerates the air flowing through the slot.

Sail interaction modifies a number of aerodynamic characteristics of the genoa and mainsail. When listed according to their primary influences, these parameters are reduced to only five in number:

1. Effective wind velocity over the genoa is increased up to 10%.

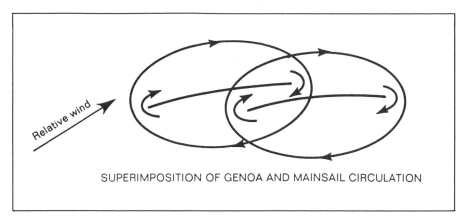

SUPERIMPOSITION OF GENOA AND MAINSAIL CIRCULATION

Figure 7

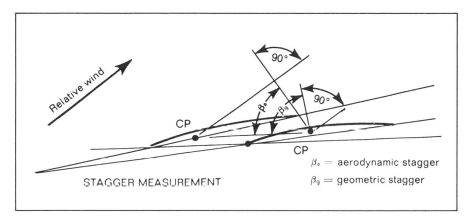

STAGGER MEASUREMENT

90°

90°

β_a

β_g

CP

CP

β_a = aerodynamic stagger

β_g = geometric stagger

Figure 8

2. A genoa's effective aerodynamic angle of attack is increased by as much as 5°.
3. Effective wind velocity over the mainsail is reduced by as much as 5%.
4. A mainsail's effective aerodynamic angle of attack is decreased by as much as 5°.
5. The angle of attack at which a mainsail stalls (severe flow separation occurs) is increased substantially.

In aerodynamics, the extent to which one airfoil leads another is referred to as "stagger". The amount of lead is measured in degrees as either aerodynamic or geometric stagger (Figure 8).

As the stagger angle β increases and the slot width decreases, the genoa and main behave increasingly as a single highly cambered airfoil. Concomitantly, the divergent angle, or decalage as it is known in aerodynamics, between the genoa and mainsail chords must increase to allow a smooth flow transition from the leech of the genoa to the lee of the mainsail.

Air passing off the genoa leech should approach the lee of the mainsail at an angle which is tangent or *slightly* convergent with the surface of the mainsail. If the genoa is strapped down too hard the mainsail will be backwinded, a situation which distorts the contour of the sail. On the other hand, if the genoa is eased too much, it loses power and the main may encounter increased separation at normal operating angles of attack.

An overlapping jib, whether a Yankee jib or a genoa, experiences an increased flow velocity which is induced by the mainsail. The close proximity of the mainsail to the jib lengthens the apparent sail chord so that the actual chord lies within the higher velocity flow region present over the forward section of any typical fore and aft sail.

The opposite situation exists for the mainsail. The mainsail chord lies in a region which has reduced flow velocity. Thus, we can credit the jib with inducing lower wind velocity over the mainsail.

The leech of the genoa and the luff of the mainsail tend to converge and thus form a huge nozzle. In order to accelerate the air through the slot, a pressure gradient must exist between the entrance to the slot and the pressure which surrounds the exit. There is only one source of pressure buildup, and that is the dynamic pressure of the relative wind.

At 15 knots, dynamic pressure is only .75 lb. square foot. The pressure immediately beyond the slot exit is slightly less than atmospheric pressure, typical of the lee side of any sail. The total potential pressure gradient along the slot will be less than 1 lb. square foot at 15 knots.

Air passing through the slot is retarded by friction with the surfaces of the sails and, most importantly, by the sperated flow which streams from the mast. As a result, the acceleration of the air through the slot is slight, and the exit velocity is only about 1 knot higher than the local velocity would be for an isolated sail (Figure 9).

As we've just seen, the increase in velocity over the lee of the mainsail is of minor consequence. This is as it should be, since increased velocity reduces the pressure on the windward surface of the genoa, thereby reducing genoa performance. The end result is what counts here. Although there is a local increase in velocity, the total effect is a small decrease in the effective wind velocity over the mainsail.

When the jib and mainsail are set in the normal manner, the flow over each sail is induced into an arc by

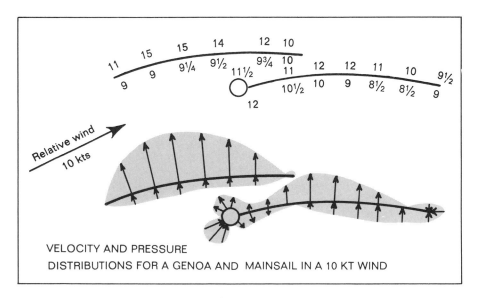

VELOCITY AND PRESSURE
DISTRIBUTIONS FOR A GENOA AND MAINSAIL IN A 10 KT WIND

Figure 9

the pressure pattern which envelops the adjacent sail. This effect is not accounted for by the section coefficient C_l.

The induced flow over the jib is due, in part, to the mainsail. The reaction on the jib is increased by an equivalent amount. The section lateral force coefficient C_l and, consequently, the aerodynamic loading, is increased proportionately.

The situation is somewhat different for the mainsail. The presence of the jib tends to resist the normal induction near the luff of the mainsail. As a consequence, the section lateral force coefficient C_l and the effective velocity are reduced. Equally important is the downwash streaming from the jib. This lateral component of flow, acting in concert with the slightly accelerated flow through the slot, forces the mainsail boundary layer to remain attached to the leeward surface well aft to the leech. The drag coefficient C_d is decreased proportionately.

An aerodynamicist uses "influence coefficients" to adjust the section coefficients for mutual induction. These factors are principally functions of the stagger, gap, and individual sail power. The analysis is a repetitive one and is best solved by digital computer.

The influence coefficients can be presented in several formats. Probably the most useful ones are the "angle of attack" ratio and the "velocity" ratio. In this way the effective angles of attack and wind velocities can be readily computed for each, configuration over wide ranges of sizes and wind velocities.

Figure 10 displays the calculated angle of attack and velocity ratios for the sloop configuration used in our example. Note that the relative effects of sail interaction are greatest at about 40% of mainsail luff height.

Figure 11 is a plot of the products of the sail interaction effects for each of the sails and the mean value for the combined sails.

Figures 10 and 11 lead us to several observations about the effects of sail interaction:
1. Overall performance and efficiency of the genoa are improved.
2. Mainsail performance and efficiency are degraded.
3. Total value of performance for the combined genoa and mainsail is

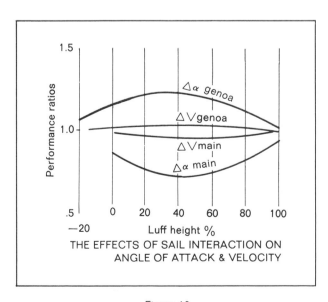

Figure 10

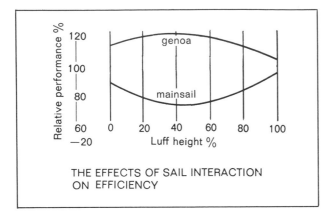

THE EFFECTS OF SAIL INTERACTION
ON EFFICIENCY

Figure 11

greater than either sail alone, but it is less than the sum of both sails.

You may find it difficult to accept the third conclusion. Let me assure you this is not contrary to the laws of physics. In nearly every technology it is accepted practice to combine elements to increase the absolute level of performance even though the efficiency of the individual elements may be compromised. This procedure is commonly referred to as "optimization" and is, perhaps, the most crucial factor in the design of a complex system.

The IOR MK III assesses 150% LP genoa and mainsail areas at about 80% and 70% respectively. The foretriangle I/J and mainsail P/B ratios are taxed at 12.5% and 20% respectively of the excess over 2:1 and then added to the basic sail area rating.

One of my studies compared the AR effectivity versus the assessed rating over a broad range of aspect ratios. A summary of the results is plotted in simplified graphic form in Figure 7.

Part 7 (a) shows that high and low aspect ratio mainsails are at a de-cided disadvantage when compared to a moderate (2:1) plan form.

Any equitable rule should have a constant aspect ratio effectivity/area ratio value. I feel the mainsail assessment under the IOR MK III should be reduced from 20% to about 12%. Furthermore, an aspect ratio credit should be given to sail plan configurations which are less than 2.0.

In 7 (b) we see that the IOR MK III genoa handicapping formula appears to be incorrectly proportioned at all I/J values also. It is quite apparent that short foretriangle configurations should receive AR credits to account for their lower efficiencies and the AR tax be raised to 20%.

There are two morals to every sail-plan story:

1. Designer and/or owner should carefully evaluate the impact of an extreme sail plan upon performance and rating before committing himself to a design which is not in harmony with the rating rule.

2. Any rating rule can and should be changed whenever and wherever it runs contrary to good design practices.

How Sails Really Work

Beginning to question old principles   Arvel Gentry

So **you think** that you know how sails work — about the slot effect, backwinding, stalling, and all that stuff. You've learned these "facts" of sailing from books and from magazine articles by the experts. Well, read on. You are in for a few surprises.

All the books give about the same explanation for how the main and jib work, and about *slot effect*. However, Marchaj in *Sailing Theory and Practice* states that "the interaction between sails is still a controversial subject and not fully understood." As a research aerodynamicist, I became very interested in this subject and set about conducting a study to, at last, resolve this problem.

In my research I made use of three important tools. First, the Analog Field Plotter, a device for accurately determining the streamlines about any airfoil shape. Second, a new sophisticated computer program that is capable of calculating the pressures and air speeds on and about any airfoil combination. And third, a water channel where the flow patterns about airfoil shapes, including separation effects, can be observed under controlled conditions and photographed. The results shown in this and the articles that follow are, therefore, based on well-proven aerodynamic analysis methods.

My research has revealed the astounding fact that all the explanations in the sailing books on the interaction between the jib and main are wrong. In fact, if the air really went like many of these explanations say, then the resulting effects on the sails would be exactly the opposite of what is claimed!

It will take a number of articles to present the complete results of the research that has led to these conclusions. However, I like to think that each one of you will share with me a little of the excitement that I experienced when all the pieces of this puzzle started to fit together for the first time: the puzzle of how sails really work, how they influence each other, and most important, how to demonstrate clearly these effects. In this series, I will try to avoid unnecessary mathematics and technical terms. And though each article will deal with a particular aspect of the problem, a thorough understanding of it will depend upon the information contained in previous articles.

To understand fully the interaction of a jib and a mainsail we must have correct information in a number of areas: (1) we must know how the air flows about the jib and mainsail when they are used separately, (2) we must know where the air flows when the two sails are used together, (3) we must know how the resulting changes in airflow affect the pressures on both sides of the sails, and finally (4) we must know how the air very close to the surfaces of the sails (the boundary layer) is affected by the changes in airflow and the changes in surface pressures.

Until recently there has been no accurate way of obtaining all of this information. Actual test measurements are difficult to make, and when they are made it is difficult to separate the effects of what happens in the airflow away from the sail surfaces from what happens in the boundary-layer air very close to the surface. The only approach in the

247

past was to use "logical thinking" and "educated guesswork." However, the proper tools are now available to solve this problem and to provide a clear demonstration of the interaction effects.

As the first step in understanding how the air flows around sails, one must be able to draw streamlines that show the paths that the air takes. The concept of a streamline is very simple and we need only to look briefly at the accurately drawn flow about a single sail (Fig. 1) to get the basic idea. The streamlines tell the direction of the airflow at different points in the flow field about an airfoil.

The airflow between two particular streamlines will always stay *between* the two streamlines. The stagnation streamline, marked (S) in Figure 1, is the streamline that separates the airflow that goes on one side of the airfoil (the lee or top side) from the airflow that goes on the other side (the windward or bottom side). The stagnation streamline leaving the trailing edge or leech of the airfoil divides the airflow coming off the top of the airfoil from the air coming off the bottom. The stagnation streamline is very important in understanding the flow about sails.

Once a complete set of streamlines is determined we can make some very useful judgments as to how wind speed and pressure vary in the flow field about the airfoil. The relationship between speed and pressure is given by an equation called Bernoulli's equation. The Bernoulli equation shows how the pressure of the air and the speed of the air are directly tied together.

Wherever air speed increases in flowing around the sails the pressure goes down. Where the air speed slows down, the pressure will be found to increase. Wind, well out in front of the boat, may be blowing at a certain constant speed (relative to the boat). However, when the air gets closer to the boat, its speed and direction begin to change.

If we look at the streamlines in Figure 1 we see that sometimes they get closer together, and at other times they spread further apart. It is quite obvious that when two streamlines get close together or close to the airfoil surface the air will have to speed up to get through the smaller area; and the air pressure will be lower. Where the streamlines get further apart the air slows down and the air pressure becomes greater.

Now this is all quite simple. but it is important to note that, before we can apply Bernoulli's equation, we must first know how the air flows about the airfoil. We must know where the streamlines go. The sailing literature is full of these types of drawings. Unfortunately, they are just that — drawings of where the particular author *thinks* the air goes.

Figure 2 is typical of the airflow diagrams used in the books to ex-

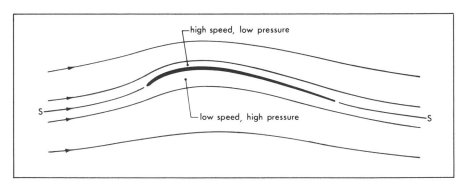

Figure 1

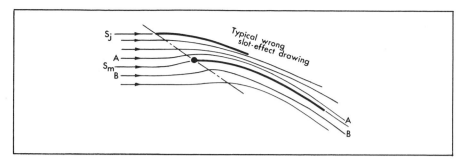

Figure 2

plain the slot effect. There are a number of things wrong with this drawing but I'll just mention the more obvious ones here. First, note that the stagnation streamline for the main (S_m) shows a slight amount of up-wash (bending of the streamline lee-ward to meet the sail). The air knows that it is approaching the sail and it starts to change direction even be-fore it gets to the sail.

However in Figure 2, the stagna-tion streamline drawn for the jib has no upwash at all. Apparently the wind knows that it is approaching the main but it doesn't know about the jib! That cannot be; and this is the crux of the problem. The streamlines for both the jib and the main must show the proper effects of upwash. This cannot be determined by guesswork.

But that's not all that is wrong with Figure 2. Look at the streamlines marked A and B on each side of the stagnation streamline for the main. Out in front of the sail the A and B streamlines are the same distance from the stagnation streamline so the air speed is the same in both tubes of air. However, by the time they reach the leech of the main the lee streamline, A, is closer to the leech than is the windward stream-line, B. We would, therefore, have high-speed, low-pressure air on the lee side of the leech stagnation streamline, and air with a lower speed and higher pressure on the windward side.

This situation cannot exist in the real flow about a sail. Instead, the entire flow about the sails would ad-just itself so that the air speed and pressures are the same on both sides just downstream of the leech. The streamlines should be equally spaced on both sides of the leech if they are equally spaced out in front of the sail.

Another important requirement is that the spacing of streamlines right at the leech of the main must be the same as the spacing of these stream-lines out in front of the sails. In other words, the airspeed at the leech of the main must be about the same as the freestream speed. I am assuming the sails are properly trimmed, and have no flow separa-tion. You will see the reasons for this leech recovery-speed require-ment in a later article (and also why it does not apply to the jib).

Check some of the drawings in your own sailing books. See whether the streamlines at the leech are drawn properly. Also, check the stagnation streamlines leading to both the jib and main for upwash. None of the drawings I have seen has both the upwash and leech streamlines drawn properly. But be-cause these erroneous streamline drawings do exist, it is easy to see why the venturi explanation of the slot effect has persisted for so long (that is, a wide stream of air seems to enter the slot between the sails and simply speed up as the slot gets smaller).

Figure 3 shows a very accurately calculated set of streamlines about a main and jib combination. Contrast it with Figure 2. Note that the stagna-

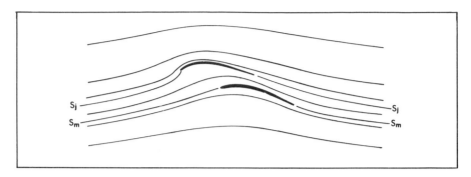

Figure 3

tion streamline for the jib (S_j) turns leeward as it approaches the luff, and that it has more of this upwash than does the stagnation streamline for the main (S_m). The stagnation streamlines for the jib and main actually spread further apart as they approach the space between the luff of the jib and the mast.

This is also substantiated in the water channel photo shown in Figure 4, and it is a very important point. It means that the air that is going to go in the slot between the two sails *actually slows down* as it approaches the sails. It slows down and only starts to speed back up as it approaches the leech of the jib.

This means that the old explanation of the slot effect in the sailing books, the venturi principle, is actually wrong. The slot does not act as a giant venturi with the air approaching the sails and then just speeding

up in a high speed jet of air in the space between the sails (as Figure 2 erroneously indicates). Instead, the air *first slows down,* and then is speeded back up in the slot.

Now, this may at first seem like a trivial difference but it is a very significant factor. The stagnation streamlines for the main and jib show how the air approaches the sails, how much air goes in the slot and, most important of all, how much air is caused to flow on the lee side of both the jib and main.

In a later article, we will see that the final airspeed in the slot near the leech of the jib is only about what it would be if the *jib were not even present* and the flow on the main does not separate. Exactly why the air behaves in this manner and how it affects the boundary layer will be described in the coming months.

Figure 4

Boundary Flow and the Headsail

Continuing to question old principles   Arvel Gentry

Most sailing books describe the primary effect of the headsail on the mainsail approximately as follows: "The jib causes an increase in the velocity of the air on the lee side of the main. This higher velocity air in the slot revitalizes the air over the main and keeps it from separating and stalling."

Well, this may come as a surprise, but if the jib did cause a higher velocity flow over the main, then it would actually *cause* the flow over the main to separate rather than prevent it. But, I'm getting ahead of my story.

When the aerodynamicist studies the airflow about a shape, he recognizes that the flow can be divided into two basic types of flow areas: the external flow region, and the boundary layer region (Fig. 1). The boundary layer flow region is the layer of air that lies very close to the airfoil and the thickness of this layer is greatly exaggerated in the figure for clarity. Air has viscosity (even though it is very small), and it

is in the boundary layer that the viscous characteristics of air come into play.

Because of this viscosity, the air that touches the airfoil is actually carried along by the airfoil (the air has zero speed with respect to the surface of the airfoil). The air just a small distance from the airfoil moves with some finite speed with respect to the airfoil, and the air at the edge of the boundary layer moves with the speed of the external air at that point on the airfoil.

The remainder of the airflow is identified as the external inviscid flow. The viscosity of the air does not affect the aerodynamic calculations for this part of the flow, but the techniques used by an engineer to calculate what happens to the air in these two types of flow are different.

The boundary layer itself is usually divided into three separate types of flow. Near the leading edge of an airfoil there is a very smooth change of air speed within the boundary layer from the airfoil surface to

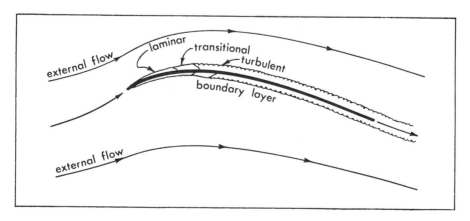

Figure 1

Figure 2

the edge of the boundary layer. This is the laminar boundary layer. Eventually, because of the development of unsteadiness within the boundary layer, and because of disturbances introduced into the flow by roughness (jib hanks, cloth seams, the headstay, etc.), and a certain amount of natural turbulence in the air, the smooth changes in speed within the laminar boundary layer start to give way to a much more erratic type of flow. This is called the transitional region of the boundary layer.

After this short transitional region, the flow in the boundary layer flow becomes very erratic, and we have what is called turbulent flow. The external flow is not appreciably affected by the change from a laminar boundary layer to a turbulent one, so the lift of the airfoil does not change very much.

The water channel photograph in Figure 2 shows another type of airflow that can exist about a sail — separated flow. We all have seen the evidence of this type of flow on our sails. As we bear-off from a close-hauled course with the jib in tight, the yarn telltales on the lee side of the jib suddenly start to twirl wildly. The telltales are responding to the very mixed-up separated flow region

that has formed over the lee side of the sail.

Note that, from the aerodynamic standpoint, we refrain from applying the word *turbulent* to the separated flow, for the word turbulent is reserved for use in describing the turbulent boundary layer. To avoid confusion, we stick to the term separated flow. Almost all our sailing time is spent trying to avoid having separated flow regions on our sails, and this is why we must learn as much as we can about the causes and prevention of separation.

We all know what happens when we get separated flow on our sails: the sail loses some of its driving force and the boat slows down. But what causes separation? It is a well-accepted aerodynamic fact that the boundary layer will separate only when the external pressure along the airfoil starts to increase too rapidly. The more rapid the increase in pressure, the more likely it is that the boundary layer will separate. We should also note that the boundary layer will not separate if the pressure is decreasing along the airfoil.

The rate of pressure change along the surface is called the pressure gradient. When pressure is increasing, the pressure gradient is called an adverse pressure gradient. Whether or not the boundary layer separates when subjected to a given increase in pressure (adverse gradient), depends upon: the character of the boundary layer (laminar or turbulent), what has happened to the boundary layer before reaching the adverse pressure gradient, and the speed of the airflow at the edge of the boundary layer. The speed-distance factor is expressed by the aerodynamicist in a term called the Reynolds number.

The most important fact to remember from this is: pressure must be increasing along a sail to cause separation and stalling. This also means that local airspeed must be decreasing (remember, when pressure goes up, airspeed must go down).

We should also know (this will be covered in more detail in a future article) that high-velocity air on the lee side of the main must slow down and return to near freestream velocity by the time it reaches the leech. It is this slowing down of the air, and resulting increase in pressure, that tends to cause separation.

Now back to my opening statement. If the slot formed by the jib caused an increase in airspeed over the main, then the air would have to slow down even more rapidly to reach the required freestream speed at the leech. This greater pressure gradient would actually cause the flow to separate rather then prevent it.

But from sailing experience, we know that the jib does help keep the flow on the main from separating. Therefore, a *smaller* speed change in the air from the mast to the leech must occur to prevent separation (a reduced pressure gradient). Obviously, the proper explanation must be that the jib actually causes *reduced* velocities over the forward part of the main if this separation is to be prevented.

A complete explanation about how the jib creates reduced velocities over the forward part of the main also will be given in a future article.

Before I leave the subject of separation, I have an interesting new idea to propose. First, some background information. Most competitive sailors use yarn telltales on their sails to indicate when the sail has stalled. The position of these telltales (12"-18" from the luff of a headsail) has been determined from experience as being a true indication of when the sail has stalled (flow completely separated). The best point of sail is located somewhere between this stalled condition and the angle where the sail luffs. Usually it is close to, but not quite at, the luffing point.

Conventional telltales are merely stall-detecting indicators that tell when you have gone too far off the wind; the luffing of a sail tells you when you have headed too close to the wind. What is needed is a luff-stall *warning* device to tell us how close we are either to a luffing or a stalling condition. The behavior of the external air and the boundary layer near the luff of the sail can provide this information.

When a sail is set at an angle where it is just on the verge of luffing, the stagnation streamline comes smoothly right into the luff of the sail, and the flow on the lee side will be attached (unseparated). When the angle of the sail is increased slightly, the stagnation streamline will actually come into the sail on the windward side. The air will have to go very fast to make the sharp turn around the luff to get on the lee side, and then it will immediately start to slow down.

The boundary layer cannot withstand this rapid deceleration so it will separate right at the leading edge. However, the flow will then quickly re-attach itself to the sail and continue to the leech. What we have is a small separation region, or bubble, along the luff. If the angle of the sail is again increased slightly, the length of the separation bubble will increase also. The complete situation where we have also started to get separation near the leech is illustrated in Figure 3, although this

253

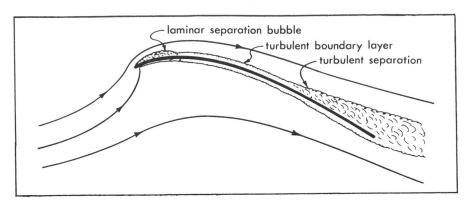

Figure 3

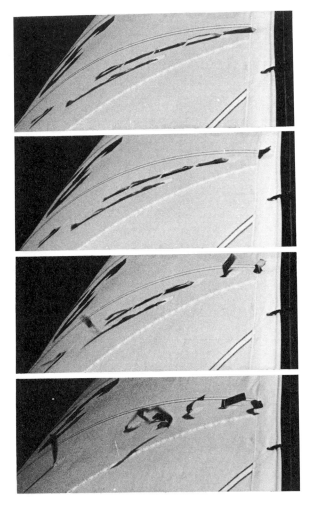

Figure 4

leech separation does not always occur in practice. If we again increase the angle of the sail, the bubble will burst and the entire lee side will be separated, as in Figure 2.

Here is my idea. The size of the separation bubble can be used to tell when a sail is between the luffing and stalled conditions. Several short three-inch pieces of yarn spaced end-to-end from the very luff to the position of the conventional telltale can be used to indicate the size of the leading-edge separation bubble. When all the lee-side tufts are lying down, the stagnation streamline is coming in right at the leading edge and the sail is right on the luffing condition (Fig. 4a).

If only the first tuft is twirling, the sail is near but not quite at the luffing condition (Fig. 4b), and the separation bubble is very small. As the boat is headed further off the wind, the separation bubble will grow larger and the first two or three tufts will twirl (Fig. 4c).

A further increase in angle will cause all the tufts to twirl (including the conventional telltale), for the sail has completely stalled (Fig. 4d). The number of tufts that will twirl before the complete separation occurs will depend upon the length of the tufts used, and the characteristics of the sail.

Some of my friends who have used these short tufts near the luff (they call them "Gentry tufts") have reported that they are very useful, both in fine-tuning the sail trim, and in staying on the best windward point of sail. It takes some practice in their use, but they provide a very sensitive warning of an approaching luff or stall. They are also valuable in improving a new helmsman's windward ability.

If I tell a beginner to sail to windward without luffing or letting the conventional telltale stall, he will do a bad job. He has several degrees of boat angle to play with, and the luffing or conventional telltale tells him only when he has already gone too far in one direction. However, if I tell him to sail with the first short lee tuft slightly agitated but with the rest all lying down, then he will sail a very good windward course.

When the first two or three leeward tufts start to twirl, he knows that he is getting too far off the wind, and he should come back up or the sail will soon stall. When all the leeward tufts settle down straight and even the first tuft is not shaking at all, the sail is on the verge of luffing. So far this tuft system has been used successfully on boats ranging in length from 23′ to 63′.

As always, tuft visibility and the problem of the first tuft's wrapping around the luff are problems, just as they are with conventional telltales. However, multiple tufts on the leading edge and the use of a plastic window close to the luff with different colored tufts on each side solve these problems. Try this setup on your own boat; you may like it.

How a Sail Gives Lift

Additional questions about old principles   Arvel Gentry

How many times have you heard that a sail gives lift to drive a boat because, "the air travels faster on the lee side for it has farther to go than it does on the windward side. So the pressures are different and you get lift." Well, that is wrong! Even a perfectly flat thin airfoil, with the same distance on both sides, has lift when it is at an angle to the wind.

So try to forget everything you know (or think you know) about how a sail gets its lift. The real explanations of how a sail gives lift may seem a bit complicated at first, but once you get the idea it is really quite straightforward.

It is true that the pressures over much of the lee side of a sail are lower than the freestream pressure, and the pressures on the windward side are higher. These pressure differences do result from the air flowing faster on the lee side and slower on the windward side (Bernoulli's principle). But, what causes the air to flow in this manner?

Early mathematicians tried to solve this problem and they derived a set of equations. The streamlines these first solutions gave are illustrated in Figure 1 for a simple flat airfoil at an angle to the flow. Their equations

and solutions were correct, but the flow lines were exactly the same on both sides of the airfoil (turn the page upside down and you'll see what I mean).

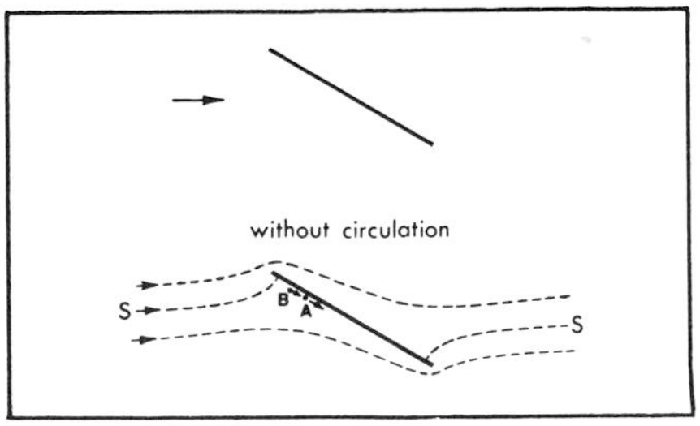

Because the flow lines are the same on both sides, the pressure forces therefore must be the same, and the airfoil would have no lift at all. This would mean that man could not fly, and birds could not fly. But bird do fly, and early man-made gliders, even with flat, uncambered wings also flew. Something obviously was missing from their solutions.

Examining the calculated flow around the edges of the airfoil gives the clue. Note that these mathematically determined streamlines in Figure 1 make sharp turns as they go around the leading and trailing edge of the airfoil (the luff and leech of our sail). For a thin airfoil this means that the air must have high velocities at these points in order to get around the sharp corners. The velocities around the luff can be reduced by bending the airfoil down into the flow (cambering the airfoil), but what about the leech?

In real life we find that the flow around the leech varies from that shown in Figure 1 as the air first begins to move past the airfoil. It changes so that the air leaves the airfoil at the leech smoothly with the same speed and pressures on both sides. This fact of aerodynamics is known as the Kutta condition (named after the man who first discovered it in 1902).

You can understand this Kutta condition requirement if you stop and visualize what would happen if the Kutta condition were not satisfied, and the air coming off of the lee side of the leech were to travel faster

without circulation

Figure 1

than the air coming off the windward side (as is implied in the flow diagrams in many sailing books). If there were different speeds, we would have different pressures (from Bernoulli's principle) on the two sides of the line dividing the lee side and windward side flows downstream of the leech. With different pressures and the sail fabric no longer separating the two different speed regions, we would have nothing to keep the high-pressure air from taking over and pushing into the low-pressure region.

What happens in a real flow is: the total region around the airfoil adjusts itself so that the air flowing off the two sides of the airfoil at the leech has the same speeds and pressures. Again, this adjusting process is called the Kutta condition by aerodynamicists. It is an important principle to remember, for it influences the entire flow field about the sail.

Mathematicians found that the Kutta condition could be satisfied by adding another type of flow solution, called *circulation*, to that already determined and shown in Figure 1. Circulation is a special mathematical flow solution where air rotates around the airfoil. The direction of the circulation flow goes forward over the windward surface, around the luff and then toward the rear on the lee side of the airfoil. The circulation flow velocities are higher close to the surface and they decrease as you get farther away from the surface.

The combination of non-circulation flow and circulation flow is illustrated in Figure 2. When the two flows are added together, both the velocities and directions are taken into account in the entire area around the airfoil. They are added together just as one adds boat speed and true wind speed to get apparent wind strength and direction.

In the mathematical solution, circulation air speeds are adjusted so that the Kutta condition at the leech is satisfied; the calculated air flow speeds and pressures are the same

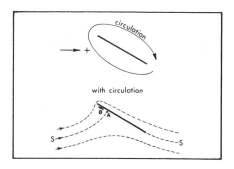

Figure 2

off both sides of the leech. The resulting air speeds of the circulation part of the flow are smaller than the non-circulation solution speeds. On the top of the airfoil, the circulation flow direction is the same as the non-circulation flow direction. This means that the two flows added together will give a higher speed flow.

On the bottom side, the circulation flow direction is against the non-circulation flow so the two flows cancel each other a little bit to give a slower speed flow.

With slow speed flow on the bottom of the airfoil and high speed flow on the top, we get high pressure on the bottom and low pressure on the top, which gives us the necessary pressure difference between the two sides of the sail to maintain the cambered shape and to give the lifting force to drive the boat.

You might ask if the results from this mathematical exercise (non-circulation plus circulation flow) are really meaningful. The answers are indeed accurate and they match test data almost exactly.

Examine the stagnation streamlines (marked S) in Figures 1 and 2. In Figure 1, the stagnation streamlines come into the airfoil close to the edges. Notice that at point A in Figure 1 the windward streamline is quite far from the airfoil surface.

At this point we should expect low speed flow in the direction indicated by the arrow. Circulation flow at this point is just equal to this speed and opposite in direction and it therefore cancels out the non-circulation flow.

Figure 3

This point becomes the place where the new stagnation streamline comes into the airfoil when we have circulation as shown in Figure 2.

At point B in Figure 1 the flow on the surface has a slower speed than point A, so the circulation flow is not only able to cancel out the non-circulation flow direction, but can actually make *the flow go in the opposite direction* around the luff of the airfoil. From this we see that the circulation causes some of the air that was going to go on the windward side to be diverted around to the lee side. We can also see this from the fact that the stagnation streamline at the left side of Figure 2 is much lower than it was in Figure 1.

The Kutta condition must always be satisfied for any lifting airfoil. However, if the flow separates from the airfoil before it reaches the leech, the Kutta condition will not be satisfied at the leech of the airfoil itself. Instead, it will be satisfied at the trailing edge of the separated region — well behind the airfoil.

However, since the flow at the trailing edge of the separated region has a smaller angle to the freestream than does the actual leech of the airfoil, the airfoil with separation has less lift and much more drag. This is shown in Figure 3.

Note that nowhere in this discussion have I said anything about the density of the air, or about the air having farther to go on the lee side, or about the air actually striking the sail. The air just does not behave like that. Also note that the airfoil used was perfectly flat and thin. Of course our cambered sail is more efficient than the flat airfoil, but, from the example given, we see that

a sail does not have to have thickness, either real or imaginary, to have lift. The air *flows* about the sail, and the way that it flows is governed by the shape of the airfoil and it is basic non-circulation flow, plus the effects of the circulation that must be added to satisfy the Kutta condition at the leech.

Air does not strike the sail like so many grains of blowing sand. Instead, air behaves like a fluid as it flows past the sail. When air sees it is approaching the sail, it starts to move and change direction in preparation for passing the sail. But air also has a certain resistance to a change in direction. It doesn't want to change direction any more than it has to in flowing past the sail.

The stagnation streamline divides the air that is going to pass on the two sides of the sail. The air that is going to flow on the lee side does not move any further to leeward than it has to to get past the sail and still satisfy the Kutta condition at the leech. The lee-side streamlines, therefore, pass very close to the forward part of the sail. They have high velocities and low pressures in this region.

On the windward side, the air is a bit lazy; it doesn't want to move up into the convex region of flow that is formed by the airfoil and the stagnation streamline. The windward side streamlines spread out a bit, the air slows down and the pressure gets higher. But, the final airspeed, pressure, and direction of flow at the leech must be the same as on the leeward surface for the Kutta condition to be satisfied.

Figures 4 and 5 show accurately drawn streamlines about an airfoil

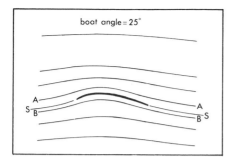

Figure 4

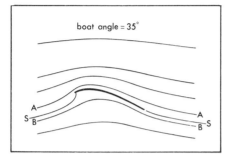

Figure 5

representing a jib at two different relative wind angles for the centerline of the boat (25° and 35°). The stagnation streamline dividing the flow that passes on each side of the sail is identified by the letter S. The first lee-side streamline is marked A, and the first windward line is B.

The detailed pressure distributions for the two boat angles are shown in Figures 6 and 7. In these drawings, the negative or suction pressures (less than atmospheric) are represented by arrows pointing away from the sail. The lower surface pressures are usually higher than atmospheric (positive pressures) and are represented by arrows pointing toward the sail.

Below each airfoil drawing is an engineering type of plot showing this same information in terms of pressure coefficient along the surface of the sail. The difference between the lee-side and windward-side pressures at a given point on the airfoil

represents the pressure difference across the sail fabric.

If you study Figures 4 and 6 together, you can see how all this information you've learned previously fits together. In Figure 4, the stagnation streamline S goes smoothly into the airfoil luff. Line A gradually gets closer to S and the airfoil surface as it approaches the maximum camber point. Line A then tends to move gradually away over the rest of the airfoil.

With this flow we would expect to have an increase in air speed to the point where streamline A is closest to the airfoil, followed by a gradual decrease in speed as the leech is

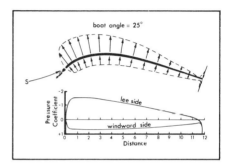

Figure 6

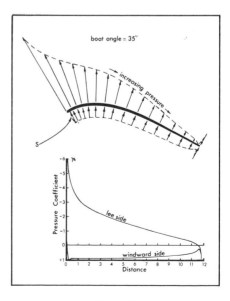

Figure 7

approached. If you remember that air pressure goes down when speed goes up (Bernoulli's principle), you therefore get a decrease in pressure over the front lee-part of the sail, followed by a gradual increase in pressure toward the leech.

In Figure 4, streamline B tends to resist moving up into the convex region formed by the airfoil and the stagnation streamline so that it gets further away from the airfoil surface. Therefore there is a decrease in wind speed and an increase in pressure in this area. Figure 6 shows how all this turns out in terms of the pressure along the airfoil surface.

For the 35° boat angle case in Figures 5 and 7, we have a higher angle of attack for the sail, and a significantly different streamline picture and resulting surface pressures. The stagnation streamline comes into the airfoil on the windward surface a little way back from the luff. Streamline A passes close to the luff and then immediately starts getting farther from the surface over the rest of the airfoil. All the air between lines A and S must pass through the little space at the lee side of the luff.

We would expect to see much higher air speeds and lower pressures close to the luff than we had for the lower boat-angle case. We would also see a rapid increase in pressure as the flow continues downstream from the luff, since streamline A moves rapidly away from the surface. The pressure drawings and plot in Figure 7 show that this is exactly what happens.

Previously it was learned that the boundary layer does not like rapid increases in pressure and it tends to separate under these conditions. In real life, the boundary layer for the high-angle case shown in Figures 5 and 7 would probably separate and the airfoil would stall. As soon as this happens, the streamlines shown in Figure 5 would no longer be true, for we would get a completely different flow picture about the airfoil (similar to Figure 3).

However, by being able to calculate the airflow with the computer as though there were no separation, we are able to study just what causes the separation to occur, and what can be done to prevent it from separating.

In the streamline drawings in Figures 4 and 5, the lines A and B are the same distance away from the stagnation streamline S at the leech as they were way out in front of the airfoil. This means that the airspeeds and pressures on both sides of the leech are about the same as the freestream speed.

The detailed calculated results show a speed, at 95% of the airfoil length, about 14% higher than freestream velocity, with the speed and pressure recovering to near freestream values by the time the trailing edge is reached. These facts will become very important when I describe two airfoils together.

Another important point can be inferred from the data presented in these figures. Because all sails are very thin, with relatively sharp leading edges, they are very sensitive to the angle of the wind.

An increased angle of attack will cause the stagnation streamline to come into the windward side of the sail. This will cause excessive pressure gradients on the lee side as the air tries to recover from its rapid turn around the leading edge and return back to near freestream values at the leech. As a result, the flow will separate and we will have a stalled condition.

As the angle of attack to the wind is reduced (the boat headed up), the stagnation streamline will shift around to the luff and then the lee side of the sail. The resulting pressure distribution will cause the sail to change its shape since there may be a higher pressure on the lee side than on the windward side. It is in a luffing condition.

Note that the air is not actually striking the sail like so many grains of sand and making it shake. It is just that the fluctuating pressures and unstable shape of the sail cause it to shake as it responds to the pressures created by the flow. Obviously, the term *backwinding* of a sail is not really a very good descriptive term, for it implies that air "strikes" the sail. And now we know that air does not behave in this way.

You should also note in Figures 6 and 7 that the higher-angle case would have higher lift — if the flow did not separate. Where does this higher lift come from? The stream-lines in Figures 4 and 5 clearly illustrate this. The higher angle of attack requires a higher circulation to satisfy the Kutta condition at the leech. Higher circulation means that more air is diverted to pass on the top or lee side of the sail. We can see this from the fact that the stagnation streamline in Figure 5 is lower (further to windward) than it is in Figure 4. Again, to get more lift we must cause more air to pass on the lee side of the sail.

Another Look at Slot Effect

Yet further questions of old principles   Arvel Gentry

The **"slot" effect,"** as we know it, is traditionally *supposed* to do three basic things:

First, the jib causes the air over the lee side of the main to have a much higher velocity, increasing the partial vacuum, and hence the sail's efficiency.

Second, the higher velocity air in the slot "revitalizes" the air over the main, which would otherwise be in a separated or stalled condition.

Third, the increased velocity in the slot results because the distance between the leech of the jib and the main is much less than the distance between the headstay and the mast, but it must accommodate the same flow per unit of time.

Sailing books, magazine articles by national champions and our leading sailmakers all have expounded on, and made use of, these ideas to tell us first, how the slot works, and second, to explain how we should trim our sails. These explanations of jib-mainsail interaction originally were derived from an aerodynamicist's description of how a wing with a leading edge slot works (Fig. 1).

But in 1971 I obtained some results from a new and sophisticated computer program that indicated that the old explanations of how a wing slot works were entirely wrong. My re-sults were accurate, detailed, substantiated by wind-tunnel data, and very conclusive.

Does this mean that the old explanations for slot effect were also wrong? The answer is yes!

My conclusion was not reached in haste for it is dangerous to say old ideas are wrong unless you have a lot of proof and can cover all the aspects of a problem. To test my theories I first made use of a device called an Analog Field Plotter that determines the flow streamlines about any airfoil combination (Fig. 2). I studied single and multiple airfoil combinations to gain a basic understanding of the directions the air takes as it flows past the sails.

A number of sail angles and relative positions were investigated and the results were then backed up by more detailed and accurate answers from the computer. Next I conducted a series of experiments in a water channel to obtain photographic evidence of my findings. On top of all this, each new conclusion and explanation was subjected to the question, do they all make sense in terms of actual sailing experience? The answer continues to be *yes!*

In the first three articles of this series, I presented a number of very important and fundamental aerody-

sail slot   aircraft wing slot

Figure 1

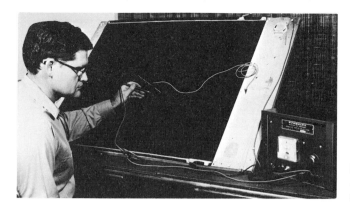

Figure 2.
Analog field plotter
equipment.

namic principles. In this fourth article, I will assume you already have studied the first three parts. However, several items should be repeated as a review.

Earlier I pointed out that most of the airflow diagrams in the sailing books violated some basic aerodynamic principles. We learned that boundary layer separation on a sail results when the surface pressure is increasing too rapidly (the airflow is slowing down too quickly). And we have learned about circulation and how lift is generated.

We saw that the airflow coming off both sides of the leech of a sail must be at the same pressure and speed (the Kutta condition). The airflow speed will be higher than freestream over the forward-lee portion of a sail, but it will return to near freestream speed by the time it reaches the leech. It is this slowing down of the lee-side airspeeds (and resulting increase in pressures) that causes the airflow to separate.

From the information I've presented so far, it is quite obvious that there are some serious misunderstandings about the old slot-effect explanations in the sailing literature. But if previous explanations for the slot effect are wrong, what are the right answers?

Until now, I've talked about general principles and about flow around a single sail. Now we'll begin the analysis of two sails together. The last article described how the flow

about a lifting airfoil may be thought of as being the addition of a circulation flow solution and a non-circulation solution. The amount of circulation on the airfoil was adjusted so that the resulting airflow was in a smooth direction off the leech. But what about a case where we have two airfoils?

Figure 3 shows that both the jib and mainsail have their own circulation fields. The strengths of the two circulations must be adjusted so that the Kutta condition is satisfied at the leech of both sails (smooth flow off each sail). In Figure 3 note that the two circulation fields *oppose* and tend to cancel each other in the slot between the jib and main. This fact gives us a hint that we will not get all the increased air speed in the slot that is claimed by the old theories.

If the slot flow did give higher velocities that increase the partial vacuum on the main, would not this same "partial vacuum" on the *wind-*

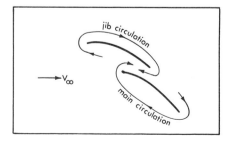

Figure 3

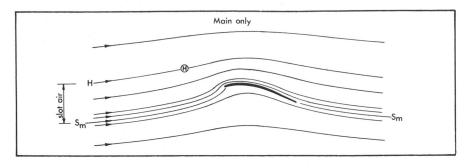

Figure 4

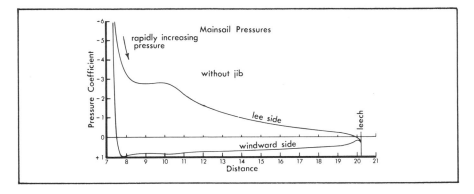

Figure 5

ward side of the jib *reduce* its efficiency? As we will see later, what really happens is that some of the air we would think might go through the slot is actually diverted by the combined circulation fields so that it goes on the lee side of the jib.

To examine the interaction between two sails, we will use a typical airfoil section of a mainsail and a matching section through the jib. The actual airfoil shapes and angles are not too important as long as they are reasonably representative of closehauled sailing conditions. In fact, for any conclusion to be scientifically correct, it must apply for almost any shape and for a wide range of angles, and I will illustrate the effect of different sheeting angles next month.

We always must check our results to see if a luffing condition would result. This check will insure that the results are correct even though the

analysis does make use of rigid airfoils instead of flexible shapes.

First, look at the flow about the mainsail airfoil without the jib in place. The mainsail will be positioned at the same angle it will have when the jib is in place; the leading edge of the main is determined by the shape of the mast. For these studies, the area right behind the mast was filled in to represent the separated region that always exists immediately behind the mast. Separation effects from the mast are reasonably understood so I will not dwell on mast effects here.

The calculated streamlines for a main alone are shown in Figure 4. Note that the stagnation streamline (S_m) comes into the lower (windward) side of the sail. The calculated pressure, if no separation or stall occurs, is shown in Figure 5. Remember from last month that low pressures (high velocities) are represented by negative pressure coefficients, and that high pressures (low velocities) are shown as positive pressure coefficients.

Since the stagnation streamline comes in on the windward side of the sail (upwash), and we have a good pressure difference on the two sides of the surface, the sail will hold its shape and not luff. Even though the forward-lee part of the sail seems to be facing the free-stream airflow direction way out in front of the sail, the upwash effect places the leading edge of the sail at a higher angle so that it will not luff. The sail only sees the local upwash flow directions.

Because the stagnation point is around on the windward side of the airfoil, we get a very high suction peak (large negative pressures) as the air tries to make the sharp turn around the mast to the lee side. The pressure then starts to increase rapidly toward the pressure it must attain by the time the leech is reached — to satisfy the Kutta condition. The boundary layer probably will not be able to withstand this steep increase in pressure, the flow will separate, and the airfoil will be in a stalled condition.

To prevent this stall, the sheeting angle of the sail is increased, either by letting out the mainsheet or moving the traveler to leeward. This is exactly what our experience is afloat when the jib is lowered. However, in the example shown in Figures 4 and 5, the mainsail is at the same angle at which it would be if the jib were present. And the pressures shown in Figure 5 are what we get if the flow does not separate.

Carefully note the shape and position of streamline H in Figure 4. This line is selected so that it goes through the point (H) that will be the leading edge for the jib (the headstay) in our next example. The distance between the stagnation streamline S_m and the headstay streamline H at the left side of the figure is a measure of the amount of air that passes between the headstay and the mast without the jib being present and without any separation on the mainsail.

Now, let's introduce the jib. The streamlines, when both the jib and main are used, are shown in Figure 6. This figure is necessarily a bit cluttered so that the flow lines before and after the jib is added can be compared.

Figure 6 is the most important figure in this whole series, so study it carefully. The solid streamlines represent the flow when both the jib and main are used. For comparison, the streamlines that existed when the main was used alone are also given (the dotted lines). A number of important points come out of this figure.

First, the stagnation streamline for the mainsail when the jib is present (the solid line, S_m) goes smoothly into the leading edge of the mast

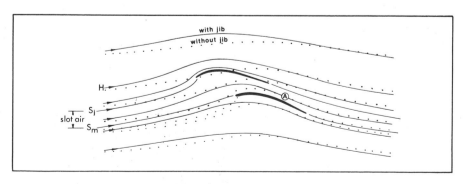

Figure 6

instead of being down around on the windward side as was the case for the mainsail alone. The air, therefore, will not have to speed up as much to get around to the lee side of the main. This means that the airspeeds will not be so high over the forward-lee side of the main and the flow will not have to slow down so much to reach the final speed that is required at the leech to satisfy the Kutta condition.

This gives a smaller increase in pressure as the air flows toward the leech (a lower adverse pressure gradient) and helps prevent the flow from separating. If the jib were placed in the picture and had it caused higher air speeds over the forward-lee side of the main, as the old venturi explanation states, then it would give a steeper pressure gradient and actually *cause* the flow to separate, rather than prevent it.

Second, the streamline H that went through the headstay point when the mainsail was used alone now goes well above the surface of the jib. The new streamline through the headstay (the stagnation streamline for the jib, S_j) now is much lower than the headstay streamline, H, in the case of the mainsail alone.

The distance between the two stagnation streamlines (S_m and S_j) at the left side of the figure is a measure of the amount of air that now goes between the headstay and the mast (and therefore into the slot

between the two sails) when both sails are present. You can see that *much less air goes between the headstay and the mast when both sails are present than it does when only the main is used.* Much more air is being deflected around the lee side of the headstay (and therefore around the lee side of the jib) than when there was a mainsail alone!

Look closely at the solid streamline for the main and jib combination that passes in the slot between the two sails at point A. Note that at this point it is exactly the same distance away from the surface of the main as the dotted streamline is for just the main at point A. This means that at this point we have about the same airspeeds when we have a jib and main as we had for the main alone! In fact, on the surface of the main itself, Figure 7 shows slightly higher pressures (less negative) and therefore *lower* velocities when the jib is used than occurs without the jib. From all this, we have to conclude that the old venturi slot-effect explanation *must be wrong.*

The calculated pressure distributions for the mainsail, both with and without the jib, are shown in Figure 7. The presence of the jib and a resulting shift in the stagnation point on the mainsail causes a drastic reduction in the high negative-pressures over the forward-lee part of the main. Since the pressure gradients are much lower, the possibility

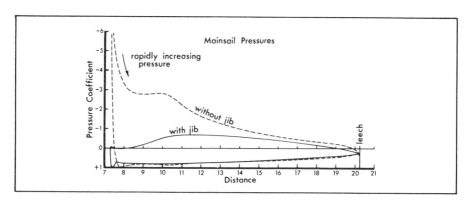

Figure 7

of complete flow separation on the mainsail is reduced, and the amount of theoretical lift being contributed by the mainsail is also reduced.

Of course, in the case of the mainsail alone, separation would have occurred in real life and you would not have been able actually to realize the amount of lift calculated theoretically when neglecting separation. You do lose lift from the theoretical non-separated value, but you now have reduced pressure gradients so the airfoil will not stall.

These findings are the keys to the often discussed phenomena of slot-flow between sails. With accurately determined streamlines, you can see that the air passing between the two sails is quite different from the old "venturi effect" explanations many of us have grown up with. With both sails set, a large percentage of the air that was going between the headstay and the mast when the mainsail was alone now goes above and down the lee side of the jib. Less air is left to pass in the slot between the sails and this tube of air *actually slows down* (the streamlines spread out) as it reaches the line between the headstay and the mast.

Then, and only then, does it begin to speed back up as it approaches the slot between the jib and the mainsail. However, by the end of the slot, the speed has only accelerated back to about what it would have been at that point if the mainsail alone were used.

These flow diagrams also verify a couple of points that we all have observed in actual sailing experience. The jib reduces the upwash on the main (gives the main a header), and the main increases the upwash (a lifting wind shift) for the jib.

Thus we see that the primary effect of a jib is to cause *reduced* velocities over the forward-lee part of the main, rather than increased velocities. The slower velocities in turn give reduced pressure gradients that help prevent separation and stall rather than some higher speed "revitalization."

The velocities in the slot are determined by the total effects of the circulation fields around the two sails necessary to give smooth flow off the leeches (the Kutta condition). The flow streamlines for this condition should never be drawn by hand or guessed. Instead they must be accurately determined by an Analog Field Plotter or computer.

More on the Slot Effect

Final questions about old principles   Arvel Gentry

In this series first we studied the air-flow around the main alone; then we added a jib, and this gave us a good picture of how the jib affects the mainsail. Now we will do just the opposite. First we will look at the airflow about the jib alone, and then add the main. By doing this, we will see that the main actually *helps* the jib to become the very efficient sail that it is.

If you have been following this series, you should be an expert at reading streamline drawings and pressure distribution plots, so let's jump right in. Figure 1 shows the streamlines about a typical jib-mainsail combination with the solid lines the streamlines when both sails are used, and the dotted lines the streamlines when the jib is used alone.

First, note that the dotted stagnation streamline for the jib alone (S_{jo}) goes right into the leading edge of the jib. However, when the main is also used, the stagnation streamline shifts to the position S_j so that it starts much lower (further to windward) and comes into the jib luff

slightly on the windward edge. In this example the jib could be pointed a little closer to the wind without luffing.

From this we see that the mainsail shifts the jib stagnation streamline to windward (a lifting wind shift) and allows the boat to sail closer to the wind. This increased upwash on the jib is caused by the fact that the circulation fields for the two sails add together to become stronger in the area in front of the jib. This is not a new fact, but at least now we see exactly how this jib wind shift occurs.

Another result is that the mainsail causes more air to be diverted around to the lee side of the jib. You can see this by comparing the levels of the two jib stagnation streamlines well out in front of the sails. The stagnation streamline of the jib when both sails are set (S_j) is much further to windward (lower) than it was without the main (S_{jo}). The distance between these two lines (L) represents additional air that the mainsail causes to flow on the lee side of the jib. Without the mainsail, this chunk of air would pass *on the wind-*

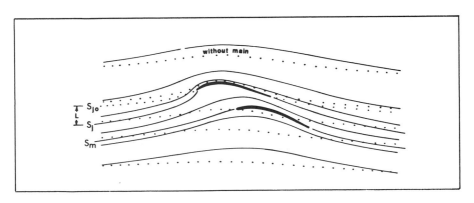

Figure 1

ward side of the jib!

This diversion of air to the lee side of the jib has a very important effect. We know that the more air that flows on the lee side of a sail, the greater its lifting force. Because we have more air flowing to lee of the jib, it will travel at higher speeds and the lee-side pressures will be lower.

With lower lee-side pressures we have a larger pressure difference across the sail and more jib lift. This also can be achieved by a higher angle of attack, or it can be accomplished at lower angles with the help of the mainsail.

All this is illustrated in the jib pressure coefficient plot in Figure 2. The negative pressure coefficients represent pressures lower than free-stream (suction pressures and high velocities); and the positive coefficients are higher than freestream (lower speeds).

Note that the negative pressures on the jib are much more negative when both the jib and mainsail are used. *The jib develops much more lift when it is operating in the flow field influence of the mainsail.* We would expect this to happen, however, for the jib is operating in the upwash field of the main. In an actual situation afloat, we can make use of this by sailing a bit closer to the wind. But this fact alone does not account for the great efficiency attributed to the jib in the presence of the main.

If we examine pressures near the leech in Figure 2, we will see a second reason why the jib is such an efficient sail. Note that pressures near the leech are slightly on the positive side (A) with a jib alone. This means the jib leech velocity, without a main, is near the free-stream value required to meet the Kutta condition on a single sail.

However, the jib leech pressures with a main present actually are negative which indicates leech velocities higher than freestream (point B). In this case, the velocity at the leech of the jib is about 30% higher than freestream speed. How has this happened?

I have mentioned before that airspeeds must be the same on both sides of a single sail at the leech to satisfy the Kutta condition. For a single sail, the leech speed turns out to be close to freestream airspeed. When we have two sails, jib and mainsail, the airspeed at the leech of the last sail in the line (the main-sail) also will satisfy this Kutta condition and be near freestream values.

Yet, the leech of the jib is in a high speed region of flow created on the lee side of the mainsail; and detailed calculations show that the air flowing around the jib adjusts itself so that the Kutta condition is satisfied *not* at freestream conditions, but at a speed that blends with the high speed flow created by the main-sail in the region of the jib leech.

This high speed region would be there even if the jib were not present

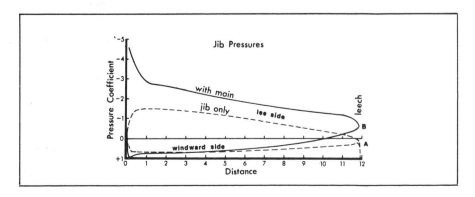

Figure 2

(providing the flow on the main is not separated), for airfoil shapes and angles used in my research show that jib leech airspeed would be about the same if the mainsail were used alone.

The Kutta condition on the jib must be satisfied in a high-velocity region created by the combined flows of the jib and mainsail (point B in Figure 2). The net result of this is that *the entire velocity distribution on the lee side of the jib is increased by a considerable amount*. These increased velocities mean lower lee-surface pressures and a resulting increase in jib lift.

In other words, the mainsail actually helps the jib, not only by giving it a lifting wind shift, but also by causing it to have much higher velocities on its lee side because of the Kutta condition requirements at the jib leech. While the aft windward side of the jib does lose some of its positive pressure, this is a small price to pay for the large increases in the suction pressure on the lee side.

This phenomenon will be referred to as the *dumping velocity* or *bootstrap* effect. The name bootstrap indicates that the main is actually helping the jib in this unusual manner.

What if a third sail were added forward and to lee of the jib, with its leech in the increased velocity region of the jib? This third sail would have an even higher leech velocity and higher lee-side velocity distribution because of what the main is doing to the jib — and what the jib, in turn, does to the third sail.

The higher velocity flow that is forced to the lee side of the jib by the main has another important effect. These higher velocities all along the lee side of the jib mean that the boundary layer will be able to withstand more rapid increases in pressure (stronger adverse pressure gradients) without separating. The boat can be pointed at a higher angle (with the jib stagnation streamline coming in slightly on the windward side) without the whole jib separat-

ing and stalling.

Now let's examine the effects of four different jib and mainsail angles. Figure 3 shows four streamline drawings with only the stagnation streamlines appearing so that you can see clearly what happens to the slot flow as the sail angles are changed. Rather large sail angle changes of five degrees were selected so that the overall effects would be easier to illustrate.

Figure 3A has the sails at the same setting used in the jib-main flow study we already have discussed. In Figure 3B the jib has been moved five degrees closer to the mainsail, and, as you can see by the number at the left, this causes a 60% reduction in the amount of air that flows through the slot.

The stagnation streamline for the jib now comes into the sail on the lower, or windward, surface, and the stagnation streamline for the main comes into the sail on its upper or lee side. This would cause higher pressures on the lee side of the main than on the windward side and the main would luff (carry a large bubble). As soon as the sail changes its shape, our nicely calculated streamlines become invalid, for the entire flow field changes a bit in response to the new shape of the sails.

But in Figure 3B we see what happens when we sheet the jib in too close. The slot-flow air is reduced; the pressures on the forward-lee side of the main become higher as the air flow becomes slower; and the mainsail loses more and more of its driving potential until we reach the point where it luffs. Even in this luffing condition, however, the main serves a useful purpose by causing an upwash in front of the jib. And it still contributes something, though less, to the bootstrap effect.

This, of course, assumes that only the forward part of the main is carrying a bubble and that the aft part of the sail is loaded up.

In Figure 3C, both the main and the jib are sheeted closer to the centerline of the boat by five de-

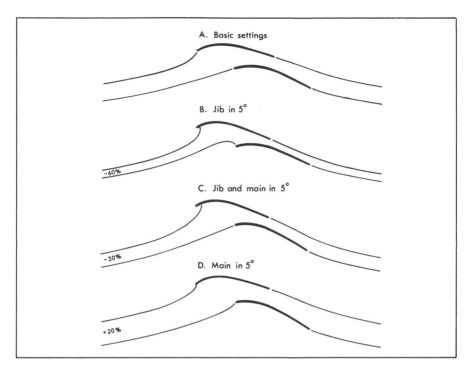

A. Basic settings

B. Jib in 5°

-60%

C. Jib and main in 5°

-30%

D. Main in 5°

+20%

Figure 3

grees. This causes a 30% reduction in the amount of slot air compared to the sails with basic settings in Figure 3A. However, in Figure 3C, sheeting both the main and the jib in closer causes even more upwash on the jib, and the stagnation streamline comes into the jib even further back on the windward side. Here the air is treated rather roughly as it makes the sharp turn to get on the lee side and will probably separate and cause the jib to stall unless the boat is pointed closer to the wind. Both sails in short, have been trimmed in too tightly for the boat angle being sailed.

In Figure 3D the jib is at its original basic setting but the main has been sheeted in five degrees to open up the slot. This causes a 20% increase in the amount of air that flows through the slot, and the stagnation streamlines for both the main and the jib have moved slightly around to the windward leading edge of the sails.

These comments do not pretend to show how sails should be trimmed for maximum speed; they are included only to show the general effects as the sail angles are changed. All these results however, clearly indicate that the amount of air that flows through the slot between the jib and main will vary depending upon the relative sheeting angles of the two sails. The angles also have a direct influence over the way in which the stagnation streamline comes into the sails. And this, of course, affects the pressure distributions and determines whether or not the lee-side boundary layers will separate and the sails stall.

All my comments to date have primarily applied to a jib-mainsail combination having considerable sail overlap. A similar situation would have occurred if the sails had less overlap. The only difference would have been in the relative magnitude of the observed effect. With less overlap, a jib would not have such a strong effect on the mainsail, and the mainsail lee-side suction pressures would not have been reduced as much.

The downwash effect of the jib on the main also would have been smaller. With less overlap, the leech velocity on the jib would have been a bit lower and the bootstrap effect not quite so strong.

Of course all these comments also would apply to a single sail combination with varying sail shape and overlap from the deck to the top of the mast. Nevertheless, the basic conclusions still would be the same.

I now would like to classify the major jib-mainsail interaction effects. Although they are for the most part interdependent, I will segregate them into the effect of the jib on the mainsail, and the effect of the mainsail on the jib.

The major effects of a jib on the mainsail are:

1. The jib causes the stagnation point on the mainsail to shift around toward the leading edge of the mast (the header effect).
2. As a result, the peak suction velocities on the forward lee-side of the main are greatly reduced. Since the peak suction velocities are reduced, the recovery adverse pressure gradients also are reduced.
3. Because of reduced pressure gradients on the mainsail, the possibility of the boundary layer separating and the airfoil stalling is reduced.
4. A mainsail can be operated efficiently at higher angles of attack without flow separation and stalling than would be the case with just a mainsail alone. This is caused by a reduction in velocities over the forward-lee part of the mainsail rather than by a speed-up in the flow which is the popular theory.
5. *Much less air* goes between the headstay and the mast when the jib is placed in the flow with

the main. The circulations of the main and the jib tend to oppose and cancel each other in the area between the two sails, and more air is therefore forced over the lee side of the jib.
6. As the jib is sheeted in closer to the main, there is a continuing decrease in suction pressure on the lee side of the main. When pressures both to the windward and leeward side of the mainsail become equal, there no longer is the pressure difference across the sail necessary to maintain the airfoil shape, and the sail begins to luff.

The major effects of the mainsail on the jib are:

1. The upwash flow ahead of the mainsail causes the stagnation point on the jib to be shifted around toward the windward side of the sail, and the boat can be pointed closer to the wind without the jib stalling or luffing.
2. The leech of the jib is in a high-speed flow region created by the mainsail. The leech velocity on the jib is, therefore, higher than if the jib alone were used.
3. Because of the higher leech velocity, velocities along the entire lee surface of the jib are greatly increased when both the jib and main are used, and this contributes to the high practical efficiency of a jib.
4. The higher lee-surface velocities on the jib mean the jib can be operated at higher angles of attack before the jib lee-side flow will separate and stall.
5. Because of all this, proper trim and shape of the mainsail significantly affect the efficiency of the overlapping jib. Anything that causes a velocity reduction in the region of the leech of the jib (such as some separation on the aft part of the main) results in a lower driving force con-

tributed by the jib.

6. The trim of the main significantly affects the pointing ability of the boat, for it directly influences the upwash that approaches the luff of the jib.

7. The mast in front of the mainsail always has been blamed for making the main less efficient than a jib. From my studies, I believe this is only part of the answer. Another, and probably equally important, factor is the increased velocity on the jib and the fact that its Kutta condition must be satisfied in a local high speed flow region that is created by the mainsail.

Contributors

Bob Barton, a Long Island Sound native, has been with Murphy & Nye Sailmakers, for whom he is corporate vice president; since 1971 he has been its Marketing Manager and Director of Offshore Development, a position involving computerized sail design and rating analysis. His racing experience includes winning the Eastern Single-handed Championship, campaigning in two America's Cup challenges, and sailing on numerous one-design and offshore boats. Winner of the 1975 Miami-Nassau race in *Country Woman* and a North American Half-Ton champion, he also crewed in a victorious North American Men's Championship, was a 1972 Olympic team backup in Solings, and took a sixth and a fourth overall in the '75 and '74 SORC, respectively. He is a member of The Chicago Yacht Club.

Charles S. Booz, Jr., had ten years' experience racing Lightnings before moving on to big boats. He now campaigns his own 30-footer, *Metaphor,* between ocean-racing crew engagements. A professional writer and photographer, he was assigned by Du Pont to produce a film on the 1967 America's Cup. Since then, he has published a number of articles on racing and sailing technology, and was the author, with Olin Stephens and Ted Hood, of the booklet "Quest for Excellence," an account of the 1970 Cup defense. He serves as coordinator of Public Affairs for the Organic Chemicals Department of Du Pont.

Bruce Cameron has been sailing all his life, being weaned on a Turnabout in Beverly, Mass. He then progressed from class competition and college racing to ocean racing and cruising. In 1969 he entered sailing professionally through chartering and delivery, and is associated with The Moorings in Tortola. He lays claim to some 200,000 miles of ocean sailing in everything from Admiral's Cup yachts to shrimp boats. As a navigator, he has raced in the SORC, Onion Patch, Jamaica Race, Fastnet, Cowes Week, and the Rio Circuit. Mr. Cameron owns a traditional wooden Herreshoff ketch.

Stephen Colgate is president and owner of Offshore Sailing School, Sail Away Club, and Steve Colgate Sailing Enterprises. Based in New York City, his businesses are primarily engaged in learn-to-sail, racing, and cruising instruction in New York, South Carolina, Puerto Rico, Texas, and the Bahamas. Since beginning sailing at age 15, Mr. Colgate has had wide experience in both one-designs and ocean racers.

He crewed in the 1968 Olympics on a 5.5 Meter and in two America's Cup trials — 1967 on *American Eagle* and 1970 on *Heritage*. He has also participated in five Transatlantics and seven Bermudas, as well as the Soling Worlds, Admiral's Cup, and Mallory Cup races, and has won numerous class championships and distance events. The author of *Colgate's Basic Sailing Theory* (van Nostrand Reinhold) and other books and magazine articles, he is a member of the New York and the Seawanhaka Yacht Clubs, the Cruising Club of America, the Royal Ocean Racing Club, and several racing associations.

Hubert Dramard is with the Bruce Banks sail loft in Sarisbury, England.

Richard duMoulin is Assistant to the President of Ogden Marine, New York. He began racing in 1955 on Long Island Sound in Lightnings and Blue Jays, and in his family's sloop *Lady Del*. From 1964-68, he was Dartmouth sailing team captain, and from 1969-72 was ocean racing coach at the U.S. Naval Academy, where he was also skipper of its 54-foot yacht *Rage*. As crew, navigator, or skipper he has participated in numerous major races, the latest to date being the '74 One-Ton Championship on *Robin* and the '74 Congressional Cup Series with Ted Turner. For the 1967 America's Cup, he served as sheet tailer on *Constellation;* in the '74 challenge, he was navigator aboard *Mariner* and, after her elimination, *Intrepid.*

Bruce Dyson is a sailmaker in Marblehead, Mass.

Arthur Edmunds operates his own yacht design office in Fort Lauderdale, where he has executed sailboats for S 2 Yachts and Allied, among other commercial and custom clients in both sail and power. His early sailing experience was on Lake Ontario and at the U.S. Coast Guard Academy, from which he was graduated in 1954. Though many designers find little time for actual sailing, since 1960 Mr. Edmunds has been an active crew member in offshore racing during the S.O.R.C. and other Florida regattas.

Steve Falk is a pond sailor first, and secondarily a blue water sailor out of Marblehead. His home club sails Sunfish and 470s at Sherborn, Mass., where he has perennially been fleet champion. A regular contributor to SAIL, he is also widely read through his books *Sailing Racing Rules the Easy Way* and *Fundamentals of Sailboat Racing* (both St. Martin's Press). Ashore, Mr. Falk heads a management consultant company, and he applies computer simulation to sailing techniques. He has developed his own supersensitive relative speed indicator, the "Falk Racing Wand."

Arvel Gentry is a research aerodynamicist at Douglas Aircraft. Putting into practice the "Gentry Tuft System" and the iconoclastic theories described in his SAIL articles, he has been quite successful in racing his Ranger 23, *Kittiwake*, in the Southern California area. Non-sailing weekends are spent in behalf of Kittiwake Enterprises dealing in sailing-related projects. Mr. Gentry's extensive theoretical and experimental studies on mast section aerodynamics led to his designing the mast section shape used on *Courageous* in the '74 America's Cup. He has also designed and built performance recording equipment for ocean racers, and serves as consultant to Telcor Instruments.

Gabriel M. Giannini is a physicist and industrialist, and holder of 58 patents in aircraft instrumentation, telephony, and plasma devices. His initial forays in racing were with one-designs and dinghies, but he soon moved to ocean racing, where, in over 35 years, he has accumulated world-wide experience. Highlights include, in the '50s on the 60-foot S&S yawl *Marie Amelie:* first, Class A, Miami-Nassau; third, SORC; four-time winner Commodore's Cup. In the '60s aboard the 49-foot S&S yawl *Pacifica:* first, class A, Miami-Nassau and winner of a number of major overseas races. From 1972, Mr. Giannini has been campaigning the 57-foot S&S yawl *Circe.*

Bernard A. Goldhirsh is founder and president of the Institute for Advancement of Sailing, Inc., and publisher of Sail and Motorboat magazines.

Bruce Goldsmith is a vice president of Murphy & Nye Sailmakers in Chicago. At age 12 he was National Nipper Champ, and proceeded to rack up an impressive racing record, as follows: Collegiate Sailing Hall of Fame, U. of Michigan, 1959; Rebel National Champ, 1957-58; Thistle National Champ, 1961; Penguin North American Champ, 1965; three-time Lightning North American Champ, 1967, 1973, 1974; two-time Lightning World Champ, 1969, 1973; Pan Am Games, Gold Medal in Lightnings, 1967; second place Soling Worlds, 1971; Olympic team backup in Solings, 1972; first place Solings, CORK, 1971.

Herbert A. Hild, a New Yorker, has spent his entire working life in sailmaking. He is president and owner of Hild Sails, makers of racing and cruising sails; Island Nautical, producers of the Island Nautical Dodger; and Hilco Marine, a yacht yard and new-boat sales firm — all of City Island, N.Y. Owner of 12 Star boats in 21 years, one of his many outstanding achievements in that class was in serving as an alternate in the 1948 Olympic trials. He has won every major East Coast Star event, including two Atlantic Coast championships. Mr. Hild is a partner in the Fair America syndicate and is a member of the board of governors of the Etchells Class and of the advisory council of the International Star Class. He belongs to the American Yacht Club, New York Yacht Club, Storm Trysail Club, and a number of racing associations. He owns a Tartan 44.

Tony Johnson established Competition Sails in St. Petersburg in 1972 when he was 26, having been in sailmaking from age 15. His first interests in racing were Windmills and Thistles, in which he captured district and interdistrict championships. In his highly modified Irwin 24 (cut to 22) he placed second in the overall MORC Station 10 Championships. In 1975 he had his own 30-foot One-Ton/MORC boat built for defense of the MORC title and the One-Ton Nationals.

Murray Lesser is an ex-aerodynamicist turned computer engineer. After better than 40 years of leading an essentially sedentary life, he took up sailing at the urging of his wife Jean. In pursuing the art of coastwise cruising under sail since that time, he has examined much of sailing's "conventional wisdom" in the light of his professional training and experience. He has written a number of thoughtful essays about the pleasures — and the pains — of sailing.

John Marshall operates the East Coast branch of North Sails, where he has rapidly become one of the country's leading authorities on sailmaking and sail trimming. The Stratford loft cut sails for both *Courageous* and *Intrepid* in the 1974 America's Cup; Mr. Marshall was a member of the latter's afterguard in charge of sail trim. He has contributed to sail inventories on numerous successful ocean racers, including *Charisma, Running Tide, Yankee Girl, La Forza del Destino,* and *Kahili II.* Twice he has been an Olympic sailor, winning a bronze medal in 1972 in the Dragon class.

Don McKibbin is with McKibbin Sails of Irvine, Ca., and has been in the sailmaking business since 1960. He has sailed or crewed in numerous dinghy and keelboat classes. His offshore racing participation includes the SORC as well as several Mexican races. He is a member of the Newport Harbor Y. C. and the St. Francis Y. C.

Peter Schoonmaker operates his own sail loft, Schoonmaker/Campbell sails, in Long Beach, Ca. His first taste of sailing was in Snipes on San Francisco Bay in 1939. He changed to Stars in 1948, racing them until 1959, in which year he helped found the Bay Area's MORA. He has since won the Cal 25 Nationals, the Banshee Nationals, and, twice, The Cyclone Nationals, among others. In 1971, he placed 2nd in the Half-Ton National Championships. Longer races have included the Mazatlan, Cabo San Lucas, and the San Francisco-Newport.

Norris Strawbridge, an architectural designer, started in racing at St. Georges school in Newport, R.I., where he was team captain in 1964. Six years later, he served as crew aboard *Intrepid* in the 1970 America's Cup trials. He has also been a several-time fleet champion of I.O.D.s out of Northeast Harbor, Me., and is a frequent ocean racer.

John Stanton is an engineer trained in aero/hydrodynamics. Associated with boats since early childhood, he became fascinated with sail aerodynamics in the late '50s, for several years thereafter conducting research into the subject. The results were published in Sail, as well as other magazines and technical papers. Mr. Stanton has worked as a design consultant to several well-known yacht designers, sailmakers, and equipment manufacturers, and has taught small-craft naval architecture. He is a member of SNAME, SAE, SSCD, ABYC, AIAA, and NAYRU, and has participated in various marine committees of these organizations. He is the author of a recent book about propellers.

Peter L. Sutcliffe is an aerospace engineer at Boeing and a small-boat racing skipper. He has won several yacht club championships in the Town Class, and placed second and third in the Town Class Nationals in 1970 and 1972, respectively. In 1973, he joined the ranks of Day Sailers and that year won the New England Day Sailer championship. He has authored a number of articles on small-boat racing technique, and has delivered scientific papers on sailing theory at professional meetings.

Peter M. Sutter has been a sailmaker for over three decades and is president of Sutter Sails, Sausalito, Ca. He bought his first sailboat, a 10-foot sloop, in 1939 for $17.00. He has since progressed through a Snipe, two Stars, a Mercury, a Golden Gate, a 38-foot sloop, and, lastly, the 33-foot S&S sloop *Spirit*, in which he races and cruises. His offshore racing career includes four Transpacs, five Mazatlans, three La Pazes, two Acapulcos, two Puerto Vallartas, and one Bermuda. Mr. Sutter is a member of the Cruising Club of America, and the St. Francis, the Sausalito, and the San Francisco Yacht Clubs.

Warwick M. Tompkins, Jr., operates a delivery and speed evaluation service in Mill Valley, Ca. His early sailing experience was aboard the 85-foot schooner *Wander Bird*, in which he made 13 Atlantic crossings, four passages to Honolulu, and rounded Cape Horn — all by the age of eight. In later years he participated in two America's Cup trials with *Weatherly* and *Nefertiti*, and successfully raced aboard *Kialoa, Ondine,* and *Tiare*, among other long-distance boats. He has also won a number of races in a variety of one-design classes.

Charles Ulmer operates Charles Ulmer Sailmakers, City Island, N.Y. He started sailing at City Island at age four, and had his own boat a year later. The following years were spent crewing for his father on Starboats, traveling world-wide to Star regattas. He was the recipient of the U. S. Naval Academy's McMillan Cup in 1961. Mr. Ulmer won national championships in the Mobjack class, and was the first national champion in the Tempest class. In 1968, business reasons drew him to larger cruising boats, where his sailing emphasis has since remained.

Donald Vaughn was introduced to racing on the schooner *Goodwill* where, wearing a hard-hat, he mastered handling her 30,000 feet of line and jibing her 72-foot spinnaker pole. After that, it was a coast downhill, participating in the 1964 and 1967 America's Cup trials in *Columbia,* and sailing aboard *Escapade* and *Bolero.* He raced for many years for Robert Johnson on *Ticonderoga* and *Windward Passage,* and lastly has been crewing for Mark Johnson on *Passage.*

Charles H. Vilas has been cruising for over 50 years, and is still on only his second boat, *Direction,* a scaled-down version of a Colin Archer redningskoite type. Since retiring in 1969, he and his wife Margaret have lived aboard out of Nova Scotia's Bras d'Or Lakes and wintered ashore in Connecticut. Their adventures and other reflections on cruising life are recounted in his book *Saga of Direction* (Seven Seas Press, 1975). Mr. Vilas is editor of Cruising Club News, house organ of the C.C.A., of which he has been a member since 1938. Other clubs of long-standing Vilas membership are Offsoundings, Essex Yacht Club, and New York Yacht Club.